D1093137

Cheerful Sacrifice

JONATHAN NICHOLLS

Cheerful Sacrifice

THE BATTLE OF ARRAS 1917

with a Foreword by
MARTIN MIDDLEBROOK

LEO COOPER

First published 1990 by Leo Cooper

Leo Cooper is an independent imprint of the
Octopus Publishing Group, Michelin House,
81 Fulham Road, London SW3 6RB
LONDON   MELBOURNE   AUCKLAND

Copyright © Jonathan Nicholls 1990

A CIP catalogue record for this book
is available from the British Library.

ISBN 0 85052 520 9

Photoset by Rowland Phototypesetting Ltd
Bury St Edmunds, Suffolk
Printed and bound in Great Britain by
Butler & Tanner Ltd, Frome and London

Contents

Introduction   1

PART I – Trenches and Tunnels   5
1   Alberich   7
2   Ant-Heap   19
3   The Men   39
4   Trench Raids   45
5   The Week of Suffering   52
6   In Praise of Infantry   57
7   Easter Sunday   64

PART II – The Day of Doings: 9 April, 1917   73
8   Vimy Ridge   75
9   Harper's Duds   91
10   Maxwell's Procession   98
11   Centrepunch   106
12   The Hindenburg Line   117
13   Forcing the Gap   123

PART III – A Victory Wasted   133
14   The Day of Delay   135
15   The Crucial Day   139
16   The Defeated Enemy   156
17   Comical Works   170
18   A Deuce of a Fight   183
19   The Right Thing   191
20   Recipe for Disaster   195
21   The Boys who Really Did the Job   209

Appendix I: Skeleton Order of Battle
(and Casualties), British Divisions   222

Appendix II: Skeleton Order of Battle,
German Divisions   225
Appendix III: Victoria Cross Awards   227

Acknowledgements   229
Bibliography   241
Index   245

Illustrations

1. Alberich (*Imperial War Museum*)
2. Siegfried Stellung (*Imperial War Museum*)
3. Sir Edmund Allenby (*Imperial War Museum*)
4. Sir Douglas Haig (*P. Scott Collection*)
5. Captain 'Pat' Blair (*Author's Collection*)
6. Sergeant Bill Hay (*Author's Collection*)
7. Corporal Alf Razzell (*Author's Collection*)
8. Private Neville Tompkins (*Author's Collection*)
9. Private Arthur Betteridge (*Author's Collection*)
10. Livens Projectors (*Imperial War Museum*)
11. Fixing ladders for the Infantry assault (*Imperial War Museum*)
12. 'Lusitania' moves up (*Imperial War Museum*)
13. Advance of the 4th Division (*Imperial War Museum*)
14. German prisoners (*Imperial War Museum*)
15. 18-pounder Battery (*Imperial War Museum*)
16. Cavalry at Monchy (*Imperial War Museum*)
17. Cavalry at Arras (*Imperial War Museum*)
18. 'The Cavalry was going up at last' (*Imperial War Museum*)
19. Monchy: 'This was the Cavalry' (*Imperial War Museum*)
20. Ditched British tank (*Imperial War Museum*)
21. Roeux Chemical Works (*Imperial War Museum*)
22. 'Onward, Joe Soap's Army' (*Imperial War Museum*)
23. 'Dead Dump' (*Imperial War Museum*)
24. Sunken Road, Fampoux, 1985 (*Author's Collection*)
25. Battery Valley, 1985 (*Author's Collection*)
26. Great blockhouse at Roeux, 1985 (*Author's Collection*)
27. Arras, 1989 (*Author's Collection*)
28. 'The boys who did the job are dead' (*Author's Collection*)
29. 9th (Scottish) Division Memorial on 'Point du Jour' ridge (*Author's Collection*)
30. Sergeant Bill Hay, 1983 (*Author's Collection*)
31. Corporal Alf Razzell
32. (*Keith Collman*)

Maps

1 Operation Alberich: The German retirement to the
   Hindenburg Line, 25 February to 5 April, 1917   14
2 The infantry attack plan, 9 April, 1917   26
3 Vimy Ridge, 9 April, 1917   77
4 The advance of the 12th (Eastern) Division to Battery
   Valley, 9 April, 1917   114
5 The attack of the 9th and 4th Divisions, 9 April, 1917 124
6 The attack of the 10th Infantry Brigade on the Chemical
   Works, 11 April, 1917   150
7 The infantry attack plan, 23 April, 1917   171
8 The attack of the 51st (Highland) Division on Roeux and
   the Chemical Works, 23 April, 1917   174
9 The infantry attack plan, 3 May, 1917   198
10 The advance of the 8th/9th Royal Fusiliers, 3 May, 1917 203

For Gregory and his generation '*Lest they forget*'.

Foreword

In writing his book Jonathan Nicholls starts with one great advantage – his heart is completely in the subject. I first made his acquaintance about ten years ago when I saw the entry he had made in the Visitors' Book of a British war cemetery on the Somme. I was so impressed by the obvious sincerity behind his words that I made contact with him on my return to England. Meetings with him in the intervening years and this book have confirmed his deep interest in the First World War and his compassion for the front-line soldiers who experienced the ghastly conditions of trench warfare and of the great set-piece battles in France and Belgium.

The written history of that war – as of any war – comes in many forms. There are the diaries, letters and personal memoirs of the men involved, most valuable because only they know what it was like to fix bayonets, go 'over the top' against bullet and shell and take part in that unique exercise of kill or be killed that civilization tolerates as war. Then there are the unit histories in which the part played by various formations – battalion, brigade, division – are described. There are what I call 'books on generalship' in which more academic authors describe the strategy of battle, the leadership of commanders and the way war and politics inter-react to produce victory or defeat.

More recently there has been added a 'new wave' of war books, detailed descriptions of individual battles based on research of original unit war diaries and studies of the ground on which the battle was fought, but with these basic components enriched with the personal accounts of a large number of men from both sides who took part. Such work is time-consuming and expensive, but these books allow ordinary men who do not have the ability to write their own memoirs to have their experiences published before the men pass away and the stories are lost for ever. Some academic writers look down upon these books and point out the weakness of reliance on unsubstantiated stories. But, if the basic research is done properly and interviewing is skilful, most excesses can be eliminated and a wealth of new detail becomes available. I feel strongly that there is no 'last word' in military history and that no one form of war writing can offer a complete study. My advice to those seeking knowledge is to read all forms of books, to study what individual soldiers did, what units did, what the generals did, and then the composite books which describe the wider experience – then make up your own mind about what should or should not have been. I have always thought that the British 'school of military history' leads the world and its breadth of range is one of its strengths.

Most of the battles fought by the British Expeditionary Force in the First World War have been covered by the new treatment, but the Battle of Arras, fought in the Spring of 1917, has been a major omission. That battle may not be quite as important as the various battles of Ypres and the Somme but it ranks very close behind them. The packed cemeteries around Arras testify to that. The still largely volunteer British Army of early 1917 was committed to action – as so often – in conjunction with a French attack elsewhere. The French failed and the morale of their army broke, and the British thereafter had to shoulder the major burden of sacrifice on the Western Front. Jonathan Nicholls will tell how the British achieved considerable success at Arras, showing how much generalship and soldiery had learned from the Somme in 1916. That complete success and strategic result eluded the British is one more testimony to the inherent nature of the stalemate of the Western Front through most of the First World War.

As a poultry farmer with little academic background, I wrote a book – *The First Day on the Somme* – which was published in 1971. Many people approached me in following years, saying that they were 'inspired' by what I had done, to write their own books and asking for help and advice. Jonathan Nicholls is the only one who has shown the perseverance and skill necessary to achieve publication and I congratulate him. For filling a gap in the history of the First World War, many will surely thank him.

Martin Middlebrook

February 1990

Introduction

The third Christmas of the Great War came and went with such alacrity that the soldiers, facing each other across the freezing wastes of the Western Front, hardly noticed its passing. The seasonal spirit of 1914, with football matches and exchanges of gifts in no-man's-land, was long dead and buried. The immediate concern of all – apart from staying alive – was keeping warm in this, the coldest winter in European memory. On the home fronts of the belligerent nations, enthusiasm for the war had long since waned, suffocated in the mud and slashed to ribbons on the cruel barbed wire of the Somme. Everyone was by now acutely aware of the cost of the terrible adventure on which they had embarked with such buoyant optimism in that golden August of 1914. The agony of the recent heavy losses had been particularly hard to bear and the word 'deadlock' seemed to be on everyone's lips, although it seemed to have little influence on those responsible for the conduct of the war. Hardly had the last tortuous blows of the Somme battle been thrown in the awful conditions of November, 1916, than generals and politicians alike were scheming as to how they could best break the back of the enemy when the weather improved.

Early in 1917 momentous events changed the conditions under which the Great War was fought. Russia dropped out and America came in. Britain had a new Prime Minister in David Lloyd George and the French had finally ditched the solid old buffer, General Joffre, who by his uncontested leadership and prestige had for so long dominated the conduct of the war. His brutally simple but wasteful strategy had worn thin. France had suffered enough. From the anvil of Verdun a new blade had been forged. A new star, who had recaptured sacred Fort Douaumont and restored French pride, had risen. He was General Robert Nivelle. He promised a glittering new vision for the spring of 1917; 'Victory is certain, I give you my assurance . . .' But it was the promise of victory in forty-eight hours that carried most weight, especially with the British Government.

1

Here was a far more attractive plan than Joffre's remorseless warfare of attrition. Nivelle was renowned for his ability to charm politicians. That, combined with his ability to speak fluent English, captivated Lloyd George.

Not so convinced were those British warhorses, Haig and Robertson. Their own plan for a massive attack in Flanders was already far advanced. Mounting shipping losses from U-boat action had seen to that. Lloyd George made no secret of his distaste for Sir William Robertson and his methods of waging war. He loathed the Western Front and, although he longed for victory, constantly sought easier methods and other theatres of war to achieve it. But he thought Nivelle's plan dynamic. For a start, the French would be doing the bulk of the fighting. The British would play a supporting and far less expensive role in attacking – in a diversionary capacity – out from the town of Arras towards Cambrai, thereby drawing the German reserves. Nivelle wanted the British thrust to precede the French attack on the Aisne by one to two weeks. Although in a secondary role, this would still be the biggest effort of the British Army so far. Lloyd George told Robertson to instruct Haig to conform to the Nivelle plan 'in the letter and the spirit – on no account must the French have to wait for us owing to our arrangements not being complete'.[1] Robertson, however, said that he 'interpreted these instructions as meaning that Sir Douglas Haig is expected to attack, whether he is ready or not'.[2]

Although the British generals were unsure of Nivelle's plan, they loyally cooperated with the new French Commander-in-Chief. Yet Lloyd George was not satisfied and resorted to trickery in order to reduce the status and authority of Haig and Robertson. Calling them to a conference at Calais on 26 February, 1917, under the pretence of discussing the lack of suitable French railway transport, he attempted to place Haig and the British Armies in France under the direct command of Nivelle. Robertson and Haig were outraged – there was even talk of resignation. However, a compromise was reached, whereby the British Army retained its identity under Haig, who was subordinated to Nivelle – junior in rank and experience – for the duration of the offensive outlined in the plan. But the notorious Calais Conference had opened a wound of mutual mistrust between soldiers and politicians which never properly healed.

By the spring of 1917, Arras was the central town and main

[1] Public Record Office (PRO) CAB 23/1.
[2] Ibid.

2

The New Conductor
Opening of the
1917 Overture

battleground of the British Armies on the Western Front and was the scene, throughout the war, of several battles fought by both the British and French Armies. Although other battles of the war exacted a higher toll in casualties, the Battle of Arras, which began on Easter Monday, 9 April, 1917, primarily as part of a joint offensive with the French, turned out to be the most lethal of any *offensive* battle fought by the British Army in the Great War. In the relatively short period over which the battle lasted – thirty-nine days – the daily average casualty rate was far higher than that of both the Somme and Passchendaele. Indeed, as many of the survivors later testified, the Battle of Arras was the most savage infantry battle of the war.

Part I
TRENCHES AND TUNNELS

1
Alberich

In the late afternoon of 22 February, 1917, while holed up in a frozen trench just south of the German-held ruins of Petit Miraumont, Lieutenant Frank Lucas of the 7th Royal West Kents, suspicious at a strange lack of enemy activity from the trenches opposite, clambered up on the slippery firestep and peered into the gloom. Squinting through field glasses only served to amplify the murk. He could not see a thing. Scrambling quickly over the parapet he decided to take a closer look. The 55th Infantry Brigade was holding the whole of the 18th Division's front at the head of the shell-torn Ancre Valley and this was not normally a quiet sector; Lucas was curious as to what the Germans might be up to. Cautiously he advanced along the battered West Miraumont road until he came to the hedges of rusty barbed wire that lay in front of the enemy trench, and, even more cautiously, picked his way through the steel briars, crawled up to the parapet and peered down. To his amazement he saw that the trench was empty. On the left he saw a lone German soldier climb out of the trench, stand up and run swiftly back towards the ruins of the village. The enemy had abandoned their trenches.

Slithering breathlessly in the cold air back into his own lines, Lucas immediately reported his findings to his dubious senior officers. No patrols could be sent out during the night to confirm Lucas's story, because of the danger of British artillery shelling the German front trenches; but at 5 a.m. the following morning Lucas obtained permission to go out again, this time taking with him Lieutenant Francis Lewin.[1] The two officers, with revolvers at the ready, then crept along Crest Trench for several hundred yards, meeting no one. There was no doubt about it: the Germans had gone.

Further south, Australian patrols had also been out exploring and tentative claims were later made that they were first to make the

---

[1] Francis Harold Lewin, MC. Killed in action 12 October, 1917.

amazing discovery, but these claims were dismissed as they were not reported at the time.[2]

On the morning of 24 February three patrols of the 21st Manchesters probed forward over half a mile into the enemy trenches and bypassed the evil ruins of Serre village which appeared to be devoid of the enemy. Their Commanding Officer, Lieutenant-Colonel W. Norman, later wrote:

> They found a series of dugouts, one of which was entered and showed signs of recent occupation. Throughout the reconnaissance, not a single shot was fired by the enemy and not a sight of them seen. I myself proceeded to move post early this morning to await the return of the patrols. I saw no trace of them until about 9.45 a.m. when I saw them returning over the crest line of the ridge which roughly follows Luke Alley and from here watched their return down Walter Trench. The above report seems almost incredible but I am of the opinion that it is reliable. If so it points to the evacuation of Serre by the enemy.[3]

Although the enemy had been pulling out in small sections locally, the cautiously advancing British soldiers soon found that they were up against tough rearguard troops who stubbornly resisted any attempts at a heavy penetration. Several sharp fights broke out for the small villages and outposts scattered along the German perimeter. But to where were the Germans withdrawing, and why?

In the latter part of September, 1916, while the Somme battle was still raging, the Germans had began the construction of a powerful new trench fortress system some distance behind the existing front. They called it the *Siegfried Stellung*, but to the British it was to become known as the Hindenburg Line. The early diggings of these new earthworks to the south-east of Arras had been spotted by the Royal Flying Corps at the end of October, on one of the few days when there had been clear visibility, but orders from high command for the RFC to make further investigations came to nothing. The onset of the winter weather made observation difficult and, although the RFC always pressed their photo-reconnaissance flights with great gallantry, they were outmatched and outfought during this period by the

---

[2] Lieutenant Lucas's report, which can be found in the Public Record Office, ref. WO 95/2047, is the earliest *reported* evidence that the enemy had started to withdraw. Frank Laurence Lucas survived the war. He became a Fellow of King's College, Cambridge, and was a prolific author. He died in 1967.
[3] PRO WO95/1668.

powerful new twin-gun Albatross and Halberstadt fighters. More-over, no particular urgency had been attached to the orders.

German resources had come under tremendous pressure during the Allied offensive on the Somme. Now, for the first time in the war, the German High Command had begun to look at the idea of a strong defensive position to which their troops could fall back should the need arise. By withdrawing to this new position, the line would automatically be shortened, thereby making a great saving in man-power which could be used elsewhere. The original plan for the *Siegfried Stellung* was that of a fortified belt in five sections, stretching from the Belgian coast to Pont-à-Mousson on the River Moselle, a distance of 300 miles. The most important part of this line was to be in the centre, behind the large salient between Neuville Vitasse, a village just to the south of Arras, and Soissons. The brain behind this new concept was a certain Colonel von Lossberg, Chief of Staff to General von Bulow and an expert in the art of military defence. He was immediately given the necessary authority to begin work; all efforts were to be directed to its early completion.

This formidable new line was to be built on the reverse slopes of hills, thereby denying observation to the enemy. Attacking infantry crossing the forward crests could be slaughtered by unseen artillery. Standard practice of packing the forward trenches with troops, who would suffer accordingly under bombardment, was out. The front line, some 600 yards deep, would be thinly held by defensive outposts and machine-gun positions. Any attacking infantry breaking through this line would then have to negotiate a second zone of defence, with inter-supporting strongpoints, which would be supported by a third line consisting of deep ditches and ferro-concrete blockhouses connected by tunnels. Here large bodies of troops could be safely kept underground in concrete *stollen*, or bunkers, until ready to counter-attack the enemy. The average position was to be about one mile in depth, but it was planned to extend this to four miles by adding a further defensive line after April, 1917. Insignificant French villages previously untouched by the war were swallowed up by the fortifi-cations. The whole system was to be protected by dense thickets of barbed wire up to fifty feet in depth, laid in zig-zag patterns in front of the fire trenches. Any attempt to get through this formidable obstacle could be enfiladed by fire from the covering machine-gun nests: 'No troops who saw it before rust had touched it will forget the sinister impression made by its blue sheen in the light of the afternoon.'[4]

[4] Official History, France and Belgium, 1917; p. 92.

The *Siegfried Stellung* was Germany's greatest engineering achievement of the war. The construction of the reinforced concrete blockhouses, by thousands of Russian and Belgian prisoners of war, was supervised by civilian ferro-concrete experts. River-washed sand and gravel was brought from the Rhine by canal barge and rail. Often surrounding earth would be heaped around the monstrous structures to a depth of twenty feet or more. Blockhouses were erected among farm buildings or neighbouring cottages, in some cases with a jacket of brickwork built around the concrete and the disguise completed with the addition of mock doors, windows and chimneys. No interruptions halted the construction programme, and, under the admirable supervision of Crown Prince Rupprecht and his Chief of Staff, General von Kuhl, the work was completed in just five months.

The ceaseless British pressure on the Somme in the autumn of 1916 had put the German Army, also fighting on the Russian front, in dire straits. Their overstretched lines on the Western Front needed to be shortened in order to accumulate reserves and give tired divisions a chance to recover, but time was needed to complete the new defence line. Time was the key: time to delay the expected Allied attack in the spring. Fortunately they were given a gratuitous gift of the time they needed by the new French Commander-in-Chief, Robert Nivelle, who, during this period, was living in a world of optimistic dreams, far from the forbidding realities of the front.

And so the momentous decision to withdraw behind the safety of the *Siegfried Stellung* was made. An organized programme of vandalism, or 'scorched earth', was to be carried out in the country they were about to vacate. The most important instigator behind the decision to pull back was Crown Prince Rupprecht, although he was initially opposed by the aggressive-minded Ludendorff to whom the very thought of retreat was inconceivable.

On 4 February secret orders were issued for the preparation of the withdrawal – which was to last over a five-week period. The main retirement would begin on 16 March, the first 'marching day', although, as we have seen, the Germans started to pull out of the Ancre valley as early as 22 February. The withdrawal has since become known as Operation Alberich, after the malicious dwarf of the Nibelung Saga, although Alberich was, strictly speaking, just the name of the sector south of St Quentin, facing the French. In view of the awesome difficulty of pulling back an army under the noses of the enemy, Operation Alberich proved to be one of the most brilliant German operations of the war.

In spite of overwhelming evidence pouring into the British HQ that

The Invaders.
'I suppose old Hindenburg
knows what he's about?'
'Anyhow, every step takes us
nearer the Fatherland.'

the enemy was pulling back, Nivelle, in overall command, stubbornly denied the irrefutable facts laid before him. 'The enemy would not retreat on his front!' he maintained. But the British assured him that the enemy would – and indeed had, leaving the whole of Nivelle's left wing, the *Groupe des Armées du Nord* (GAN), about to attack into a void. Incredibly, Nivelle refused to make any changes in his plan of attack, even though his troops were straining at the leash to pursue the enemy. Eventually, on 15 March, GAN was given the order to advance – but it was too late. The enemy had escaped. To Allied propagandists, however, this was a good omen, and Nivelle was proclaimed hero of the hour; at last the 'hated Boche' was on the run.

The men of the 18th (Eastern) Division had emerged from the Somme battle with a fine fighting reputation. Under the leadership of Major-General Sir Ivor Maxse, who had trained them to perfection, they had seized all of their objectives on 1 July, 1916, captured Trones Wood on 14 July and, with these two successes under their belts, had been assigned the formidable task of capturing the notorious fortresses of Thiepval and Schwaben Redoubt. On 25 September, 1916, Maxse confidently announced to his soldiers: 'The 180th Regiment of Württemburgers have withstood attacks on Thiepval for two years, but the 18th Division will take it tomorrow.'[5] His confidence was not misplaced. On 26 September Thiepval fell, to a brilliantly executed flank attack. This fine achievement was crowned the following day with the attack on the Schwaben Redoubt and its subsequent capture.

The 18th Division was probably the best fighting division possessed by the Army in September, 1916, and was a typical 'Kitchener' or 'New Army' division, consisting entirely of civilian soldiers from London and the south-eastern counties. Their ranks had been sorely depleted by the merciless Somme fighting, but the replacements or 'draftees' as the troops called them had been of good quality although a lot of them were conscripts.[6]

Sergeant Jack Cousins, of the 7th Beds, a farm labourer before the war and typical of the lads of dependable county stock that made up the ranks of the division, was one of the survivors of the Somme. As he later reflected:

> Seven of us boys from Redbourn had joined the Army together on the same Saturday in August, 1914, when we had walked from Redbourn to the recruiting office at St Albans, but at the end of the Somme battle I was the only one left. I was lucky and came through the whole lot unscathed. It was simply a matter of self-preservation. I was paid to kill Germans and I did it to the best of my ability . . . It's either you or them, don't wait to be asked, just get stuck in. I remember General Maxse's words when he pinned the medal on me: 'Kill Germans.'

Sergeant Cousins was awarded the Military Medal after the attack on the Schwaben Redoubt, won by skilful use of the Lewis gun in clearing a particularly dangerous section of trench.

The daring exploits of Maxse's men had not gone unnoticed by the Army hierarchy and by Christmas, 1916, Maxse had been promoted Lieutenant-General and given an Army Corps. The new leader of the 18th Division was Major-General Richard P. Lee, who had arrived at Divisional HQ while the division was suffering the worst of the winter weather. His first major success had been the capture of Boom Ravine in the Ancre Valley on 17 February, albeit at a cost of fifty-four officers and 1,135 other ranks. Now, as a result of Lieute-

[5] PRO WO95/2041.
[6] Conscription had been introduced in May, 1916.

nant Lucas's discovery that the Germans had pulled out, the division was back on form and raring to go; if necessary they would chase the enemy back to Berlin. But it was now that the legendary adversary of the British soldier, the weather, came into play – in the shape of a sudden thaw. Trenches collapsed, huge pot-holes appeared in the few serviceable roads, and everywhere there was mud, mud and more mud. Men sank up to their waists in it, guns and waggons sank up to their axles, horses got stuck and had to be shot.

But clawing its way slowly forward, the 18th Division seized the villages of Miraumont, Irles and, by 10 March, Achiet-le-Grand. Now the men of the 18th began to encounter the results of the Germans' 'scorched earth' policy. As Private Horace Ham, of the 12th Middlesex, later recalled: 'We stood in the road at Achiet-le-Grand and counted seven fires blazing in the distance; seven villages were on fire.' Not only were the 'Jerries' setting fire to the country-side, they were felling trees to block the roads. But the British continued to edge forward, and among the advance guard was Private Ham:

> We stuck to the side of the road and got through
> Achiet-le-Grand and into a deserted redoubt on the other side
> of the village. When it was daylight, I saw in the distance a
> patrol of Uhlans, coming towards us. Now this was the first time
> that we had ever seen the buggers, so we set up our Lewis gun
> and waited. I tell you, if our Sergeant had kept his head we
> would have had the lot but he opened fire at 400 yards. We saw
> one fall forward in the saddle but the rest scattered and
> disappeared behind a low hill. That was the first and only time
> in the war that I ever saw German cavalry. The next day our
> Sergeant, a little Cockney fellow, stood up and looked over the
> edge of the trench. He yawned, stretched and said, 'Roll on
> death, let's have a nice long sleep,' then *Wallop!* A sniper got
> him right through the chest as he finished uttering the words.
> He fell back into the trench, coughing up blood, and was gone
> just like that. Talk about tempting fate!

After an improvised but successful withdrawl from the Ancre valley, the main German retirement began on 16 March when thirty-five divisions left their positions and pulled out. By 19 March they were safely established in the new line. The whole operation had been completed in just three days, without a hitch. But in their wake, obeying the order that *'Der Gegner muss en vollig ausgesogenes land vorfinden'* (The whole zone between the present fighting line and the new position will be made a desert), the Germans left a terrible legacy.

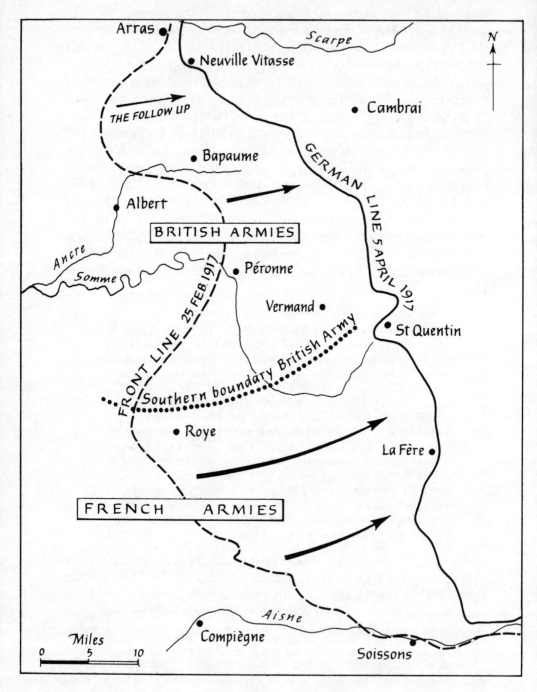

1. OPERATION ALBERICH.

The German author Ernst Jünger, who described his wartime experiences in his book *Storm of Steel*, was a *leutnant* in the 73rd Hanoverian Fusilier Regiment who took part in the retreat; it was, he said, 'an orgy of destruction'. After ransacking the contents of the local villagers' homes, the troops – 'arrayed in the abandoned wardrobes of the population, in women's dresses with top hats on their heads' – set about demolishing them:

> With positive genius they singled out the main beams of the houses and, tying ropes round them, tugged with all their might, shouting out in time with their pulls, till the whole house collapsed. Others swung hammers and smashed whatever came in their way, from flowerpots on the windowledges to the glasswork of conservatories. Every village up to the Siegfried Line was a rubbish heap. Every tree felled, every road mined, every well fouled, every watercourse dammed, every cellar blown up or made into a death trap with concealed bombs, all supplies of metal sent back, all rails ripped up, all telephone wires rolled up, everything burnable burned. In short, the country over which the enemy was to advance had been turned into utter desolation.[7]

One can sense an element of pride in Jünger's vivid description of the destruction wrought by his comrades. That pride was not shared, however, by one German soldier who served with Jünger until he was wounded in May, 1917, and who kept in contact with him after the war. Requesting that his comment remain anonymous, he said:

> I still feel ashamed at what we soldiers did during the march back to the Siegfried position. I have never set foot in France since I went home wounded in 1917, and I have no desire to do so. Myself and four comrades were billeted with a French woman and her two young daughters for eight months. During that period we were treated with great kindness. In my spare time, I carved a small table for the woman as a gift. When it was complete she placed it in the middle of the room and covered it with a small lace cloth. On this table she would place cakes and biscuits which she had cooked for us. Can you imagine our feelings when we were ordered to destroy the cottage which had been our home for so long? The woman and her daughters were led away before we started. The first thing I smashed was my table. We smashed up the whole house. We had to do it but felt very sad. So perhaps this sounds soft, but nothing caused me more pain in the war than this.

[7] Jünger, The Storm of Steel, p. 126.

15

Great excitement at the prospect of open warfare rippled through the ranks of the British and French armies. The French, when finally allowed to do so by Nivelle, were quick to pursue the retreating enemy, as did elements of Gough's Fifth Army, but in general the British follow-up was pedantic and slow. The main problem was that everyone had to be in on the act. The cavalry and the artillery were ordered forward by a Staff inexperienced in advance-guard warfare, and promptly blocked the roads. Huge traffic jams built up, with the Engineers and Pioneers working furiously to clear the roads of cut-down trees and mines planted at every crossroads. Soon the British advance was at a standstill. If the German artillery had turned and opened fire the result would have been catastrophic. As one British officer recorded (Captain Geoffrey Christie-Miller, 2/1st Oxford and Bucks):

> On 18 March, 1917, it was discovered at dawn by the Warwicks who were occupying our front that the enemy had cleared out, so off they went in pursuit with patrols. Very soon after, we were ordered forward to Lihons and great was the excitement at the prospect of an advance. At Lihons we found things in the state of a most glorious confusion which continued for the next week or more. This state of affairs was the direct result of the most muddle-headed staff work that ever our divisional staff had succeeded in perpetrating. The chief hindrance to our work was the presence of the whole of our divisional artillery who had pulled out of their battery positions and been ordered to push through Chauldes, quite regardless of the fact that their advance could not be commenced until an approach had been prepared. So the whole artillery of the Division, with their transport, completely blocked the road through Lihons towards Chauldes for twenty-four hours, during which time I doubt if the maximum progress was over a hundred yards.

Everywhere, British troops were horrified at the destruction wreaked by the retiring enemy. Whole villages had been laid waste and wells fouled. In his memoirs, Ludendorff claimed that he had not ordered the wells to be poisoned; but, on the Fourth Army front, captured instructions dated 14 March clearly directed that a cavalry regiment stationed just north of Bapaume should ensure that 'plenty of horse-dung should be left near the wells'.[8] The Crown Prince disapproved of the extensive destruction carried out by his army, fearing that it would further blacken Germany's name throughout the world – as indeed it did. It also gave the Allied propaganda machine plenty of wholesome material to work on.

[8] Official History, France and Belgium, 1917, p. 113.

Meanwhile, however, the British advance was meeting sporadic resistance in the form of snipers and machine-gun crews. Some of them, after delaying actions, ran back to safety. Others, fighting to the last, were surrounded and killed. A few of these last-ditch defenders were captured and often came in for rough treatment. One of the tasks of the Military Police, when they were not being blamed for causing the traffic chaos, was to escort these prisoners to the rear, through throngs of advancing British troops – an unpopular but necessary duty. Sergeant Lionel Charles, of the Royal Mounted Military Police attached to Third Army HQ, remembered one occasion when he was sent forward to collect some German prisoners. They had been flushed out by some Red Indians with the Canadian cavalry, and when Sergeant Charles arrived on the scene he found the Red Indians indulging in some blood-thirsty entertainment:

> With whoops and shouts, they were chasing [the] Germans, swords in hands, with many of the weapons already red with blood. To all intents they were back home on the prairie hunting the buffalo. It took me all of two hours to collect just six Germans and start back.

With the captives rounded up at last, Sergeant Charles delivered them to 'the mound of stones which was our advanced HQ – the Germans having destroyed everything for miles around'. He noticed that they 'seemed to know this place' and locked them in a cellar to await interrogation the next day. After an uncomfortable night and breakfast of 'black tea and a rasher of bacon on a hard biscuit', the weary Sergeant was directed to take his prisoners to another cellar where a senior officer would interrogate them. One of the prisoners promptly started shouting at the officer, jabbing his finger towards Sergeant Charles. Helpfully the officer translated the prisoner's words:

> 'He is Major So-and-So, and he accuses you of making him spend the night in a latrine instead of a suitable place befitting his rank.'
> 'Well, sir,' [Sergeant Charles replied] 'he should have told me he was a Major – and secondly, with respect, he should have known that his men were using that particular cellar as a shithouse!'

Slowly the British troops continued their advance into that devastated wilderness. If there was one consolation for them in what

17

Sergeant Charles described as the 'utter desolation left by the retreating enemy', it was that here at last there was an abundance of firewood – a much-needed commodity in that bitter winter – in the form of smashed furniture, cupboards, doors and window frames. But the half-demolished buildings held hidden dangers: booby-traps arranged by the Germans to kill or maim any unsuspecting or careless Allied soldier. The roads, too, were mined, often with delayed-action fuses timed to go off many days, even weeks, later.

On Saturday, 17 March, while Sir Douglas Haig was meeting his Army Commanders to discuss the problems caused by the German withdrawal, the 2nd Australian Division was entering Bapaume, which had been in enemy hands since 1914. The whole town had been totally demolished, apart from the ancient town hall which had been left largely undamaged. Suspecting that the building could have been mined, a thorough search was made and a large mine found in one of the cellars. It was disarmed and removed. But it was a ruse. One week later, on the night of 25 March, while thirty Australians were sleeping in the building, a second hidden mine exploded, killing a number of the soldiers as well as some non-combatants employed at the coffee stall of the Australian comforts fund.

On the whole, the majority of booby-traps left by the enemy were discovered and many lives saved thanks to the bravery and ingenuity of the Royal Engineers. Many deadly devices were left, but the most common of all, and the one most remembered by the soldiers, was the 'souvenir'. This might be in the form of a *pickelhaube*, a German spike-topped helmet much valued by British soldiers, or perhaps a Mauser pistol left in a holster as if abandoned, or even an innocent-looking packet of cigars. All were tempting prizes. When the victim picked up the object a wire attached to a charge or a pin in a grenade would be pulled. A shovel leaning against the side of a trench was another favourite trick; when moved it would trigger a hidden mine. The simple iron stove in a dugout with a piece of the chimney lying beside it might be another trap, or the lumps of coal nearby might contain detonators. As Sergeant Lionel Charles wrote:

> The hand of death was always present, for our enemy was a
> master at setting booby-traps. You did not dare touch any left
> object until you were sure it would not blow up in your face.
> Were you trained in this? No! You trained yourself.

2

Ant-Heap

By 1918 Arras, Albert and Ypres had become household names. Honourably defended by the British Army throughout the war, only Albert fell to the enemy for a short period in 1918. The ancient city of Arras, destined to lend its name to the forthcoming offensive, was the most important French town held by the British Army throughout the war. Its importance was twofold: firstly, it held the central and most important strategic position on the British line; secondly, the close proximity of the town to the front line made it a potential springboard for any offensive.

Arras lies in a gentle depression in the Artois plain, overlooked from the east by a semi-circle of low rolling hills from which, in the spring of 1917, the entrenched German Army enjoyed an uninterrupted view into the town. This beautiful city, fortified in the seventeenth century by the great French engineer, Vauban, was no stranger to war – or to the British. With a pre-war population of some 30,000 inhabitants, it boasted a rich and interesting history. Arras was an early Roman settlement, then called Nemetacum, to which all roads, with typical Roman straightness, seemed to lead. Built alongside the deep and navigable River Scarpe, which ran from west to east, cutting a deep valley through the surrounding hills, Arras had always been a major centre of communications – and a valuable asset to any would-be conqueror or defender.

By the onset of winter in 1914 Vimy Ridge, the shield of Arras, was in enemy hands. They had paid dearly in blood to take this commanding position and had no intention of relinquishing it. It lies just over three miles to the north-east of the town, the highest point of the semi-circle of hills which had stood silent guard over it through the ages. From the Allied side the ridge appeared as a long blue-grey bluff, not very dramatic; but in such a war, when the slightest hummock could cost the lives of thousands, it was a colossus. From the German side – that is, approached from the east – the ridge appeared far more formidable, being visible for miles and plunging dramatically 200 feet or more down to the Douai plain. To the south-east the ridge slopes gently down towards the River Scarpe before the land rises again towards Monchy-le-Preux. Stretching over seven miles, this great whale-backed ridge was destined to become the most powerful German fortress on the Western Front.

Beneath its loamy clay topsoil Vimy Ridge is made of chalk – ideal for tunnelling, as the Germans had quickly discovered. Indeed, as they burrowed deep into the ridge to improve its natural defensive position, they found huge caves and tunnels believed to have been dug in medieval times. Adapting the old workings to their advantage, the German infantry soon had an extensive system of deep trenches and tunnels where they could shelter in complete safety from enemy artillery fire. They were going to take some shifting.

Meanwhile the Germans' own artillery was already in position, their heavy guns concealed in the folds of Vimy Ridge, and they seemed intent on destroying Arras and its many beautiful Flemish buildings. Fleeing from the terrible rain of shells, the citizens sought shelter in the deep medieval caverns.

Throughout that miserable first winter of the war, the French troops suffered in vain, up to their waists in freezing slush in their totally inadequate trenches, while watching the systematic destruction of Arras. Then, in May 1915, the French infantry launched an assault on the German positions, but were quickly cut down by artillery and machine-gun fire. From May to November the Germans withstood all attacks on Vimy Ridge, inflicting casualties of 150,000 killed or wounded on the French. And still the Germans were digging in, constructing ever deeper earthworks and concrete strongpoints. Their iron grip on the ridge grew tighter.

The British Third Army arrived on the Arras front in March, 1916, relieving the troops of the French Tenth Army, who were sorely needed at Verdun. Immediately, the British soldiers set about tidying up the mess left by the French, practically overcome by the smell of dead bodies; it was impossible to dig into the trench walls without uncovering some fragment of humanity. In a depression to the west of Vimy Ridge, appropriately named 'Zouave Valley', lay hundreds of dead French Algerian Zouave troops, killed in suicidal frontal attacks the previous November, their rotting bodies still in the scarlet pantaloons and dark blue tunics of 1914.

The French had also started tunnelling into the ridge, and now the British took over, burrowing towards the enemy workings. Sometimes the opposing saps ran so close that one would collapse into the other – and soon the two sides learnt to assist nature by using explosives to destroy the enemy's tunnels. It was a race against time: whichever side completed its tunnel first could undermine the other side's efforts. The digging was done by specialist tunnelling companies, usually highly paid civilian miners drafted into the army and working in shifts at the tunnel face. The chalk refuse was collected in sandbags and manhandled to the rear for disposal by the infantry, care being taken lest its location alert the enemy to the miners' intentions. By means of an instrument called a geophone, similar to a doctor's stethoscope and used at the tunnel face, the Germans could be heard working. As long as the steady picking and scraping of their tools could be heard, all was considered safe; but when the noise stopped, the worrying started. Were the Germans about to set off an explosion? Whenever they did, the ground would rock as if in a violent earthquake. Soldiers in the nearby trenches referred to the experience as 'joyriding'.

One of the miners with the New Zealand Tunnelling Company was Jim Williamson, a tough forty-two-year-old from Auckland. The New Zealanders had arrived in France on 9 March, 1916, and quickly won a name for their skill and hard work. Within five days they had relieved the French 7/1 Company Territorial Engineers in the galleries east of the Lille road, under the southern slopes of Vimy Ridge. But according to Jim Williamson, who in 1948 wrote a humorous account of his adventures underground, the New Zealanders also became known for their disrespectful attitude towards authority – especially British authority. One English officer asked Williamson to take him along a gallery nearly forty feet below the surface, to inspect the New Zealanders' progress:

> Lofty and a chap named Collins were working it and Leith was filling the sandbags. I took the officer down and, getting to the face, Lofty was picking in hard ground. The officer said, 'Do you think Fritz can hear you?' Quick as lightning came the reply from Lofty: 'They'll have to be bloody fucking deaf if they can't.' That satisfied the officer that it was no place for him and he left straight away, saying, 'Fearful language your men use.' He didn't ask to go down again.[1]

Happily, the enemy did not discover Williamson and his team, who shortly afterwards succeeded in blowing their first mine under the German trenches.

Indeed, the Allied tunnellers soon began to gain the upper hand.

[1] Williamson papers, Imperial War Museum.

By the middle of May, 1916, the Germans were smarting from the heavy losses they suffered as a result of mine explosions. Then, on 21 May, they launched a day-long artillery barrage which caused havoc in the British positions and followed it up that evening with a ferocious assault. Attacking on a 2,000-yard front, they captured the British front line and support trenches, and dug in to await the expected counter-attack. It duly came two days later when General Sir Henry Wilson launched his IV Corps against the new enemy positions. But the attack was a failure; over 2,500 casualties were incurred in the three days' fighting. Wilson immediately made arrangements for another attack, but this was shelved by Sir Douglas Haig, already committed to his plans for the Somme campaign. The next attempt to capture Vimy Ridge would have to wait until the spring of 1917.

Up on the ridge the Germans spent the winter nervously expecting another attack at any time. While continuing to shell Arras, they stepped up their efforts to strengthen the defences behind the ridge and to the south, to coincide with the completion of the *Siegfried Stellung*.

The terrain was to the Germans' advantage. One key village in German possession was Monchy-le-Preux, three miles behind the German front line and completely dominating the central battlefront. Standing on a high plateau, with its odd, sentinel-like church spire surrounded by a tight cluster of red-brick houses, Monchy appeared safe, serene and remote. To the north-west it was protected by two natural barriers, first Orange Hill and then Observation Ridge, and between the two lay a deep depression which the Germans called *Artillerie Mulde* – 'Battery Valley' to the British. From this sheltered spot, German batteries lobbed shell after shell into Arras.

Another village in German hands, and even more of a natural fortress, was Roeux. High on the wooded northern bank of the River Scarpe, standing over a system of deep caves, Roeux was protected on its southern flank by the river and its lakes and marshes, while to the north the embankment of the Arras–Douai railway provided a man-made barrier. But the Germans were not content to rely on natural defences alone. Cleverly concealed amid the outbuildings of an old château, they had built one of the largest concrete *mebus* (blockhouses) yet seen on the Western Front. Moreover, near the railway station, a derelict dye factory had been fortified and connected to the château blockhouse by tunnels. This jumble of old vathouses, engine sheds and chimney stacks – the Chemical Works,

22

as it was known, soon to become all too familiar to British soldiers – overlooked an open plain to the west; evidently fearing attack from this direction the defenders further dug deep trenches in two small copses, Roeux Wood and Mount Pleasant Wood. And on Balloon Hill (Greenland Hill to the British) they raised several observation balloons.

To the south of Monchy, German defences were concentrated in a redoubt called Hubert's Farm, or Cavalry Farm, overlooking the shallow valley of Cojeul Brook and the little hamlet of Guémappe; in an old windmill known as Fasbender Tower, near Wancourt, dominating the high ridge to the south from where the defenders could observe every inch of land towards Monchy; and in Fontaine-les-Croisilles and Bullecourt, two villages that the Germans now turned into bastions of the *Siegfried Stellung*.

But the Germans did not have it all their own way. Straddling the front line to the south-east of Arras was the old health spa of Neuville Vitasse, separated from the British lines only by level ground. Looking across the new no-man's-land from their positions in Beaurains, recently destroyed and abandoned by the Germans, the British could clearly see the village, protected by thickets of barbed wire and a blockhouse known as Neuville Mill, built under an old windmill. While held at bay further north, the British artillery released their frustration on this one exposed village in the enemy line. Their orders soon amounted to an adage: 'If in doubt, strafe Neuville Vitasse.'

When General Sir Edmund Allenby's controversial plan of attack for the Arras offensive arrived at GHQ in early February, 1917, it caused nothing short of uproar. But then Allenby was a controversial soldier and often caused uproar. Claiming to be a direct descendant of Oliver Cromwell, he was known throughout the British Army as 'The Bull'. A balding, square-jawed six-footer who sported a military pedigree every bit as good as Haig's, he terrorized generals and colonels alike with his bursts of temper; Allenby was unable to suffer fools gladly. Lord Wavell, who served under Allenby, described him thus: 'His manner was often gruff and abrupt; his questions were straight and sharp; and he demanded an immediate and direct reply. Any attempt at prevarication and indefiniteness, even hesitation, might provoke a sudden explosion of anger that could shake the hardest.'[2]

Back in 1916, on the opening day of the Battle of the Somme, Allenby's Third Army had been given the unenviable task of launching a diversionary attack against the powerful fortress village of

[2] *Allenby, Soldier and Statesman*, Wavell, p. 166.

Gommecourt. Allenby's ambitious plan of using two territorial divisions, the 56th (London) and the 46th (North Midland), to encircle and cut off the village had failed. Rumours in the lower echelons of the British Army had spread rapidly, to the effect that 'Allenby had fallen out of favour with Haig because of his failure to capture Gommecourt on 1 July,' as Trooper Charles V. Taylor of the South Irish Horse later wrote. 'We all respected [Allenby],' Taylor added, 'but the rumour soon went around that he was finished and would be sent home.' Contrary to popular gossip, however, Haig retained his confidence in Allenby, placing the responsibility for the Arras offensive on his broad shoulders.

This time Allenby was determined that his plan should not fail – but he needed to get his ideas over to Haig. Brigadier-General John Charteris made this observation:

> Allenby shares one peculiarity with Douglas Haig, he cannot explain verbally, with any lucidity at all, what his plans are. In a conference between the two of them it is rather amusing. D.H. hardly ever finishes a sentence, and Allenby's sentences, although finished, do not really convey exactly what he means. Yet they understand one another perfectly; but as each of their particular staff only understand their immediate superior a good deal of explanation of details has to be gone into afterwards and cleared up.[3]

Allenby had built up a loyal and extremely efficient Staff, who had worked ceaselessly through the winter months to prepare a worthy plan for him to put before his Commander-in-Chief. It was basically a simple plan, but it introduced some refreshingly new, if somewhat controversial, ideas. Working on Allenby's well-known saying, 'The principles of war are eternal, but there are no rigid rules for their application,' the planners carefully incorporated an element of surprise.

The offensive would begin with an intense artillery bombardment of continuous rapid fire, lasting forty-eight hours. This would be possible, according to Allenby's Commander of Artillery, Major-General E. A. E. Holland, if a strict rota system was imposed on the respective gun teams. The bombardment would then be followed by a powerful infantry thrust which, for the first time, would include supporting infantry divisions to 'leapfrog' through the central assault divisions, thereby maintaining the momentum of penetration deep

[3] *At GHQ*, Charteris, p. 210.

into enemy lines. Meanwhile, General Sir Henry Horne's First Army, which included four Canadian divisions, would assault Vimy Ridge, and elements of the Fourth and Fifth Armies would support the main attack by attacking the right flank. The main objective was to take Monchy-le-Preux by nightfall on the first day.

But the very thought of launching such an offensive against the strongest positions yet prepared by the enemy on the Western Front after a mere forty-eight hours' bombardment caused many Staff officers at GHQ to choke on their port. As the Official History comments, 'Nothing of the sort had been projected by the British Armies since warfare on the Western Front had assumed its present complexion.'[4] GHQ considered that Allenby's plan was impossible; the massive preparations and short barrage would without doubt reveal the attack to the enemy. Haig himself, after studying the plan, considered that the continuous rapid-fire bombardment would put both the guns and their crews under too great a strain.

Disappointed at the reaction from GHQ, Allenby argued that he had conducted experiments in rapid fire and was totally confident that his plan would succeed. Neither side would back down; at one stage it looked as if the forceful Allenby would have to be removed from his command. To avoid this embarrassment, GHQ found a sly way to bring him to heel. Major-General Holland was conveniently promoted and removed from the scene, and in his place Allenby was given an artillery commander of more orthodox views. He was now obliged to take the advice of the new man and thus was forced to lengthen the barrage from two days to four (an extra day was added later).

The enemy withdrawal to the Hindenburg Line, however, had caught the Allies napping and spoilt their careful plans for the new offensive. The area in front of the Fourth and Fifth Armies had been turned into a wilderness; therefore the scale of their assistance to the main attack had been practically negated. The situation had also changed on the Third Army's right flank, where an exceptionally strong section of the Hindenburg Line now faced the attacking troops. After a hurried reorganization of Allenby's plan, it was finally decided that the infantry attack would go in on 8 April, 1917 – later changed to 9 April, Easter Monday, at the request of Nivelle who was not ready.

The Third Army attack was to be launched on a front of almost ten miles, using ten infantry divisions to make the initial assault with two

---

[4] Official History, p. 177.

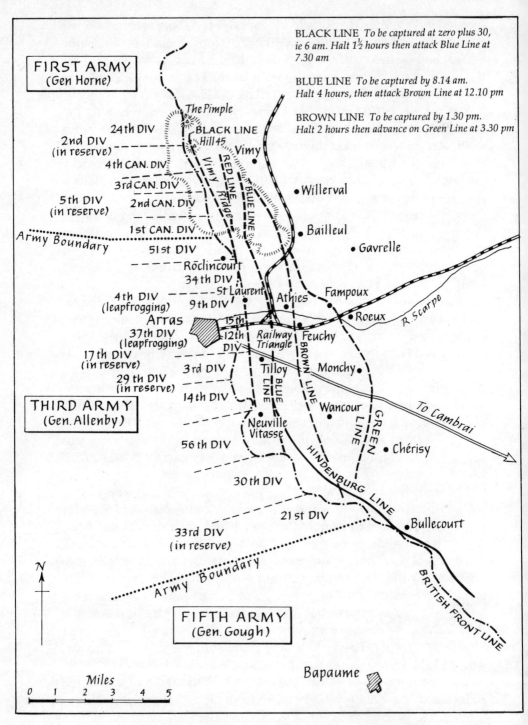

FIRST ARMY
(Gen Horne)

BLACK LINE *To be captured at zero plus 30,
ie 6 am. Halt 1½ hours then attack Blue Line at
7.30 am*

BLUE LINE *To be captured by 8.14 am.
Halt 4 hours, then attack Brown Line at 12.10 pm*

BROWN LINE *To be captured by 1.30 pm.
Halt 2 hours then advance on Green Line at 3.30 pm*

The Pimple
24th DIV
2nd DIV
(in reserve)
BLACK LINE
Hill 45
4th CAN. DIV
Vimy
3rd CAN. DIV
5th DIV
(in reserve)
2nd CAN. DIV
Willerval
1st CAN. DIV
Bailleul
Army Boundary
51st DIV
Gavrelle
Roclincourt
34th DIV
4th DIV
(leapfrogging)
St Laurent
Athies
Fampoux
9th DIV
Arras
15th
Roeux
R. Scarpe
37th DIV
(leapfrogging)
12th
DIV
Railway
Triangle
Feuchy
17th DIV
(in reserve)
3rd DIV
Tilloy
Monchy
29th DIV
(in reserve)
14th DIV
Wancourt
THIRD ARMY
(Gen. Allenby)
Neuville
Vitasse
56th DIV
Chérisy
30th DIV
HINDENBURG LINE
To Cambrai
21st DIV
33rd DIV
(in reserve)
Bullecourt
Army Boundary
BRITISH FRONT LINE
FIFTH ARMY
(Gen. Gough)

N

Bapaume

Miles
0 1 2 3 4 5

2. THE INFANTRY ATTACK PLAN, 9 APRIL, 1917.

in reserve (see infantry attack plan, opposite). The intention was to break through the enemy's defences between Croisilles in the south and Farbus in the north, thereby taking the Hindenburg Line 'in flank and rear', and then to press on towards Cambrai. The day of the attack was to be known as 'Z-Day' and was to be preceded by four days of bombardment. The consecutive lines of German trenches to be captured were given code names: the first was the Black Line, the second the Blue Line and the third the Brown Line. Each line was due to be taken by a set time, followed by a pause to allow time for consolidation and for organizing the next stage of the advance. It was hoped that Monchy-le-Preux would be captured on the first day, and the Monchy line was code-named the Green Line. The Cavalry Corps, consisting of three divisions, was to be ready to exploit success and burst out through the gap created by the infantry.

Of the twelve infantry divisions involved, all had seen much action on the Somme. Three of the divisions were Scottish – the 51st (Highland) Territorial and the 9th and 15th Divisions – which, with a scattering of Scottish battalions throughout some of the other divisions, meant that over one third of the troops attacking on Z-Day would be Scottish.

To safeguard the Third Army's northern flank, it was vital to capture Vimy Ridge. This task fell to the four Canadian divisions of the First Army, assisted by the 13th (British) Brigade and the 24th (British) Division. Their assault was timed to start simultaneously with the Third Army offensive: at 5.30 a.m. on Z-Day. If all went according to plan, elements of the 4th (Canadian) and 24th (British) Divisions would then secure a little wooded knoll dubbed 'The Pimple', to the north of Vimy Ridge and dominating the valley of the River Souchez, together with a small wood called Bois-en-Hache.

In command of the 'Canadian Corps' was Lieutenant-General Sir Julian 'Bungo' Byng, a stocky, sad-eyed, English cavalry officer of fifty-four. Byng's preparations for the capture of Vimy Ridge had been most thorough. Assisted by an all-British staff, he had drawn up a water-tight plan to deliver his men to their jumping-off trenches: he was going to send them through the subterranean network of tunnels.

Back in October, 1916, an ancient system of large underground caves had been discovered below Ronville and St Sauveur, the south-eastern suburbs of Arras. It was thought that they, like the tunnels up on Vimy Ridge, had been formed by the removal of chalk for building work in the Middle Ages. Again like Vimy Ridge, these caves had rapidly been exploited by the British Army.

The caves alone, when properly levelled off and cleared, were able to accommodate 11,500 men. Further large caves and cellars were found beneath the centre of Arras, under the two squares called Petite Place and Grande Place, capable of housing 13,000 men. Someone immediately had the idea of connecting all these caves, and a plan was drawn up to link them; via the Crinchon Sewer, eight feet high and six feet wide, the central caves would be connected to two long tunnels extending south-east through the caves under St Sauveur and Ronville. The aim was to drive the tunnels out into no-man's-land, where British troops could launch an attack on the enemy through concealed exits. It was an ambitious scheme. Could the work be done before the Arras offensive began?

Major Jack Durgan, commanding the New Zealand Tunnelling Company, was summoned. He in turn called for the advice of one of his most experienced miners, Sapper Jim Williamson, MM:

> What the Major wanted was for me to give him my opinion as to whether the Tunnelling Company could connect them all up by the beginning of April. Going through the plans and estimating the footage to be driven, and other parts of the scheme, I considered that we could do it in time. But I advised him, if it were possible, to get some more reinforcements. I thought some of the men were a bit worn out and new blood would make all the difference.[5]

Major Durgan agreed. He promptly submitted a request to Third Army HQ for extra men, and work on the Arras subways began on 10 October, 1916. The new men soon arrived, but, much to the surprise of the brawny New Zealanders, they were from a Leeds 'Bantam Battalion', the 17th West Yorks, part of the 35th (Bantam) Division. The diminutive Bantams were just as surprised by the New Zealanders, whom Private Chas Rowland described as 'big beggars who worked like hell . . . digging big tunnels too'. Private Rowland remembered how

> We had just come out of the front line to the reserve trenches, hoping for a sleep and perhaps some hot food, when a call came from HQ asking for volunteers for a hush-hush job – but this was limited to ex-miners. One incentive was added, that there would be double rations. Who could miss an opportunity like this? . . . All of a sudden the whole platoon, in fact I think the whole company, became ex-miners – until pay books were produced stating your civilian work. That put paid to it.

[5] Williamson papers, Imperial War Museum.

But the New Zealanders and Bantams soon took to each other and shed much honest sweat together, the former cutting the tunnels while the latter performed fatigue duties, assisting with the heavy task of removing the spoil.

The work was gruelling, and not infrequently dangerous. As the New Zealanders broke into caverns that had been abandoned hundred of years before, the roofs sometimes collapsed on the tunnellers. But their progress was remarkable. On 6 November Captain Vickerman recorded in the War Diary that the New Zealanders had completed 268 feet and 3 inches that day alone; 'total footage for week . . . 1,742 feet. This I feel safe in saying is a record for the British Army.'[6]

Not only did the tunnels have to be dug, but some of them also had to be laid with tram lines for hand-drawn bogies which would be wheeled right up to enemy lines. And even more important: the miners had to prepare the exits. As these could not be completed without giving the game away, the miners hit on a clever scheme to bore a series of holes and fill them with ammonal, ready for exploding when the time came. In Sapper Jim Williamson's words:

> The holes, starting twelve or fourteen feet below the surface, were gradually bored upwards till they got within four or five feet of the surface. When exploded and cleared out, they left a trench for the infantry to walk right through the German front line.

But that was still many weeks away.

In December, 1916, Jim Williamson was working on the all-important Crinchon Sewer, linking the tunnels with the vast medieval caves – some over sixty feet square and twenty feet high. He came across several dates scratched into the chalk by miners of a bygone age: 'One date I remember was 1314. I thought of something that had happened in our own history on that date.' That same month, Williamson recorded, an unofficial work-to-rule was staged by the New Zealanders on behalf of their colleagues, the Bantam fatigue men:

> On our night shift, 11 to 7, the Bantams would be brought up to our shaft at about 7 o'clock and have to wait in the cold there until 11. Of course, the officer who brought them up would go away and have a pleasant evening. The Bantams had no

[6] PRO WO95/407.

evening meal and no crib (tucker) for their 1 o'clock snack, so
of course we had to share with them. We were very short of
rations ourselves, so we all got together and decided to lessen
our footage until the Tommies got better conditions.

Major Durgan quickly noticed the drop in progress and sent for
Williamson to ask what was going on. Williamson duly explained and
found the Major sympathetic:

He evidently had a straight talk with some high official, for the
next week the Tommies arrived at 10.30 p.m., had had tea, and
each one had a small snack. They thought the world of the
tunnellers after that.

On another occasion, too, Major Durgan seems to have proved his
sympathy for his miners. The New Zealanders had little time for
tiresome regulations, such as saluting an officer, and, again according
to Jim Williamson:

I believe a complaint came in from General Allenby that we
weren't saluting officers. Durgan is said to have asked Allenby
whether he wanted discipline or work, telling him that if he
insisted on saluting the footage would drop and the caves would
not be ready in time. Allenby gave in.

Throughout that winter the tunnelling work went on, until a
veritable maze of subways took shape beneath Arras. Entrance to
this subterranean network was through manholes in different parts of
the town. The main entrance to the sewer tunnels was in the yard of
the French barracks; other entrances were in the basement of the
shattered town hall, the Hôtel de Ville, and down a 100-feet shaft in
front of Arras railway station. Eventually it would be possible to
walk, in complete safety from shelling, right up to the front line. But,
in spite of comprehensive maps, men still managed to get lost in the
tunnels. One day Captain L. Gameson of the Royal Army Medical
Corps, attached to the 71st Infantry Brigade, found himself in a
'hideously narrow dark passage' and realized he was lost:

Happening upon another solitary troglodyte, an Australian
[New Zealand] tunneller, I asked him the way. He told me the
way, and I said that I thought he was wrong. He was a good
chap; grinning, he drawled, 'Well, I guess you oughter know. I
only made the bloody tunnel!'[7]

[7] Gameson papers, Imperial War Museum.

In early January, 1917, work began on the installation of an electric light system, powered by five engines and dynamo sets erected in the Ronville powerhouse. Six weeks later, all the central tunnels had been connected and one major tunnel had been completed, the Port-de-Fer, measuring ten feet in diameter, which had been part of the town's old fortifications. A sixty-centimetre railway track had been laid through the Ronville Tunnel. But by now the Germans were growing suspicious. On 15 March they launched a raid which blew the entrance to one of the tunnels. Luckily the damage was slight, but a few days later there was a potentially more serious sequel. A British heavy mortar shell exploded halfway across no-man's-land, causing a roof-fall in one tunnel that was still under construction. Seven men were trapped in a tiny area: three New Zealanders, three Bantams and Second-Lieutenant Rutherford. However, the air pipe had not been severed and it was soon established that the men were still alive. In just nine hours their comrades managed to dig a 'rabbit hole', a small gallery measuring just two feet by two feet six, bypassing the roof-fall and extending fifty feet. Their frantic efforts paid off, and the entombed men were finally released.

Soon the tunnellers were putting the finishing touches to their work. On 3 April the lighting system was completed and switched on and, for a rehearsal, a battalion of infantry was successfully passed through the St Sauveur tunnel from the cellars under the Grande Place. All that remained to do was to blow the exits into no-man's-land just before zero hour. On 5 April Lieutenant-General A. Haldane of VI Corps wired the following message to Allenby:

> I wish to bring to the Army Commanders' notice the excellent work done by the New Zealand Engineers Tunnelling Company . . . First under Major Durgan and now under Captain Vickerman, the work of the Company has been excellent. Not only have the men worked extremely hard and well, but the excellent relations that have been maintained with the various divisions shows a first-class organization.[8]

The underground tunnels of Arras were complete. In total the network comprised 10,901 yards of subways. Designed as a protective system of tunnels, it clearly fulfilled its purpose: between 5 and 11 April, through one subway alone, it was later estimated that the traffic amounted to an amazing 9,700 men. It was a unique engineering achievement and, in the history of the British Army, never

[8] PRO WO95/407.

equalled before or since in the field of protective tunnelling on the scale accomplished at Arras and Vimy Ridge.

As work was completed below ground to conceal a strike force of 25,000 British soldiers, the massive preparations above ground were no less hectic. 'Arras was just one great ant-heap,' Corporal Tom Bracey recalled later. 'I'd never seen so many bleedin' troops.' On the Third Army front alone, some 4,000 Nissen huts had been erected, and with so many thousands of soldiers now concentrated into such a small area, many of the frost-damaged roads had to undergo hasty repairs. However, the rail transport situation had improved as a result of the Calais Conference, and out of the 659 trains requested for conveyance of munitions, a creditable 463 were supplied between 17 March and Z-Day. In fact, the artillery now had all the ammunition they required, and great munitions dumps were set up on the outskirts of town to hold the surplus until required.

A massive weight of artillery fire was to be concentrated on the German defences on Vimy Ridge, smashing the tunnel entrances, cracking concrete pill-boxes and collapsing dugouts. The Canadian troops were amazed at the vast collection of artillery pieces being assembled behind their lines. To support the Vimy attack, 245 heavy guns had been positioned to the west of Arras, in the Scarpe valley. In addition, 132 extra heavy guns of I Corps were arranged on the northern slopes of the Souchez valley and 720 medium guns of the Royal Field Artillery were dug in forward – one medium artillery gun for every ten yards of frontage, compared with one in twenty on the opening day of the Somme. In total 1,097 'big guns' were ready to pave the way for the Canadian infantry, the preliminary bombardment being due to start on 20 March.[9]

Altogether, on the Third Army front, a total of 1,720 heavy and medium guns, one to every twelve yards, were ready to blast the German front line. When the infantry attack began, a creeping barrage of shrapnel and high explosive was to be fired by eighteen-pounder guns, following an elaborate fire plan with each gun firing two rounds a minute. A dense curtain of fire would thus precede the advancing infantry, lifting every hundred yards at four-minute intervals, to ensure that it was safely ahead of the troops. This main bombardment was due to start at 6.30 a.m. on 4 April. Supported by thousands of light, medium and heavy trench mortars together with harassing heavy machine-gun barrages, it would be the greatest artillery bombardment the world had ever seen.

[9] Figures taken from Official History.

There was one small doubt, however, concerning the efficacy of this artillery attack. Some of the gun-crews had been issued with shells featuring the new 106 fuse, which was designed to explode the shell on immediate contact rather than when it had buried itself in the ground; these shells, it was hoped, would cut through barbed wire more efficiently. But several accidents had been caused by the new shells. Apart from the gunners' lack of experience in their use, the shell sometimes 'wobbled' in a gun's worn-out barrel – with terrible results. Gunner George Goodbody, of 133 Siege Battery, Royal Garrison Artillery, remembered seeing one gun that had been destroyed in this manner: 'It was ghastly,' he said, 'the barrel split like a half-peeled banana and all or most of the crew killed.'

In addition to the artillery fire and due to start at the same time, the British planned to launch a massive gas bombardment. Here again they were using a new weapon, the Livens Projector, which was merely a hollow iron tube, sealed at one end and attached to a small baseplate. The whole tube was buried up to its neck in the ground, in batteries of twenty-five, and pre-set at an angle in order to lob a hollow metal bottle containing 30 lb of liquid phosgene gas into enemy lines. The projectors, loaded with an explosive charge at the bottom of the tube, were electrically fired simultaneously and when each metal bottle landed a small charge of TNT split it open to release the deadly contents. Depending on the size of the explosive charge in the tube, it was possible to obtain ranges of up to a mile; but because of the inaccuracy of the weapon, the targets selected to be saturated with gas were villages and valleys honeycombed with dugouts. The Third Army had 2,340 projectors in all, ready to lob over 50 tons of gas into the enemy's positions.

Sometimes the Livens Projectors were used to launch bombs of 'liquid fire', according to Sapper James Greenwood of the Special Brigade, Royal Engineers, 'the bombs being filled with a highly inflammable liquid, such as petrol mixed with oil, which was ignited and spread about when the bombs burst – not unlike napalm.' Whatever their contents, the effect of these Livens bombs was soon being felt by the enemy. On 8 April, 1917, one unknown German sergeant of the 8th Reserve Infantry Regiment noted in his diary, later found by British troops, that this was the fourth consecutive day on which gas shells had landed on his regiment's positions:

One officer has already died and several are very ill. The sad point is that the English gas is almost odourless and can only be seen by the practised eye on escaping from the shell. The gas

steals steadily over the ground in a bluish haze and kills
everyone who does not draw his mask over his face as quick as
lightning before taking a breath. The prospects look terrible.
Our people say that things weren't as bad at Verdun as here.[10]

Yet another new weapon of war was the tank. The Heavy Branch
of the Machine Gun Corps (later the Royal Tank Corps) already had
some experience of them, as forty-nine tanks had been used – for the
first time in history – during the Battle of the Somme on 15 September, 1916. There they had achieved little, apart from frightening
the enemy and assisting in the capture of some insignificant strongpoints. This was mainly due to understandable lack of experience in
their use, but also because there had been too few of them (only
thirty-two actually reached their starting point). However, Sir Douglas Haig expected great things from the tank and had made urgent
requests for production to be stepped up. Unfortunately a serious
hiccup in tank production ensued and six months later, despite Haig's
requests, only sixty tanks were available for the Arras offensive.
Forty of these were allotted to Third Army, twelve to Fifth Army and
eight to the 2nd Canadian Division to assist in the capture of Vimy
Ridge.

Almost all the tanks were Mark 1 and 2 machines, repaired after
use on the Somme but still mechanically unreliable. In particular they
suffered from a design defect which placed the radiator inside the
vehicle; that, coupled with a poor fan belt, caused the temperature
inside the machines to rise well above comfortable levels. The tank
crews, largely volunteers selected from the infantry, were forced to
suffer the most terrible working conditions. Apart from the heat
problem they were nearly suffocated by carbon monoxide fumes and
the noise from the engine rendered even a shout inaudible. The
maximum speed of these ungainly ironclads was just over four miles
an hour – considerably reduced while crossing a cratered battlefield,
when the tanks were usually left behind by the infantry.

Following preliminary reconnoitring of possible objectives for the
tanks, advance parties of the HBMGC arrived in the Arras area on 10
March. Suitable locations were found for the 'tankdromes' and
construction work soon began. Battalion workshops and personnel
moved up on the 20th and, ten days later, the tanks themselves. With
six supply dumps established, the crews now started loading their
machines, six-pounder ammunition on the 'male' tanks and machine-
gun ammunition on the 'females'. The problem was where to store it

10 PRO WO157/151.

34

all. Cans of water for the engine cooling system, tins of petrol and oil were essential, but space also had to be found for rations, flares and – much to the consternation of the crews – a box of dynamite which had to be stored on each tank, to destroy it if it looked like falling into enemy hands. And that wasn't all: each tank had to carry a pigeon basket and four carrier pigeons, the only reliable means of communication in those days, before radio 'walkie-talkies' were invented and when telephone lines were cut by shellfire.

There are few references to the Carrier Pigeon section of the Royal Engineers in books on the First World War and yet the contribution made by this unit to front-line communications was immeasurable. The Officer Commanding this unique little branch of the army was Captain Alec Waley, a racing pigeon enthusiast whose expertise was to prove invaluable and who spent many hours, prior to the battle, lecturing infantry and tank crews in the use of the pigeon as a means of communication. Large lofts were placed in the Arras *gendarmerie* and over thirty mobile lofts – converted double-decker buses, painted black and white in the mistaken assumption that the pigeons would see them more easily – were brought up to the battle area. Over 24,000 valuable winged messengers were trained and made ready for use on the Third Army front. Meanwhile, the Germans were also relying on pigeon communications; occasionally a 'hostile' bird flew into one of the British lofts, immediately recognized for what it was because the Germans dyed their birds bright red.

More so than pigeons, the most important inhabitants of the Arras skies during this crucial period were the men of the Royal Flying Corps, for supremacy in the air was vital if victory was to be achieved. But the RFC faced a daunting challenge. The Germans by this time had reorganized and re-equipped themselves with the fast new Albatross DIII fighter, the 'V' strutter, whereas the RFC was still saddled with obsolete aircraft that had barely been able to hold their own against the Fokker monoplane back in 1915. Now, on the First and Third Army fronts, there were twenty-five British squadrons with 365 serviceable aircraft, a third of which were single-seater fighters, mainly DH2s and FE2bs – 'pusher' types, where the pilot sits in front of the engine. Their main task was to defend the hopelessly slow and cumbersome two-seater BE2c spotter planes. Altogether, on the First, Third, Fourth and Fifth Army fronts, by 9 April there was a total of 754 British planes, including 385 fighters. By contrast the Germans had 264, of which 114 were fighters. But while the British had numerical superiority, the Germans enjoyed the advantages of quality – and not just in the machines themselves, for on the whole the Germans possessed much better pilots. Due to heavy British losses in February and March, the demand for new pilots for the Royal Flying Corps and Royal Naval Air Service resulted in men being pitched into aerial combat with as little as ten hours' solo flying experience, and often with no experience at all of the particular planes at their new squadron.

Major-General Hugh ('Boom') Trenchard, commanding the RFC, insisted right from the start on an aggressive flying policy to support the Arras battle. He knew, however, that his young flyers, some of them mere boys fresh out of school, would suffer accordingly when they came up against the skilled and aggressive enemy pilots. The average flying life of an RFC pilot in April, 1917, was officially calculated at seventeen and a half hours. It was with sublime courage, therefore, that the crews of the shaky observation machines went about their daily patrols, weather permitting, over enemy lines. In temperatures well below freezing and often reduced to a snail's pace against face-chafing headwinds, the boy pilots held their flimsy planes on a straight course, while the observers loaded and re-loaded the cameras, photographing enemy trenches, strongpoints and battery positions – often given away by muzzle flash. These photographs, which were of priceless value to the artillery, were used to produce over 50,000 excellent trench maps for use by the attacking infantry.

The arrival of Germany's crack air-ace, Baron Manfred von Richthofen and his famous 'Flying Circus' on the Arras front was bad news for the RFC. With a highly skilled team of pilots, who decorated their planes in a variety of bright colours (Richthofen's was all red), they tore into the formations of RFC planes and shot them from the sky. Between 4 and 8 April, 1917, seventy-five British aircraft were shot down, twenty-eight on Easter Sunday alone, with the loss of 105 aircrew killed, wounded or missing; and in the same period, fifty-six British planes were accidently crashed by inexperienced pilots. This dismal time was forever known in the RFC, later the RAF, as 'Bloody April'.

To counter the Red Baron's mastery of the air a special 'Anti-Richthofen' squadron had been formed back in February – No. 56 Squadron, at London Colney, in Hertfordshire. They arrived in France in the first week of April. The squadron's leading pilot was Captain Albert Ball, and, with the squadron equipped with the new SE5 fighters, these hand-picked young pilots were ready to take on Germany's best.

The daily air battles soon became a familiar sight to the troops of both sides, but they were not always one-sided, the British sometimes gaining the upper hand through sheer tenacity. With an audience larger than the biggest cup final crowd, the antagonists fought out their grisly encounters like gladiators in the arena of the sky, cheered on by thousands of up-turned heads with ears tuned to the faint crackle of machine guns. One battle in particular made a vivid impression on Sub-Lieutenant Tom Lawrie, of Howe Battalion, Royal Naval Division:

> Two of our spotter planes were overhead when out of the blue
> sky arrived a Fokker. The spotters were pretty helpless and
> they tried to make off. Alas, one was shot down and in the
> course of the machine coming to pieces, the pilot fell apart from
> the wreckage. All eyes on the ground were rivetted on the
> events above when seemingly out of nowhere, the other British
> plane arrived and swooped down, missing the body of the
> hapless airman. Again it swooped down, obviously trying to
> catch the falling pilot on one of the wings in the outside chance
> of perhaps saving his life. The excitement among the troops was
> terrific, their shouts of encouragement might have been heard
> in Berlin! Alas the attempt failed but it was certainly
> spectacular.

A similar tragedy was witnessed on Easter Sunday by Musketier Herman Keyser, of the 84th Reserve Regiment, who had been enjoying a stroll with one of his comrades:

> The weather was clear and soon there were planes about. We
> saw the usual dog-fight which regularly happened in the
> afternoon and saw an English plane fall out of the sky, and then
> another one which somersaulted over and over before hitting
> the ground about a kilometre away . . . Unfortunately it was
> one of ours, with the well-known Leutnant Frankl, with his
> 'Pour le Merite' (Blue Max) and Iron Cross, 1st and 2nd Class
> on his chest, lying still in front of us.[11] Solemnly we went back
> to the village.

Another dog-fight, over Arras itself in March 1917, was later recalled by Private Arthur Betteridge of the 4th South African Scottish Battalion:

> One German aircraft, a Halberstadt, was shot down in flames,
> the pilot jumped and his body hit the main cobbled road. The
> aircraft pieces fell over a wide area half a mile away. The

[11] Leutnant W. Frankl had been awarded the 'Pour le Merite' on 12 August, 1916, and was credited with nineteen victories. He was killed in action on 8 April, 1917.

German pilot was fully dressed in flying kit but his boots had come off in his descent. The cobblestones where he fell were pushed at least an inch lower than the others.

Such horrors were to become increasingly common, with daring young men on both sides meeting sudden and violent death, as the Battle of Arras began.

3

The Men

Vimy Ridge was held by the new *Gruppe Vimy*, led by General Ritter von Fasbender, which consisted of the 79th (Prussian) Reserve Division, the 1st Bavarian Reserve Division and, newly arrived from the Somme, the 14th Bavarian Division. His area of command stretched from the highest point of the ridge (the northern tip held by the 16th Bavarian Division of *Gruppe Souchez*) to a point just north of the River Scarpe. Here was a force to be reckoned with – for the Bavarian troops were highly respected by the British soldiers.

Von Fasbender knew the ridge like the back of his hand and, moreover, had every confidence in his battle-seasoned troops, the majority of whom had been there since its capture and had ruthlessly hammered both French and English in defence of the ridge. However, von Fasbender had recently been ordered, in accordance with General Ludendorff's new theories on 'elastic' defensive methods, to redistribute his garrison on the ridge. Instead of two battalions of each front-line regiment, now only one would hold the front trenches, the other being distributed in fortified positions in the centre and rear of the battle zone. Furthermore, the reserve battalions, instead of being in the centre of the battle zone, were to be moved back a mile or so behind it. Reorganizing a solid defence that previously had held up well caused von Fasbender serious misgivings, compounded by the new aggression in evidence from the opposing Canadian troops. The persistent harassment could only mean one thing: the Canadians were going to try to take the ridge.

South of the Scarpe to Bullecourt, four divisions formed *Gruppe Arras* under the command of Lieutenant-General Dieffenbach. These two groups were part of the Sixth Army and the officer in overall command was General von Falkenhausen. It soon became common knowledge that there was going to be an offensive. This was confirmed by Field-Marshal Crown Prince Rupprecht, according to whom: 'Detailed information was obtained from a Canadian

39

prisoner, which left no doubt.'[1] Consequently, five divisions were placed behind the threatened front with the intention of rushing them up to counter-attack should the British break through (this number was increased to nine by the day of the attack).

An acute food shortage in Germany caused by the potato crop failure and the British naval blockade had given cause for grave concern among the war leaders. There were now serious doubts that Germany could win the war militarily; to save face, therefore, conditional peace proposals had been made to the Allies in December, 1916. But the Allies had responded with a stern rebuff. In answer to this, Germany had launched a policy of 'unrestricted submarine warfare' in an attempt to break the British stranglehold. The German Admiralty Staff calculated that they could bring Britain to her knees within six months; all shipping, whether hostile or neutral, would be indiscriminately sunk by roving U-boats. The risk that this would bring the USA into the war was irrelevant; at German High Command they merely shrugged their shoulders – was Germany not fighting half the world anyway? Even General Falkenhayn declared that this was 'the only remaining measure capable of saving the situation'.[2]

It seems self-evident that success for an infantry attack depended on each man having a sound knowledge of the task that lay in front of him. In the German Army, the NCOs almost always ensured that their men were fully briefed, but a justifiable grouse of British soldiers of the First World War was that they often had no idea what they were supposed to be doing or where they were going. The officers knew, and that was considered sufficient. Oliver Lyttelton, an officer in the Grenadier Guards, later commented:

> The more highly educated soldier of today must be given much
> more information than we used to give to our men: he must be
> told why he is ordered to do something. We did not do that. On
> the other hand it must be remembered that the men of 1914
> were often those swept into the Army by unemployment or
> starvation, the two press gangs of those days.[3]

He does not explain what was meant to happen to the men if their officer was killed.

In the Canadian and Australian battalions, officers were more

[1] *Mein Kriegstagebuch*, vol. 2 (1929), p. 127.
[2] Von Kurenberg, *The Kaiser* (p. 273).
[3] Viscount Chandos, *Memoirs* (p. 35).

Sergeant: Keep yer point up like yer doin' now, can't yer? You won't never get yer man If yer don't keep yer point up. Have yer never done no bayonet practice before?

Private (*just out of hospital, very bored*): I've done this 'ere to the bloomin' Bosches, I 'ave.

Sergeant: Oh, you 'ave, 'ave you? No wonder the war's lasted two and a 'alf years!

familiar with their men and often on first-name terms when off duty – a thing unheard of in British regiments. Consequently, there was a better sharing of knowledge. The rank and file trusted and respected their officers; and if an officer was wounded then everyone knew what was going on. Dominion troops often regarded the British with mild contempt. 'We called all English troops "Imperials" and I think they referred to us Canadians as "Colonials",' remembered Private Campbell C. King of the 44th (Manitoba) Battalion, who also noted their common expression of 'Hast thou a fag?' The attitude of the 'Colonials' sometimes caused trouble for the British, as reported by L. G. Plumridge, a private with the 1st Somerset Light Infantry:

> I was on guard duty with my pal when four Canadians came along. I asked them for their passes and the reply was 'Pass? Pass my bloody arse; we came over here to fight, not to be dominated by you imperial bastards,' and they pushed us aside and went through.

41

Despite the occasional friction, however, the Allied troops were united in their preparations for the assault on Vimy Ridge. The Canadians in particular were rehearsing hard. They had laid out a large training area behind the lines, on which – thanks to aerial photographs – whole sections of the German trench system were recreated, marked out in a field with tape, and the troops were issued with 40,000 trench maps indicating the various objectives. The 24th Battalion, according to Private Andy McCrindle, had to practise manoeuvres in the field 'about three or four times, until the tapes were obliterated by our muddy boots'. McCrindle was then picked to join the Rifle Grenadiers, who were issued with Mills hand grenades – not, however, for use in the normal fashion, but for launching from special attachments to their rifles which would propel them a greater distance. 'They gave us some training with live bombs,' McCrindle remarked, 'and so we had to be darn careful, but it was good to have the experience before the actual battle.'

'The work was hard and constant,' as the war diary of the 42nd (Royal Highland) Battalion recorded, but 'all ranks entered into the training with a cheerfulness and spirit that augured well for efficiency in results.'[4]

The Canadian divisions included a very high proportion of soldiers born in the UK, British immigration to Canada having reached record levels just before the war. The following enlistment figures were given by Brigadier-General James Mason to the Canadian Senate on 14 March 1916, (they apply to the Canadian Army on 15 February that year):[5]

Native-born Canadians	73,935	30%
British-born (in UK)	156,637	62%
Others	18,899	8%
Total	249,471	100%

Thus, by joining locally raised battalions, the men of British stock, while representing the New World, were still fighting for the mother country. The 'others' cited by Brigadier Mason included French-Canadians; despite anti-British feeling whipped up by Henri Bourassa, leader of the French nationalists in Quebec, the Canadian Army now fielded a French battalion – the 22nd Infantry Battalion, or 'Van Doos' as they were better known. In addition, the 'others' included Americans, over 9,000 of whom had crossed the border by

[4] PRO WO95/3898.
[5] J. Castell-Hopkins, *Canada at War, 1914–18* (p. 80).

January, 1917, in order to fight with the Canadian Army, as well as Russian, Italian and Greek immigrants – and, surprisingly, Japanese. Victor W. Wheeler, a sergeant with the 50th Battalion, later wrote of one Japanese-Canadian NCO, Sergeant Kaji, who sought special dispensation to go into battle carrying the traditional *katana* and *wakizashi* (respectively, sword and stiletto-type dagger) that his father had used in the Russo-Japanese War (1904–05). His wish was granted, but it didn't do him much good. One night he took part in a raid, and in Victor Wheeler's words:

> He was last seen by us mounting the parapet, proudly grasping his naked *katana*, flashing in the light of a bright half-moon, and his *wakizashi* swinging loosely from his web belt – heading across no-man's-land. The Japanese-Canadian Sergeant was never seen again.[6]

Also scattered throughout the Canadian ranks were many Red Indians, and while Sergeant Wheeler and his chums of the 50th Battalion were rehearsing for the forthcoming battle, one of their number was given special authority to pursue his skill as a sharp-shooter on Vimy Ridge. His name was Henry 'Ducky' Norwest, a Metis Cree Indian from the Buffalo Lake area, north-west of Red Deer, Alberta. Working independently and armed with a Ross rifle and telescopic sight, this legendary and much respected sniper was soon the terror of the Germans on the ridge. Concealed and expertly camouflaged, often in freezing weather, Norwest waited in no-man's-land for many hours with just his official observer to confirm his 'kills'. When a suitable target appeared he fired a single head-shot – and he never missed. He often found his chances when all heads were upturned, watching aerial combat. The Germans, aware of the menace caused by Norwest, brought up their best snipers in an attempt to kill him, but all efforts failed. Norwest outwitted and outshot them all.[7] The Army quickly realized the value of such men, whose sharpshooting activities raised their battalion's morale; but in contrast to the glory heaped on RFC aces such as Ball, Bishop and Mannock who became national heroes, their daring exploits were soon forgotten.

The green fields behind Arras echoed to the continuous crackle of

---

[6] Wheeler, *No Man's Land*, p. 122.
[7] Awarded the Military Medal and Bar, Private Henry Norwest's luck finally ran out when he was shot through the head by a German sniper whom he simultaneously killed, on 18 August, 1918, near Fouquescourt Crucifix Corner. He is buried in Warvillers churchyard extension near Amiens. His official record of 115 observed 'kills' was unmatched.

musketry as battalion after battalion struggled to improve their shooting skills. Over and over again, the infantry went through their paces in rehearsing for the great attack. At least it was a pleasant change from the front line, as Captain Robert d'A. G. Monypenny of the 2nd Essex recalled:

> Towards the end of March, 1917, our division, the 4th, was sent back for a long 'rest' and special training. Spring was coming now and so we marched away from the battle area and came back to civilization with green trees and fields amidst the delightful little untouched villages, nestling in the hills and valleys. We billeted each night in a different village and by day as we marched along the men's spirits seem to cheer up as they broke into song, singing all the latest catch songs. We finally settled ourselves in farm houses and barns halfway between Aixes-le-Château and St Pol. After a day or two clearing up and bathing, we got down to the serious matter of battle training which included tactical training and assault practice. For the latter a regular plan was made over the surrounding countryside to the exact formations, positions and defences of the German Army in front of Arras which we were to attack in one grand assault in the near future. The officers studied special maps issued to them and, more than once, the whole division advanced together in rehearsing its part. A line of runners in front, waving white flags, acted as the moving barrage. And so the pleasant days passed all too quickly and we gradually moved up to the front behind our objective. This was the biggest drive yet and the Divisional commander held a parade of all officers and gave us a final lecture, adding that the concentration of guns and ammunition was the heaviest yet made and to remember that all possible would be done to support us. We were given definite objectives which we were told we should be able to take easily, owing to the sheer weight of our attack, but the General added he hoped we would not stop there but keep on moving gradually for the Rhine!

Such stylish training practice was all very well in the safety of the rear, but life was a great deal more perilous at the front. For while the cheerful Captain Monypenny and his fellows were enjoying their 'special training', all along the First and Third Army front the soldiers were taking part in a grimmer kind of preparation: trench raids.

4

Trench Raids

The object of trench raids, carried out night and day, was to throw light on what sort of defences the Germans had prepared, to identify the enemy units opposite, to kill and capture as many Germans as possible and generally to wreak havoc in their lines. Large or small, trench raids were much hated by the soldiers. Larger raids were assisted by artillery, which rehearsed for the main attack by cutting lanes in the enemy wire, the raiders entering the enemy trenches as soon as the barrage lifted. More often than not, however, the forays into German lines were smaller affairs, usually at platoon strength. The men, faces blackened with burnt cork, would creep across no-man's-land in the darkness and silently cut through the enemy wire. Armed with a variety of weapons for close-quarter fighting, in addition to Mills bombs, revolvers and rifles, a variety of home-made 'persuaders' were often carried.

The Mills bombs alone were no match for the deep German dugouts; even after the explosion the defenders were still in fighting form, ready to shoot their way up the dugout steps and into the open. Therefore more drastic measures were devised. Phosphorus bombs, attached to gallon tins of petrol and 20 lb mobile charges of ammonal, usually in a square metal tin with Mills bomb fuses attached, would be lobbed down the dugout steps. Fire and suffocating smoke would immediately fill the dugout, while the ammonal charge blew in the entrance and collapsed it. After several unfortunate incidents when the raiders were buried by their own explosion, they learnt to lengthen the fuse. And, where ammonal charges were not available, Stokes mortar shells were used as grenades, sufficiently powerful to stun the Germans in the dugout and collapse the entrance. Yet even then, the raiders found extra effort was often needed, as Company Sergeant Major Albert G. Anderson, MC, DCM, of the 4th Gordon Highlanders later recalled:

> On one particular raid I was in, I managed to get the shoulder straps naming the regiment from one of the German sentries.

He refused to come back with us, so I had to put him out of
action with my dirk . . . It was the safest policy. Kill them all.

During another raid, on 7 April Second-Lieutenant T. B. Ashburner of the 1st South African Infantry found the Germans equally
reluctant to surrender. The raiders threw two Stokes shells down one
dugout and, Ashburner commented tersely, 'The explosion brought a
man's leg and a boot out.' Ashburner went on:

> I then saw another Boche run towards a dugout. I called upon
> him to surrender. He snatched up a bomb and attempted to
> throw it at my party. I shot him dead and he fell and rolled
> down the dugout. We put another shell down this dugout. I
> then heard the whistle to retire. After this we made our way
> back to our front line.[1]

Although Ashburner and his men returned safely, that same raid had
been a disaster for some of their fellow South Africans. While
crossing no-man's-land they were caught by the short firing of a
British gun. This was not uncommon, the gun barrels being so
overworked and worn; only the day before, an identical mishap
occurred involving the 27th Brigade, a neighbouring brigade of the
same division.

Commander of the 27th Brigade was Brigadier-General Frank
Maxwell, VC, DSO,[2] a brilliant soldier who had recently been
promoted and transferred to the 9th Division from the renowned 18th
Division, where he had commanded a Middlesex battalion on the
Somme. Totally fearless, Maxwell was never a general to command
from the rear and continually exposed himself to danger in the front
lines in order to find out first-hand what was going on. On 6 April,
Maxwell was right up front to watch a raid by some of his troops. As
he later reported:

> Under cover of a smoke barrage put up by the artillery, a party
> of one officer and thirteen other ranks, 9th Scottish Rifles, left
> the vicinity of Cuthbert Crater at 6 p.m. this evening, with
> orders to enter the enemy trenches and secure identification.
> Six of the party were killed and one wounded as they left our
> trench by a short smoke shell. The remainder carried on,
> entered the enemy's trench and travelled down it some fifty
> yards until they reached an undamaged dugout. Here a German

[1] PRO WO95/1777.
[2] Brigadier-General Francis Aylmer Maxwell, VC, DSO, killed in the front line by a sniper on
21 September, 1917, at the third Battle of Ypres. Buried Reservoir Cemetery, Ypres.

was found coming up, and the officer unwisely but perhaps naturally shot him before he came quite out, with the result that the man fell back dead into the dugout. It was not possible to go back down to secure this identification as others of the enemy fired up the stairway. The victim wore a green and white cockade in his cap. The party returned without casualty from the enemy. They saw none of the enemy on the parapet during their advance to the German trenches. The smoke barrage was very effective, but several shells (smoke) fell very short including that which unfortunately burst just to the south of Cuthbert Crater and killed half the party.[3]

Unhappy with the artillery direction, Maxwell further commented:

I submit that until FOOs [Forward Observation Officers] of heavy artillery abandon their present observation posts for nothing short of the front line . . . short firing will and must continue. From a perch in the 'Refugees' in Arras the most experienced FOO would fail to distinguish between a German shell and one of our own falling in our lines. From the front line or somewhere in its vicinity a proper judgement is quite easily attained, provided the owner of it is not destroyed by one of his own battery shells. Infantry would, I think, welcome the advent of FOOs as their guests in the more forward regions of the trenches and I beg leave to extend to them, through the GOC, an invitation from this Brigade to enjoy our hospitality. I personally can recommend our craters as particularly good points for close observation.[4]

Maxwell's caustic criticisms of the FOOs may be deemed somewhat unfair, however, considering that this raid took place on a sector of the front that was to be the centre of the main attack just three days later. Here FOOs would be fully committed as the main bombardment had already started. Their role, which was to spot the fall of shot for their respective batteries and to direct them on to several different targets, was the most important on the entire battlefield. It was also one of the most dangerous.

Up on Vimy Ridge, the Canadians soon turned trench-raiding into a personal mission, each battalion endeavouring to outdo its neighbour in harassment of the Germans. With growing confidence the Canadian 4th Division now began to plan a more elaborate raid, involving four battalions of infantry: the 72nd (Seaforth Highlanders), 73rd (Royal Highlanders), 75th (Toronto) and the 54th

[3] PRO WO95/1770.
[4] PRO WO95/1770.

(Kootenay) who were on the left of the Canadians on the ridge and facing the highest and strongest point, Hill 145. This was to be a 'big show', with a total of 1,700 troops attacking the German positions. It would also involve the use of poison gas, to soften up the enemy before the infantry went over. Two types of gas would be released; one was a form of teargas called White Star, and the other was chlorine. The gas cylinders would be dug into the front-line trenches, with short rubber hoses leading into no-man's-land.

The raid was planned for the end of February, but had to be postponed several times as the wind direction was not favourable. Finally, in the early hours of 1 March, the coded signal was given: '*Cat*'. At 3 a.m. exactly the White Star gas was released. By this time, however, the wind on the ridge had changed. The gas was blown straight back into the faces of the Canadians. The resulting clamour alerted the Germans, who opened up with heavy rifle and machine-gun fire. The sky was lit up by hundreds of flares, while a heavy artillery bombardment of high-explosive and gas shells descended on the Canadian trenches, shattering some of the gas cylinders and adding to the confusion. The bombardment lasted just over an hour and then died down. Because of the débâcle with the White Star gas, the release of the chlorine was cancelled. The infantry attack had been timed to start at 5.40 a.m., but, due to large amounts of gas still drifting around the Canadian trenches, many of the attacking companies formed up in front of, and behind, the front-line trench. This chaotic last-minute reorganization was soon spotted by the Germans; they sent up an SOS rocket which immediately brought down a bombardment on the exposed Canadians, causing many casualties. Promptly at 5.40, the British artillery barrage opened and the assault got under way – but before the Canadians could reach the enemy wire, many were killed in no-man's-land by their own shells falling short.

It was truly a nightmare. The survivors pressed on, slithering and sliding over the mud through a storm of machine-gun bullets. Almost before they saw it, they were on the German wire. The stakes uprooted, it was smashed and tangled but not well cut. One man who was caught up in the nightmare was Private Andrew McCrindle:

> We had already got a whiff of gas so had put on our respirators, then Jerry started shelling us so that we kept our heads down. A little while later we took our masks off when we heard shouting from the left, and there we saw a terrible sight. It was our lads from the 4th Division being slaughtered by enemy machine-gun fire and I could see some of the 73rd in their kilts stretched out

on our wire, some of whom were dead but alas, some who wished they were, struggling among the wire. So one may say we had ringside seats for this tragic attack, which was nothing but a farce.

In spite of the bloody chaos at the wire, some of the first wave of the 72nd Battalion had managed to get through. The enemy front-line trench they found to be only thinly held, but the German support was not slow in coming and a vicious bombing fight ensued. On the 54th Battalion's front, the disorder in no-man's-land as the men attempted to form up was watched by their Commanding Officer, Lieutenant-Colonel Arnold Kemball. Kemball was an English officer of fifty-six, formerly of the Indian Army, who had officially retired in 1910; at the outbreak of war he had rejoined the Army as a so-called 'dugout', or veteran. Horrified by the panic and disorder he was now witnessing among his young Canadians, he decided to lead them on himself, contrary to orders that COs were to remain in the trenches. His body was later found in the enemy barbed wire, at the head of his battalion.

The 75th Battalion fared no better. Upon reaching the wire, the bewildered troops found that the gaps they had cut in the wire the previous night had now been mined by the Germans; and to add to their misery they found themselves in a crossfire from pre-set machine guns trained on the gaps. Some broke back in disorder. Lieutenant-Colonel Sam Beckett of the 75th, after trying desperately to get the attack cancelled, had obeyed orders and taken up a position in the front-line trench to watch the progress of his battalion. The war diary of the 75th records:

> Seeing the attack break down on the right and men returning, he at once mounted the parapet, which was swept with heavy fire, and advanced boldly and endeavoured by his example and command to check the retirement. He had proceeded only some forty yards when he fell. His death was instantaneous, a rifle or MG bullet entered the left breast, just over the heart. Corporal Schissler, 75th Btn, at once went out at great personal risk to render aid, but finding his colonel dead, devoted his attention to bringing in other wounded.[5]

Some of the 72nd Battalion, meanwhile, were still in the enemy trenches when they discovered that their colleagues of the 73rd and 75th on their flanks had withdrawn. Now they retired too, fighting their way out and back to their own lines. By 6.25 a.m. it was all over.

[5] PRO WO95/3903.

There now arose the problem of the wounded, a great many of whom were lying out in no-man's-land in front of the Canadian trenches. At 8 a.m. the situation was considered quiet enough for a rescue mission, preceded by an artillery barrage to subdue the enemy front line. But again the artillery fire fell short, slaughtering many of the wounded. The Canadian losses totalled 687, including two battalion commanders, many of them killed by their own guns. The Germans, in contrast, had suffered no casualties from the gas although thirty-seven were taken prisoners. The raid had been a complete failure.

Urged on by pitiful cries for help, continuing attempts were made to recover some of the wounded on the nights of 1 and 2 March, but at 10.30 a.m. on 3 March there occurred a strange event. According to the war diary of the 26th Battalion, three German officers walked across no-man's-land towards the Canadian lines carrying a flag with a red cross:

> It appeared an armistice had been made with the 4th Division and Huns opposite for the purpose of evacuating many of our men killed lying in Hun areas. The agreement was that the Huns would carry our dead to the 'halfway' line and that our men would take them back to our lines. This armistice lasted until 12 noon, or 1 p.m. German time, at which hour both parties returned to their lines.[6]

The war diary added that the German soldiers seemed to have been deliberately picked with the intention of causing most chagrin to the Allies; all 'were of exceptionally good physique, looked well fed and very clean' and one officer happened to mention that he had been educated at St Paul's School in London.

And so the bodies of Colonel Arnold Kemball and his men were recovered, the Germans carrying over the gallant Colonel's body and treating it with 'all due respect and tenderness'.[7] Forty-six of the fallen were taken to the village of Villers-au-Bois, HQ of the 4th Division, for burial at Villers Station cemetery, including Colonels Kemball and Sam Beckett.

Following the disastrous '1st of March Gas Raid', as it became known, the trench-raiding was stepped up but never on the grand scale attempted on that fatal day. The total cost of these raids to the Canadians was enormous. For the fortnight 22 March to 5 April 1917,

[6] PRO WO95/3825.
[7] J. B. Bailey, *Cinquante-Quatre* (a history of the 54th Battalion).

71 officers and 1,582 other ranks in the Canadian Corps were killed, wounded or missing. The Canadians' confidence had been severely shaken. If they were to dislodge the stubborn Germans from Vimy Ridge on the 'big day', then better preparation, better staff work and better artillery observation was necessary. They had just forty days to get their act together.

5

The Week of Suffering

Behind the German lines all was quiet. The gunners of 405 Field
Artillery Battalion, newly arrived on the Arras front, had just been
given their firing programme for the day, Wednesday 4 April, 1917.
There was a freezing wind, enough to cut a man in half, laced with
intermittent squalls of snow and the leaden early morning sky gave a
sombre appearance to the four grey 15 cm Krupp field guns of No. 1
Company. Each gun crew had been ordered to fire one shot every five
minutes for a one-hour period starting at 8 a.m. Nineteen-year-old
Kanonier 'Fritz' Godry and his five mates on No. 1 gun all came from
Berlin and considered themselves an efficient team. They had already
agreed that only two men would operate the gun for the firing
programme; the rest would try to keep themselves warm by removing
empty shell cases to the rear and generally tidying up the gun
positions. In spite of the rotten weather they were happy. As they
stamped their feet and rubbed their hands together, conversation
drifted towards home and food. Soon breakfast was brought up by
two of the crew, a large jug of black coffee and some spicy sausage
and bread. The crew thought themselves lucky; some mornings they
got only coffee, some mornings nothing at all.

As the gunners sat around chewing at the tough sausage, Fritz
clambered into the battery dugout to gain a brief respite from the
biting wind. Suddenly there came a noise like an express train rushing
through a station; with an ear-splitting roar, the ground shook and
erupted in fountains of earth and smoke. The British bombardment,
signalling the opening of the Battle of Arras, had started.

As Kanonier Godry later recalled, the effect was devastating:

> Our shelter had wooden beams with boards across as main
> support for the roof and a shell must have landed directly
> above, for the lot collapsed and I was buried in complete
> darkness under the debris. Although stunned by the explosion,
> I presently heard somebody say, 'I suppose Fritz will be dead by
> now.' But Fritz was not dead! And, regaining my senses, I

scrambled out of the hole left by the shell in the roof. We soon got out of this position as it was too dangerous. The enemy had zeroed in on us with incredible accuracy. Although two of our guns had been destroyed and several of our men killed, we were ordered to immediately move the guns to a safer place. This had to be done in a hurry. Our main bunker was on the reverse slope of a hill and we were ordered to move to that position. The guns were hurriedly limbered up. Being the last to leave I decided to take a short cut and run across the hill. Halfway across, a gas shell exploded with a 'pop' about three metres away and I clearly saw the shell break up into a few large fragments from which a large blue foggy cloud emitted and engulfed me. Although I held my breath and carried on running, some of the gas got down me. When I reached the new position I laid my head on the bridge of the gun, feeling awful. Then came the reaction. From out of my eyes, nose and mouth, water was discharging, as if my whole body was trying to get rid of all its liquid matter. But my comrades thought it funny and were rolling about laughing.

The laughter soon stopped, however. All along the German lines, tons of high explosive, shrapnel and gas shells fell as the British batteries searched out hostile gun positions, ammunition dumps and strongpoints. A steady tempo of shells began to fall into the dense hedges of barbed wire, including some with the new 106 fuse, which blew it into tiny shreds of metal. Front-line trenches collapsed and men were buried alive in the dugouts. Shards of red-hot metal sang through the air, dismembering and disembowelling fragile human bodies. There was no respite.

Rehearsing their tactics for Z-Day itself, the Allied infantry had now developed several vicious new ploys. One was the 'Chinese barrage', a fierce bombardment punctuated by moments of calm. As the barrage lifted, the Germans rushed up from their deep dugouts, expecting the infantry assault – only to be caught in another sudden rain of shells. The same ploy worked time after time, until soon the majority of defenders in forward positions were cut off.

After the two weeks of preliminary bombardment, this ferocious assault was almost too much to bear for the unfortunate Germans on Vimy Ridge. Relief was well nigh impossible. Cold, hungry and thirsty, they could only wait for their luck to change. Adding to their misery was the release of gas, launched by the new Livens Projectors, which crept silently down dugout steps and choked the hapless residents to death. Over 400 men were killed by this means in Blangy alone. According to the history of the 51st Prussian Infantry Regiment, defending the Railway Triangle near Arras: 'The English artillery was so effective that any movement behind the lines during the day was out of the question. Even at night, movement was only at great risk. However, every man did his duty in typical "old Prussian" style, right up to the last breath.' For the German soldiers, this was their worst experience of artillery bombardment since the war began. For ever after it was known to the survivors a 'the week of suffering'.

And the English artillery was not the only cause of their misery. Far to the south of Arras, the massive array of French artillery had also launched a preliminary bombardment of the German lines, in preparation for the mighty offensive upon which General Nivelle had staked his carrer. The whole of France was buzzing with the excited expectancy of a great victory – the final glorious push to win the war. But as usual, according to the soldier's legend, whenever the Allies decided to attack, that unseen enemy, the weather, also went on the offensive.

On 5 April, after a meeting with Nivelle, Sir Douglas Haig decided that the British attack at Arras, planned for 8 April, would have to be delayed for twenty-four hours. The French were not ready; besides, the weather was deplorable – freak conditions for that time of year, with heavy falls of snow and sleet, totally rejecting the warm hand of spring. Consequently Z-Day was now Monday 9 April, with zero hour fixed for 5.30 a.m. Many British soldiers believed that the date was changed in order to preserve the sanctity of Easter Sunday; indeed, that was the reason they were given at the time.

But Nivelle's great plans had already suffered a heavy blow. On 4 April, as the British were unleashing their artillery at Arras, the Germans at Sapigneul had launched a massive raid into the French trenches, and among many unwary French soldiers captured in this brilliantly-executed affair was one NCO carrying a document that detailed the battle orders for Nivelle's attack on 16 April. In that daring foray into the French trenches, the Germans had hit the jackpot. Nivelle's scheme was blown.

It seems incredible that such an important document should have found its way into the front-line trenches, but this had been part of Nivelle's flamboyant planning, to keep every single man of his army informed of the victory he was about to exact on the Germans. Unfortunately, every German soldier was also now informed and solid preparations were made to meet the French head-on. The Army Group Commander, Crown Prince Wilhelm, the Kaiser's son, issued a proclamation to his soldiers announcing that

His Majesty the Emperor has sent me the following telegram: 'The Armies are being subjected to a violent artillery bombardment. At any moment the great French attack may be expected. All Germany awaits it, her eyes fixed on her valiant sons; salute them for me, my thoughts are with them, God will be with us.'

I bring these words of our supreme Lord to the notice of my Commander and troops, with the firm assurance that we should give to His Majesty and our beloved country the reply which they expect.[1]

Two days later the French held an urgent top-level conference at Compiègne, where General Nivelle and his senior army commanders were summoned to meet President Poincaré, Prime Minister Ribot and the Minister for War, Painlevé. At this meeting Nivelle faced some bitter criticism, not only from his political superiors but also from one of his subordinates, General Micheler. He offered to resign. Poincaré, however, persuaded him to stay on, although he too had grave doubts about Nivelle's plans.

News of this disarray behind the French scenes, at a time when the British Army was already committed to the offensive, soon reached the ears of General Sir William Robertson. He promptly informed the British War Cabinet in a letter describing what he saw as the French Government's 'unstable nature' and tendency to 'serious vacillation'. 'As an example of this,' he went on,

It has been reported by our liaison officers with the French armies that on the 6th instant – after we had commenced our artillery bombardment in the offensive operations which were proposed by the French Government, and agreed to by the War Cabinet – a conference was held at Compiègne with the object of considering the desirability of not undertaking these operations.[2]

Robertson further noted that Nivelle's position as French Commander-in-Chief was in jeopardy – which must have been dismal news to Lloyd George, Nivelle's loyal admirer.

One of the liaison officers mentioned by Robertson was Major Edward Spears, who later described the episode in his book, *Prelude to Victory*. Summing up, he said:

[1] PRO WO157/151.
[2] PRO WO158/23.

The Compiègne conference was the inevitable result of the earlier one held at Calais. The seed planted at Calais bore fruit at Compiègne. The British forces were under the orders of the French Commander-in-Chief, but the French Commander-in-Chief was under the control of the French Cabinet, who in an emergency such as had occurred, did not hesitate to use their powers without reference to the British Government. It was now quite evident that our Cabinet had abdicated its powers in favour not of a French general but of the French Government.[3]

Lloyd George and the British Generals had been warned. French indecision and reluctance to confer with their allies would have serious consequences in the forthcoming offensive.

---

[3] Spears, *Prelude to Victory*, p. 437.

6

In Praise of Infantry

The most congested place in Arras was the Baudimont Gate, a massive structure divided by a central wall into two small tunnels. There was no getting around it and the road was continually blocked by traffic heading for the front. In fact, it made a perfect target for enemy shelling. The St Pol road from the west was under constant observation and in spite of camouflage netting screens, the Germans on the ridge could clearly see the long convoys of lorries, guns, horses and men, worming their tedious way into the town. At one consistently shelled danger point known as Dead Man's Corner, the carcases of dead horses and mules, lying amid the debris of smashed gun limbers and wagons, served as a warning to the curious not to loiter. Among the many hand-painted notices of impending danger and one remembered by many soldiers who entered Arras by this route was *'For Fuck's sake don't Fuck about here . . . signed D. Haig, Field-Marshal.'* (The offending notice was soon taken down, it is said, by order of a furious Allenby, who laid the blame on New Zealand Tunnellers.)

But, from 4 April onwards, the Baudimont Gate and the St Pol road became safer places; the intense search and destroy tactics of the British artillery to knock out their enemy counterparts had largely succeeded. The British infantry, upon whose shoulders the fortunes of the forthcoming battle depended, began to trudge through the town, above and below ground, to their respective positions near the jumping-off trenches. And, although the occasional shell still fell, thousands of men were safe and dry in the deep catacombs and tunnels beneath Arras and Vimy Ridge. The whole battle area was buzzing with expectancy.

As proud as the Canadians, that their objective on Z-Day was the formidable Vimy Ridge, were the 'Jocks' of the 51st (Highland) Division, whose task was to capture the right-hand flank of the ridge. The commander of this legendary territorial outfit was Major-General George M. Harper, a lanky, white-haired man of fifty-two, with a black moustache. He was fiercely proud of his 'little fellers' as he affectionately called his Highlanders. Some of them, with a natural disrespect for anyone in authority, thought Harper a 'silly old sod' and referred to him as 'Uncle', although he was better known throughout the army as 'Old 'Arper'. The 51st Division had built up a solid fighting reputation during the Somme battle; they had been the captors of Beaumont Hamel, and now they were more than ready for Vimy Ridge. Jealous, perhaps, of the Highlanders' reputation, other units knew them by their distinctive divisional badge – featuring the letters 'HD', for Highland Division – and referred to them disparagingly as 'Harper's Duds' or 'Highway Decorators'.

One battalion of the 51st Division was the 9th Royal Scots, 'Edinburgh's Own' or – because this was the only battalion of Royal Scots wearing the kilt – 'the Dandy Ninth'. Although Lowland Scots, and sometimes called imposters by the Highland battalions, they were proud to be serving with the 51st, in 154 Brigade. In command of 'A' Company since the second Battle of Ypres was the debonair Captain Patrick Blair, MC. 'Pat', as he was known to his company, was thirty-seven years old, formerly the senior partner in a firm of Edinburgh chartered accountants and still a keen rugby football fan. A brave and steady leader, he was much loved by the boys of 'A' Company for his fatherly manner and the way he lent a sympathetic ear to their perpetual grousing. Likewise, he took immense pride in his youngsters – even though they were all soccer mad and Blair needed a firm hand to keep them under control, as footballs were often produced for a 'kick-about' in the most dangerous of places. 'We'd play whenever we got the chance,' said Sergeant Bill Hay of 4 Platoon, 9th Royal Scots:

> We had Bill and Jimmy Broad, two brothers who were
> professional footballers with Manchester City, and that made
> the 9th Royal Scots the best team in the division – although the
> Argylls would probably disagree. But without a doubt, the most
> full-blooded games were 'friendly' ones and whenever we
> played 2 Platoon I'd end up fighting with a stroppy sergeant
> called Willocks. I used to annoy him by calling him 'Bollocks'.

Hay was the son of an Edinburgh coach-maker; now aged twenty-two, he had served with the battalion since February, 1915. On and off the football field, he never quite saw eye to eye with Johnny Willocks, a fiery twenty-six-year-old. There was always a rivalry as to who had the smartest platoon. Hay was particularly proud of his platoon – besides, they were all close mates; they had been through

58

the Somme together and could rely on each other to the full. Hay describes some of the characters:

> We were a typical infantry platoon, and made up with lads from all walks of life, the sort of boys you would find on the factory floor; we had the joker, the womanizer, the swearer, the drunk, the gambler, the barrack-room lawyer, the nitwit, the God-botherer and the nancy-boy. On the Lewis gun were two brothers from Edinburgh, John and George Campbell. The youngest, George, was twenty and he was a bank clerk in civvy street so we called him 'Doey'. John was a butcher in the family firm of Campbells the haggis-makers, known as 'Niffy'. Then there was George Flynn, 'Porky' because he was skinny, and his close mate George Davidson. These two were the platoon 'shit-wallahs' or sanitary men. My other great pals were Sergeants Jock Leishman and Lawrie Smith, both of whom had been 'over the bags' with me at Beaumont Hamel. I also had an unofficial batman in a lad called Sandy Walton, a good boy who came from Manchester. He stuck with me like glue. Of the other lads in the platoon at this time whom I particularly remember, there was a poof who was a professional dancer – he was terrified of getting wounded in the feet – and a lad called Richard whose father was a horse trader from Lancashire; he was known as 'Donkey-Dick'.

The 9th Royal Scots had been relieved in the trenches near Ecurie on 3 April by the 4th Seaforth Highlanders, and had marched back to Maroeuil huts for three days 'rest' before going back into the line in readiness for the attack. They had been in a rough and muddy sector of the line and were glad to be out of it. The NCOs of 'A' Company had been allocated a hut between them, and that night they had lived it up at a local *estaminet*. The following morning, with a sore head, Hay was called to one side by Pat Blair and ordered to introduce a new officer to his platoon. Hay immediately recognized the baby-faced Second-Lieutenant as nineteen-year-old Jimmy Adams from his home town. He had not yet been in the trenches, and so Hay decided to take the fledgling officer under his wing.

The veteran Hay had only recently returned from home leave in Edinburgh himself, where he had met Adams's worried mother who implored Hay to 'keep an eye on Jimmy'. One day while in Edinburgh, Hay went for a walk along the towpath of the Union Canal, one of his favourite boyhood haunts. Dressed in civilian clothes, for he had sent his filthy uniform to be laundered, he was enjoying his quiet stroll when a pretty young woman approached him and pressed an envelope into his hand. When he opened it, he found that it contained a white feather.

**The United States
of Great Britain
and America**
John Bull (to President
Wilson): Bravo, Sir!
Delighted to have you
on our side.

On 6 April there came the long-awaited and welcome news that
America had declared war on Germany. 'Unrestricted Submarine
Warfare' had been the last straw. In Britain, many people viewed the
news with indifference, but they had no conception of its significance
to the 350,000 British soldiers crammed into the Third Army area. It
was a tremendous tonic, even though the more realistic knew that it
would be many months before America could make its presence felt.

On the same day, however, the attack that was due to be launched
on 8 April was postponed for another twenty-four hours. This news
was of more immediate significance for the anxious men of the Third
Army: the wait must go on.

Above and below ground, Arras was jam-packed with men. 'The
town has been badly knocked about,' wrote Major Walter Vignoles,
DSO, of the 10th Lincs, in his diary:

> The outside walls of most of the houses are standing, but many
> buildings are mere shells with the whole of the inside gone,

while nearly all the houses seem to have been hit at one time or another – the French will NEVER forgive the Boche, even if they live in peace with him for 200 years. A few houses are more or less habitable and we had quite a good one for our headquarters. It had no doubt been a decent place at one time, for there was a good deal of furniture left, including an easy chair. There was a number of cupboards locked and sealed by the town Major, containing, I presume, more furniture and perhaps clothes left by the unfortunate owners when they fled in haste.[1]

Not all of the town's people had left, however, as Private John Coupland, MM, 42nd Machine Gun Company, later recollected:

We took over our trenches at Ronville, a suburb of Arras, and I was pleased to see trenches partly brick-paved and real dugouts. (Our last trenches in front of the Yser Canal had been waist-deep in water.) One day in Arras, I saw a man in French uniform; he was wearing a medal and was often seen around. I was not fluent in French but reasonable, so one day I spoke to him. He was a veteran of the War of 1870 and his function was to record the damage. It made me think, but then 1870 was only forty-six years before and if he was twenty years old then, he would be in his mid-sixties.

Beneath the town the infantrymen who were destined to spearhead the assault quickly settled into their temporary new billets. Accustomed to the long hours and days of waiting before a battle, the men carried cards and board games with them to keep boredom at bay. Poker was the most popular card game, but 'Housey Housey' and 'Crown and Anchor' sessions soon produced gusts of laughter echoing through the chilly passageways and tunnels. In each small cellar or cave, in the dim light and through the haze of cigarette smoke, the men made themselves as comfortable as possible. As Z-Day loomed closer and tensions began to mount, many men wrote letters to their loved ones and exchanged them with friends, everyone promising to forward the letters should disaster overtake – though the swop was usually accompanied by reassuring comments.

Long metal troughs had been provided in some of the underground caves for washing purposes, cold water being pumped down through pipes, but they were too few for the number of men who needed them and were usually attended by long, grumbling queues. As in the trenches, most men had to make do with a bowl or bucket, as many as

[1] Vignoles papers, Imperial War Museum.

a dozen of them using the same water for washing and shaving. The more experienced among them, 'old sweats' as they were called, usually waited till last; they knew that, after four or five people had used it, the water gradually became warmer.

Cigarettes, the great comforter of the soldier, were always in demand, especially during the nervous waiting periods. Sergeant Bill Partridge, of the 7th Middlesex, had smoked since the age of eleven – and continued to do so throughout his long life, until warned by his doctor at the age of ninety-three that it would 'do him no good':

> Our usual fag was the army issue: Three Wishes – we called 'em 'three bitches' – Half-a-Mo, Ruby Queen and Red Hussars. They were all dreadful fags and we called 'em 'gaspers'. Woodbines were the best fags, but they were rare. Under stress smoking really helped, especially when the battle was on.

Private Edward Burtenshaw, of the 10th Sherwood Foresters, comments:

> Nowadays, they keep on complaining about smoking, but I'm sure if another war came the canteens would do a ripping trade selling cigarettes – it was so *boring* in the trenches, but if you had a cigarette in your mouth, oh, it was lovely!

The soldiers were all given a ration of two packets of ten per week, whether or not they smoked; those who didn't could use the cigarettes as a form of currency to 'buy' more food or rum. There was never a shortage of customers for extra 'gaspers'. Apart from anything else, the smoke helped to disguise the smell of death so prevalent in the front line.

The food situation was generally good, for General Allenby in his meticulous planning for this battle had realized the need to feed his troops well. In particular he had recommended that the men be given a 'satisfactory breakfast before attacking – care is to be taken that this meal is a good one'.[2] Hot stew was continually produced from the subway kitchens but, with so many mouths to feed, long periods would elapse between meals. Ever hungry, the men sometimes went in search of supplementary rations – like Private Carson Stewart of the 6th Cameron Highlanders, who ventured out of the caves to visit a small bakery. In his 'best French' he begged 'Madame' for some bread, 'but she refused, saying she had to store it all up for the

[2] PRO WO95/362.

forthcoming battle'! Stewart was just about to leave when Fate intervened:

> A Jerry shell blew the chimney clean off the houses, leaving us covered in dust and rubble. She immediately ran downstairs, so I went into her storeroom and tried to get 'du pang' off the shelf. But she came back up again and caught me, chasing me out of the shop, calling me a 'brigand'!

And a dispatch rider with the Royal Engineers, Corporal Fred Poulter of the 9th Division, remembered an even more dramatic incident:

> Some bright spark of a Jock said there was salmon in the River Scarpe and there was a much quicker way of catching salmon other than using a line; so they chucked a Mills bomb into the Scarpe and when it went off, salmon floated to the top. Now this went on for some time until one day some fool brought up a trench mortar bomb and blew such a hole in the river bank that it actually changed the direction of the bloody river!

Bored by the long wait, for they had spent four days in the caverns under Arras, one group of men from the 8th Royal Fusiliers broke into a locked cellar they had found. Among its contents was 'a bottle of plonk' – or so they thought – which they promptly drank. In fact the bottle had contained absinthe, a very strong liqueur. According to Private Tim Collior, 'They ended up absolutely paralytic and were taken to hospital and so, fortunately for them, missed the attack.'

7

Easter Sunday

After a sharp frosty dawn on 8 April, Easter Sunday bloomed into a beautiful, sunny spring day. Men watched with wonder the antics of the toy-like planes as they looped and swooped like swallows chasing flies, high in the clear blue sky. The reality of the grim battle raging high above was only brought home to the troops by the distant crackle of machine-gun fire, or the screaming of a sick engine and the dirty splash of oily smoke as one or more of the combatants flamed to earth.

Everywhere on this Easter Sunday, along the length of the front, congregations gathered, large and small, for divine service. Many services were held in the open, the men kneeling bare-headed to receive Holy Communion and make their peace with God. Familiar English hymns echoed among the French villages, fields and barns, lifting the hearts of the men. 'When I survey the wondrous cross', 'O Jesu lover of my soul', 'Onward Christian soldiers': the well loved words were sung with particular feeling on this day before the great attack.

Captain the Reverend Martin Andrews, Chaplain to the 4th Royal Fusiliers, wrote this moving description of one such service in a cellar in Arras:

> A sergeant helped me clear up the place and make it ready. A Tate sugar box was the altar and the French lady who owned my billet gave us a beautiful embroidered spotless white cloth on which we put two candlesticks and a cross. When we started the cellar was packed. Fortunately I had a fresh box of wafers with me, for when I got to the end of the passage it was full of men standing and kneeling, continuing up the steps into the road outside; an unforgettable sight such as I have never seen before or since. Looking into their faces while they knelt, reverent and war-scarred, I knew many had never partaken of the Blessed Sacrament. Those divine words which have comforted dying men down the ages, first spoken in the upper room and now repeated in the Arras cellar, touched the hearts of all waiting

and wondering in the silence. However Godless the age may seem, deep down in the hearts of men, sooner or later, there is revealed some sort of faith in Christ and a hazy belief that death cannot be the end. During the following days I saw several of those men lying dead on the battlefield gazing up to heaven. So often there comes to my mind the words of Studdert Kennedy (the brilliant and devoted prophet, poet and padre of the 1914 war) who wrote in the trenches:

> O God of beauty and ugliness,
> O God of tenderness and terror,
> O God of life and death,
> What art thou like?[1]

With men's religious beliefs stirred by the nearness of death, the padres were in great demand that Easter Sunday morning; in fact, there were not enough of them to satisfy demand, so in some cases the men conducted their own makeshift services. Private Tim Collior recalled that as the padre to the 8th Royal Fusiliers was absent, the Easter service was arranged by 'one of our stretcher bearers who was rather religious'. Twenty or thirty men with two of their officers duly gathered together in a cellar to attend the little service. It was, Collior said, 'very moving. Our stretcher bearer did us proud and we sang "Onward Christian soldiers".' Another makeshift service was arranged for the Canadians of the 24th Battalion by a soldier who had been a theological student at McGill University. 'We facetiously called him "the Rev",' said Private Andy McCrindle, who also remembered him as 'a good sport' with language as ripe as anyone's. In the event, however, only three men turned up for the service. The Rev was bitterly disappointed:

> He said it would be difficult to have a service worthwhile, so suppose we just say the Lord's Prayer and bugger off back to the cave? At the time it didn't seem incongruous to me, his language, but later on, in thinking it over, it brought a smile to my face.

Sadly, however, Private McCrindle added a postscript to the story:

> It is in regard to the roll-call after the battle – which is always a poignant affair. When the Rev's name was called, he didn't answer. He had answered a higher calling on April 9th.

[1] Martin Andrews, *Canon's Folly*, p. 85.

Although the sunshine of Easter Sunday did much to lift the men's spirits, the clear blue sky spelled bad news for the long convoys of ammunition and supply lorries standing nose to tail in the Arras suburbs. Forever inquisitive, the enemy spotter planes were nosing high above the town, although the RFC pilots did their best to deter them, and managed to pinpoint some irresistible targets for their artillery. Just south of Arras, in the village of Achicourt – part of the 56th Division's sector – one German shell scored a direct hit on a lorry laden with 9.2 shells. The exploding ammunition set off a chain reaction of explosions among the other lorries of the convoy; soon the whole village was ablaze, with a column of smoke rising thousands of feet into the sky – signalling to the Germans the extent of their success. It was ample evidence, if such were needed, that the British bombardment had not silenced all the enemy batteries. Indeed, the German guns were still causing death and destruction in Arras itself, as Gunner Albert Taylor, 128 Battery, RFA, recalled:

> We were in positions in and around an old candle factory on the
> outskirts of Arras, and one of my lasting memories of the day
> before the battle was to see a press photographer, when we
> were all taking cover, high up on one of the buildings, taking
> photographs, completely regardless of the exploding shells. He
> survived them all!

Meanwhile, the last-minute preparations continued. General Allenby had decided that the infantrymen of the Third Army should leave their greatcoats behind when they went into battle, reasoning that they would become too heavy and cumbersome if wet, and ordered them to be collected at designated dumps. However, some divisional, brigade and battalion commanders countermanded this order, anticipating the onset of colder weather. But Allenby's reasoning had not been entirely at fault; his infantrymen had a heavy enough burden of equipment to carry as it was.

The weight of equipment carried by each man varied slightly from division to division. 'Specialists' such as Lewis gun-teams, signallers and bombers carried equipment peculiar to their needs; but in general, the equipment carried by the average British infantryman for this battle consisted of a rifle, bayonet, entrenching tool, full water bottle, haversack (with a waterproof sheet in place of the pack), two days' rations, 170 rounds of ammunition, two Mills bombs, one ground flare and three sandbags – in addition to which, many troops carried picks, shovels and wirecutters. Lieutenant-Colonel Croft of the 11th Royal Scots thoughtfully issued each of his

Major-General (*addressing the men before practising an attack behind the lines*): I want you to understand that there is a difference between a rehearsal and the real thing. There are three essential differences: First, the absence of the enemy.
Now (*turning to the Regimental Sergeant-Major*) What is the second difference?
Sergeant-Major: The absence of the General, Sir.

men with a small bottle of rum, and directed that each man was to carry in his haversack 'one complete iron ration with five fresh biscuits, one large meat sandwich, one packet of chewing gum and the unexpended portion of the day's ration'.[2]

At the onset of darkness on Easter Sunday, the remainder of the assault troops moved through heavily congested communication trenches to their allocated jumping-off positions. Some, like the 4th Seaforth Highlanders, had been marched past newly-dug burial pits together with piles of wooden crosses – a reminder that they were not going on a picnic. Soon after midnight the weather changed dramatically and the temperature plummeted. Already in position and many without greatcoats, the troops huddled together for warmth, heads drooping under heavy steel helmets as showers of freezing rain and sleet lashed into the exposed trenches. Luckiest of all were those underground, safe and dry in the tunnels and subways – the exits of which had now been opened into no-man's-land – although no less apprehensive as to their fortunes in the approaching battle. In the crowded assault trenches, many snatched a last-minute bite to eat,

[2] PRO WO95/2882.

some enjoying the not altogether hot meal which had been prepared for them further back; but, in spite of General Allenby's orders, many others got only a mug of tea, brought up to them by those unsung heroes of the war, the ration carriers, and some got nothing at all.

Eighteen-year-old Private Fred Hollingworth and his pals of the Manchester Church Lads shooting team had enlisted together in the 4th Seaforth Highlanders when the Battalion held a recruiting drive in the city at the end of 1915. Now, as a kilted 'Highlander', Fred found himself trying to snatch some sleep while lying on the floor of a tunnel, the exit of which was close to the Lille road on the flanks of Vimy Ridge. Here he describes his last anxious moments before the attack:

> 'Equipment on, everybody. It's 2.15 a.m.!' yelled our platoon sergeant. Well, this was my first action and my stomach turned. He led us up the steps but we didn't stop in the front line, we went further forward, and I realized that we were going into an advanced trench. When we got there, there was a Royal Engineer sapper and one of our officers, who was saying that we had to be quiet, there was to be no talking and as we passed through the water at the bottom of the trench we had to be jolly careful that we didn't make a great splash, because if Jerry knew we were there, by jove, we would have caught it in the neck. Although it was dark I could just see, and we communicated by sign language. With my feet against the front of the trench and my backside against the other side, with bayonet fixed, we were motioned to try to keep our arms dry and useful. That sent another shiver through me . . . I didn't like it at all.

Further up on Vimy Ridge, the Canadians were in position too. Serving with the 26th Infantry Battalion was another youngster, eighteen-year-old Private Neville Tompkins from New Brunswick. 'All one could do was trust to luck and the guidance of the good Lord,' Tompkins remembered. 'I took the view that "The other fellow might get it, but not me," ' he went on; but even so:

> There were occasions, in tight spots, when I asked for a little divine guidance and protection, in the belief that my pleadings might do some good, and certainly could do no harm. As a body of troops cannot move without noise, it seemed strange that while waiting for zero hour on the ridge we underwent only scattered shelling, sporadic machine-gun fire and sniping. We arrived at our jumping-off trenches at around 4.30 a.m., with

the barrage scheduled for 5.30 a.m. Just prior to the opening of the barrage, which was the heaviest of the war to date, I heard an explosion in the trench-bay next to mine, and later learned that my good friend Ned Mullaly from Newfoundland, in hitching up his equipment, had in some manner loosened a pin of one of the grenades in the bag he was carrying on his back, with the result that the grenade exploded and he was killed instantly. This, I believe, was the first casualty of our company in the attack.[3]

'On Zero Day, the Canadian Corps will capture Vimy Ridge'[4]: General Byng's calm and historic announcement, circulated in operation orders, instilled further confidence in the Canadians. The ridge was theirs for the taking. Not all were going over the top, however. In both the First and Third Armies, a minority of officers and men – usually a senior battalion officer, a second-lieutenant and NCOs from each assault battalion – were left behind in the rear, to form the nucleus of a new battalion should the worst happen and the battalion be wiped out. This forced one disappointed officer, Major Walter Vignoles, DSO, to write in his diary:

> It's rotten being left out of it and having to stay back here, but no doubt I shall have a chance one of these days. Besides, I went over on 1st July and although the Colonel has been out here most of the war, he has never taken part in a big attack. As a matter of fact we were given no choice. The Colonel had orders to go over and I had orders to stay behind.[5]

Doubtless, most soldiers due to attack at zero hour would have been glad to be 'out of it'. Also 'out of it' were the British Generals and Staff. The outcome of the forthcoming battle was now in the hands of the ordinary soldier. The fortunes of the day would be decided by the captains and lieutenants, some mere boys barely out of school, and of course the NCOs, the majority of whom had come straight to the war from all walks of civvy life.

At midnight on 8 April, as the men of Princess Pat's Canadian Light Infantry shivered in their jumping-off trench, up to their knees in mud and lashed with icy rain, their Colonel received a message from Brigadier-General A. G. Macdonnell, commanding the 7th Canadian Infantry Brigade. It said: 'I cannot go to bed without

[3] Edward Francis Mullaly, age twenty-five, of Northern Bay. His name is on the Vimy memorial to the missing.
[4] PRO WO95/169.
[5] Vignoles papers, Imperial War Museum.

wishing you and your gallant lads God speed, best of good luck and victory.' By midnight, indeed, most of the Generals were in bed.

The British infantry, upon whose shoulders fell the greatest burden of hardship throughout the war, now faced the ultimate test: going 'over the top'. It was at times like this that the comradeship of the trenches was strongest. Reassuring themselves with a fervent conviction that they would be all right, many solemnly shook hands and wished each other luck. Some of the old stagers hid their fear and tried to bolster the confidence of the youngsters, quietly offering them cigarettes or sweets. Where silence was not enforced, some tried lifting the spirits of the others with bawdy jokes. Bound together by the trivial experiences they had shared in the long months of boredom, in and out of the lines, they waited with dry throats and thumping hearts. The most important thing was not to let their mates down.

In front of the village of Roclincourt, 'A' company the 9th Royal Scots waited quietly for zero hour. The young subaltern, Jimmy Adams, sat close to Sergeant Bill Hay on the firestep of the trench; nearby was one of the wooden ladders which would enable the troops to climb out into no-man's-land at the given time. Dressed, as ordered, in the uniform of a private soldier, although he carried his Webley revolver instead of a rifle, the young officer was grumbling nervously. 'He was complaining that his kilt was wet through,' Hay remembered. 'I noticed that he was shaking like a leaf, so I made him have some rum. He said he had never tasted spirits before. That squared him up a bit.'

'A' and 'D' Companies of the 9th Royal Scots had been ordered to be in position by 2.30 a.m.; but, delayed by congestion in the communication trenches, they didn't make it until 3.30. They had already suffered casualties of four killed and nine wounded from shellfire on the way up. The old football rivals, 2 and 4 Platoons of 'A' company, were due to go over first – each company attacking on a two-platoon frontage. Their main objective was 'Poser Weg', a strong fire trench set in the enemy's third line. Both companies were waiting in a new trench, dug only a few days previously by the divisional pioneers, the 8th Royal Scots. Although the form of attack had been well rehearsed, Bill Hay, after arranging his men in the planned order, convinced himself that his counterpart in 2 Platoon, Sergeant Willocks, had arranged his men in the wrong order:

> I went over to him and told him to get his lads in the right order
> as rehearsed, spread them out properly like. They were all

hanging around any-old-how. Bill Ferguson, his officer, was talking to Jimmy Adams back in our end of the trench, so I says to this idiot Willocks, 'You bloody pratt! Get yourselves sorted out.' He told me to 'fuck off' and mind my own business. So we squared up to each other and Jackie Renwick, the CSM, steps in and says 'For god's sake pack it in. You'll be fighting the Germans in a few minutes.' But I knew I was right, for I heard Renwick giving Willocks an almighty bollocking and telling him to 'straighten his platoon out'. I was in a foul mood by then.

Shortly after the obstreperous sergeants had been sorted out, Captain Pat Blair, the company commander, together with Colonel Green, came down the trench where they remained to see the rum ration distributed. After some quiet words of encouragement to the men of each platoon, the two officers moved on. At 4.30 a.m. the order was passed along: 'Fix bayonets.'

Sitting on ammunition boxes close to Bill Hay, with raindrops dripping from the rims of their steel helmets, were the Campbell brothers, 'Doey' and 'Niffy', who were part of the platoon's Lewis gun team. Doey, the corporal and No 1 on the gun, was protecting the temperamental weapon from the rain with his ground sheet. His brother had placed several panniers of ammunition in a niche in the trench wall. Hay recollected that both men were 'silently smoking and trying to keep their feet out of the sludge in the bottom of the trench'. Hay's young 'batman', Sandy Walton, was nearby, too, as was his old mate, Jack Leishman. 'We're all in this together, boys,' Hay reassured those within earshot. Jimmy Adams was studying his watch, nervously fidgeting and licking his lips. Silently they waited in the drizzle and gloom for the last few minutes to tick away, each man alone with his thoughts and suffering equally in the gathering shroud of fear.

From the northern tip of Vimy Ridge to Croisilles, fourteen miles to the south, the British Army waited for zero hour. The last sporadic shelling of enemy lines slackened off and, apart from the occasional crash of a German shell, an eerie silence descended on the battlefield. Those last few minutes were etched for ever on the memory of many survivors. Here are some of their recollections:

I remember how I felt just before going over; It was the first time, and it was 50% curiosity and 50% wind-up. After the first time, it was curiosity nil, wind-up 100%! Another funny thing I remember was some shells falling nearby and we all hit the deck. One of the lads said, 'It's OK . . . they're ours!' (*Private Leslie Dunn, 1st East Yorks*)

We had a sort of sweepstake, a gamble if you like. We done the same on the Somme. Everyone in the platoon pooled the money they had left – and we gave it to a cook to look after, who of course wasn't going in with us, the idea being to share out the money after the attack amongst those who'd survived. A little 'bonus' for coming through. And, I'm sad to say, I made a few bob that day. (*Private Harry Brown, 11th Middx*)

'I don't want to be mutilated, I don't want to be mutilated,' I told myself over and over again . . . A nice 'Blighty' will do me, or failing that, one clean through the nut; lights out, no fuss! And I think that was the attitude of all of us. (*Private Bill Partridge, 7th Middx*)

I have to say I was frightened before going over. What with the cold, well, I was shaking like a leaf. Then to cap it all, old Major Impey comes down the trench and says, 'I'll give you lot your rum when you get back, there'll be more then 'cos you ain't all coming back.' I ask you! . . . Then our ambulance man, a young lad, comes along the trench distributing bandages to cheer us up. We were all sitting on the firestep waiting, so he squeezes in and sits down. Just then a shrapnel shell burst high above the trench and a big piece of shell casing comes whirring down and hits the poor chap right between the legs, in the groin, and although the light was poor, we could see the blood arcing six or seven feet up in the air. There was nothing we could do for him. 'Oh Mum!' he screamed. 'Oh Mum!' . . . And in less than no time at all he was dead and rolled off the firestep . . . What a start! (*Private Bert Taylor, 7th Sussex*)

I was seventeen at the time and I could not stop my teeth from chattering. We were lying in no-man's-land at 5.15 a.m. and the sergeant passed along rum in a small wine glass and I asked him for a double measure. This he gave me and I swallowed it in one. Immediately, my teeth stopped chattering; I looked at my watch – two minutes to go! . . . I said a final prayer and thought of my dear mother, brothers and sisters back home in Canada. (*Corporal Jules de Cruyenaere, DCM, 1st Canadian Mounted Rifles*)

While waiting to go 'over the top' I saw behind me a fellow with four pigeons in a cage. That was all he was carrying and I assumed he had just brought them into the trench for one of us to carry over. I thought to myself, 'The lucky devil, I bet he's a brigade wallah,' and I really envied what seemed to be a cushy job. Just then a shell exploded nearby and a lump of metal took his head off. (*Private Les Belston, 17th King's*)

But the waiting was nearly over. It was Z-Day, Monday 9 April, and the great infantry offensive was about to begin.

Part II

THE DAY OF DOINGS:
9 APRIL 1917

'April 9th. The day of doings. Boys over about 6 a.m.'
Diary, Private Harry Fowler
(1st London Scottish)

8

Vimy Ridge

Just before zero hour, all along the battle front many of the attacking troops crawled out into no-man's-land and lay down in long rows beyond the British wire. Others lined the steps of the deep dugouts and tunnels, while some waited, as they had done all night, in the congested assault trenches, eyes straining at the luminous hands on watches as the last seconds slipped away. As the darkness slowly lifted, each man became imbued with a sudden alertness, mingled with a certain relief that the hour had come.

At 5.30 a.m. precisely, a distant boom from a signal gun near St Eloi denoted the start of the attack. Instantly, the ears of the assault troops were serenaded by an unearthly music as salvo after salvo of shells hurtled, shrieking and whining overhead, to burst like a thunderous surf on the German trenches. The British barrage had opened and the concussion from the initial blast of this mighty array of artillery shattered allegedly every pane of glass in Douai, fifteen miles away. Its rumblings could clearly be heard like a distant storm in southern England. For a few seconds its awe-inspiring intensity distracted the infantry from the task ahead. As a private in the 4th Seaforth Highlanders, Fred Hollingsworth, later recalled:

> This damn big gun went off at the side of us somewhere. That was the signal for every bit of artillery for miles around, they all fired at once, it was pandemonium. I wondered afterwards how we had managed to keep our ears protected; it was shocking and the whole of the ground in front of us seemed like it was blazing. One can't describe it, it was out of this world.

As the barrage smashed into the first German line, tossing and tangling the wire defences and sending great flying fragments hissing and whirring through the air, the defenders scurried for cover, falling over each other in their desperate haste to get down in the dugouts where they cowered, taking shelter from the monstrous storm of shells. This time the British were really coming. All along the

German lines distress rockets were sent up, begging for artillery support and adding a variety of colours to the fantastic flashes of the exploding shells.

The grey dawn was brilliantly illuminated by the firestorm as thousands of British soldiers scrambled out of their trenches, rushed from the tunnel exits and formed up in no-man's-land, every man thoroughly rehearsed in his task. Quickly they were in position, shepherded along by the raucous shouts and bellows of NCOs. Before the barrage had made its first lift, the leading companies were away through the icy drizzle, skating and sliding through the slippery mud and trying to avoid the many water-filled shell-holes. But the terrain was the least of their problems, as Sergeant David Gardner, 9th Royal Scots, recorded:

> The very first thing I noticed, upon getting out of the trench, was that the first salvo of shells from the British barrage fell *behind* us! I thought, here we go again, Fred Karno's Army is on the march!

In the main, however, the barrage was accurate – and devastating. But the enemy wasn't going to give in without a struggle. As the British dodged and skidded across no-man's-land, the defenders prepared to receive them . . .

Meanwhile, the Canadians were attacking Vimy Ridge. Four divisions went forward as one, to dig the Germans out of their trenches. At first the going was relatively easy, remembered Private Neville Tompkins of the 26th Battalion: 'In fact many of us covered the 1,000 yards or so to the *Zwischen Stellung* with our rifles at the sling, meeting only a few Germans who had surrendered.' But soon the enemy shells and machine-gun fire began to take a toll on the advancing Canadians. Noting sadly that there was no time to stop 'to assist a friend or foe who had become a casualty', Tompkins went on:

> As our objective was ten to fifteen degrees to the left of our jumping-off trench, my principal difficulty was keeping in line with the troops of my own battalion, as a result of which I found that I and some of the others of the 26th were inclining to the right and intermingling with other troops of our division.

But Tompkins was lucky, unlike Private Winston Pearson of the 15th Battalion (48th Highlanders):

> Soon after the attack started, I was hit in my left arm by a machine-gun bullet. At first it felt as if I had been kicked by a

76

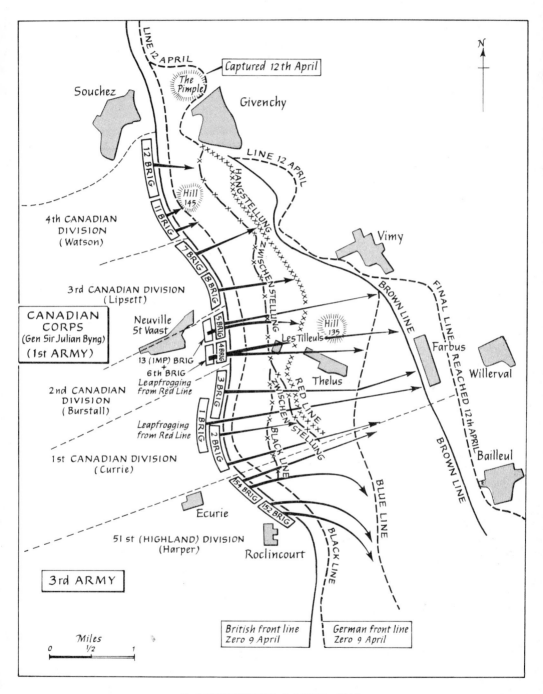

N

Souchez

Captured 12th April

The Pimple

Givenchy

LINE 12 APRIL

LINE 12 APRIL

HANGSTELLUNG

12 BRIG

11 BRIG

Hill 145

Vimy

4th CANADIAN
DIVISION
(Watson)

ZWISCHENSTELLUNG

7 BRIG

8 BRIG

3rd CANADIAN DIVISION
(Lipsett)

BROWN LINE

FINAL LINE REACHED 12th APRIL

CANADIAN
CORPS
(Gen Sir Julian Byng)
(1st ARMY)

Neuville
St Vaast

5 BRIG

4 BRIG

Les Tilleuls

Hill 135

Farbus

13 (IMP) BRIG
+
6th BRIG
Leapfrogging
from Red Line

Thelus

RED LINE

Willerval

2nd CANADIAN
DIVISION
(Burstall)

3 BRIG

ZWISCHENSTELLUNG

1 BRIG

BLACK LINE

1st CANADIAN DIVISION
(Currie)

Leapfrogging
from Red Line

2 BRIG

BROWN LINE

Bailleul

154 BRIG

BLUE LINE

51st (HIGHLAND) DIVISION
(Harper)

152 BRIG

BROWN LINE

Ecurie

BLACK LINE

Roclincourt

3rd ARMY

Miles

0   ½   1

British front line
Zero 9 April

German front line
Zero 9 April

3. VIMY RIDGE, 9 APRIL, 1917.

mule. A few seconds later the pain started. It was if I were
repeatedly jabbed with a red-hot poker. The bullet entered my
left arm just below the shoulder joint. It made a very small hole
where it entered but hit the bone, breaking it into many pieces,
and the bullet shattered, tearing a great hole in my back. It bled
plenty of course, but I couldn't see this and later found my
clothes stuck to me from shoulder to foot.

Pearson collapsed into a shell crater from which he was later retrieved
by the stretcher bearers. 'At the tender age of seventeen,' he
concluded, 'that was my total contribution to the capture of Vimy
Ridge.'

The 1st Canadian Division, commanded by Major-General Arthur
Currie, was attacking on a two-brigade front, on the extreme right
flank of the First Army offensive. Most of the casualties taken by the
48th Highlanders were caused by the machine guns of the 3rd
Bavarian Infantry Regiment, to which young Winston Pearson had
fallen an early victim. The Bavarians had held Vimy Ridge since 1915
and were well dug in. The concrete emplacements they had built for
their machine guns were carefully sited and sometimes almost hidden, lying flush with the ground and covered with straw, well back in
the *Zwischen Stellung* (the Red Line) – the objective of the 48th
Highlanders. The first two lines of German trenches, obliterated by
the artillery barrage, caused the advancing troops little problem; it
was in crossing to the third line of defences, the *Zwolfer Weg* or Black
Line, that men began to fall. Here, pockets of the enemy were
winkled out, many surrendering readily, others resisting to the end.
Bombs were tossed into dugouts and any surviving occupants
emerged in the grey light of dawn to find themselves surrounded by
Canadians. Infuriated by the still-chattering machine guns that felled
their men, some of the Canadians took their revenge on the unhappy
captives, as seventeen-year-old Private Hector Owen of the 15th
Battalion (48th Highlanders) later testified:

Two terrified Germans jumped up in front of me with their
arms raised and their faces contorted with fear. '*Kamerad,
kamerad!*' they shouted. A friend of mine shot at one of them.
The German ducked and the bullet hit the back of the trench
where his face had been a split second before. I had no stomach
for this. One man ahead of me was engaged in the most grisly
bit of action. A German had come out of his trench to meet him
with the bayonet; he then chickened out and was trying to
surrender. Our boy would have none of it and lunged at the
German again and again, who each time lowered his arms and
stopped the point of the bayonet with his bare hands. He was
screaming for mercy.

After clearing the dugouts and trenches of the enemy, the remainder of the 48th Highlanders now paused as planned at the Black Line for forty minutes. Some of the enemy who had not been killed in the Highlanders' onslaught were set to work cleaning up the newly captured trenches, while others were sent back to the Canadian lines with their hands on their heads. The 'moppers-up' now arrived at the Black Line and continued to scour the dugouts for any remaining enemy. The stretcher-bearers were busy, too; although exposed to fire from the Red Line, they went about the business of picking up their badly wounded comrades, many of whom, like Winston Pearson, were lying in shell holes. The 48th Highlanders, exhilarated though exhausted by their efforts, now sat back and watched as their artillery hammered the Red Line, or checked their equipment ready for the final advance. The pause was welcome, but all too short.

At 6.55 a.m. they set off, stumbling over the uneven shell-pocked ground. By now it was broad daylight; but from the leaden skies there fell a steady rain, intermingled with snow. The men were soaked through. The occasional German shell exploded in their ranks, like the one that caught Hector Owen and his chum:

> My friend fell on his face, dead. Realizing that I had a wound
> on my thigh, I fell back a few paces into a shell hole and applied
> a dressing. It wasn't much of a wound and I was much too
> excited to quit, so on I went. Soon I came to a rifle pit, or
> observation post. A rubber ground sheet was pegged to the
> sides; it sagged down on the seated occupant's head, his
> jackboots showed at the other side. I shot straight down on the
> top of his head. His body rocked violently back and forth and
> finally was still. Everything was exactly the same as it was
> before except for that little black hole in the ground sheet. His
> failure to collapse surprised me so much that I shot him again,
> with the same result as before, only now there were two holes.
> Yes I know, I know, I should have given him a chance to
> surrender, so I'm sorry already. We had been told to shoot first
> and talk afterwards. Life was cheap that day anyhow.[1]

But soon the 48th Highlanders had reached the Red Line, already battered by their artillery, and after a brief flash of bayonet work their task was done. Ahead of them lay the crest of the ridge and the next line of German defences, the Blue Line; but this was the objective of the 3rd Infantry (Toronto) Battalion. So now the Highlanders waited, as the weather cleared a little, for the men of the 3rd Battalion

---

[1] From the papers of Hector Owen (died 1972), published by kind permission of his son, Evan Owen, of Vancouver.

to come up through their ranks and join them in the newly won trenches. The assault troops now halted for two hours, as ordered, waiting for the barrage to lift before pressing on up the ridge.

So far the Canadians of the 1st Division had made excellent progress, finding little hindrance at the first few lines of German trenches – for which the infantry paid due acknowledgement to their artillery. 'A shrapnel barrage was laid down so as to explode about fifty yards ahead of us,' explained Private Gordon Liddle of the 3rd Battalion. 'As we advanced, the barrage was lifted so as to always be the same distance ahead of us. There was hardly a square of ground that had not been shelled.' And in the 3rd Battalion's war diary Lieutenant-Colonel J. B. Rogers, the Commanding Officer, recorded that:

> The morale of the German infantry was found to be poor. No doubt this bad impression was obtained through the severity of our barrage, stunning them and rendering them stupid.[2]

In fact, Liddle's group encountered very few of the enemy. Assuming that 'they had all been withdrawn', he went on:

> One exception was a lone German soldier who was unarmed and in a state of extreme hysteria from shell shock and was getting down on his knees and putting up his hands, over and over again. Somebody said, 'Shoot the son of a bitch,' and somebody did. I concluded that not all sons of bitches were in the German ranks.

Another unit of the 1st Canadian Division, leapfrogging through the Highlanders, was the 1st (Western Ontario) Battalion. They had reached the Red Line at just 7 a.m., and shortly after 9 a.m., following the planned two-hour pause, they launched their assault on the Blue Line and rushed the crest of the ridge. But their progress was so rapid that they ran into their own artillery barrage. General Thacker of the 1st Divisional artillery telephoned HQ to complain they were 'pressing forward too soon'.[3]

Despite Thacker's complaint, however, Major-General Arthur Currie was delighted by the reports flooding into his HQ. His men had succeeded in taking all their initial objectives. They had advanced over two miles and hundreds of prisoners were arriving in the

[2] PRO WO95/3762.
[3] PRO WO95/3727.

rear areas. He wired them a simple message of congratulations: 'Well done, 2nd and 3rd Brigades.'[4]

The 2nd Canadian Division – commanded by Major-General H. E. Burstall – advanced in similar style, attacking on a two-brigade front just north of the 1st Division, but with an extra support brigade. This extra brigade of infantry, 13th Brigade, had been provided by the British 5th Division, whose artillery would also support the attack. Their task was to fan out over the crest of the ridge, having leapfrogged through the leading two brigades once the Red Line had been taken. Their opponents would be the Prussians of Regiment 263, the 79th Reserve Infantry Division, which was holding an area known as Sector Arnulf with its northern HQ in Schwaben Tunnel, deep underground near Bonval Wood.

The 2nd Division had further support from tanks – the only ones allocated to the Vimy attack – eight in all and belonging to 12 Company, 'D' Battalion of the Heavy Branch Machine-Gun Corps. They were to be used in two echelons of four, assisting the infantry in their attack on a feature known as Hill 135, knocking out strongpoints and rolling down wire. They had assembled some days previously in a sunken road called Elbe Trench, in front of Neuville St Vaast – where, unbeknown to anyone, the Germans had spotted them. By Z-Day the enemy had summoned a special anti-tank battery – 204 Nahkampfsbatterie, consisting of four 77 mm field guns firing armour-piercing shot – which they hurriedly positioned at Les Tilleuls, only 500 yards from the Canadian front line. In the event, however, two of the guns were knocked out by the preliminary bombardment, and the crews of the other two guns abandoned them after only twenty minutes, fleeing from the advancing Canadian infantry.

But in fact the tanks proved a major disappointment to the British technicians – and a major headache to the men on the ground. They were slow and clumsy and had difficulty negotiating any uneven ground. It had been decided that their advance should be covered by a smokescreen, laid down by rifle grenadiers. One soldier who volunteered for this task was Private Edward Francis, of the 16th Royal Warwicks:

> A few days before the attack there was a call for men with experience of car engines for a special job with tanks. As I had a knowledge of this, like a fool I stepped out of the ranks and was accepted with seven other men. We reported to the Tank

[4] Ibid.

Battalion and next morning we were told by an officer what our job consisted of and got the shock of our lives. At zero hour we were to put a smokescreen down in front of the tanks, by walking behind them and firing bombs by a special attachment fixed to our rifles . . . two men behind each tank. This was a suicide job as the tanks always attracted a lot of heavy shell fire and my friend and I thought we had had it. On the morning of the battle we stacked the smoke bombs on the back of the tank and we started to climb a little hill, getting ready with our bombs. For the first hundred yards or so things were quiet but as we came to the top of the hill, every kind of shell was directed at the tank, but we sent our smoke bombs over as directed and kept close to the back of it. After we had fired all our bombs, the officer in charge stopped the tank and we were bundled inside, much to our great relief – but oh, inside that Tank . . . ! It was like getting into a hot oven with a terrific noise and an oily smell, but we felt reasonably safe. We had not gone much further when we struck a tank trap or a deep ditch and down we went on our side. We were all thrown to the side · of the tank and the crew struggled to get the door open as they were afraid we would burn. Well, we got out safely but were out of action and how that officer swore! We helped to salvage the guns and then made our way back to the Tank Depot some eight miles away, totally exhausted. The next day we were congratulated by the CO of the tanks for our work and he gave us a written citation. He also told us that of the eight men who had gone in, three were killed and three wounded. My pal and I were the only two to come out unscathed.

When the eight tanks had started at zero hour, they were immediately overtaken by the infantry in their dash to get forward. On Vimy Ridge the tanks proved to be totally useless as they chugged and slithered over the impossible terrain. The patchy smokescreen laid down by the frightened volunteers of the 16th Royal Warwicks only served to confuse and blind the drivers as they squinted into the murky haze. In spite of special attachments called 'spuds' to help them cross ditches, they all became stuck, four in a sunken track known as Blenpense Ditch and the remaining four in the Red Line trenches; the maximum distance covered was about 500 yards. The disappointed CO of 12 Company, Major Robert Ward,[5] blamed the failure of his tanks on their narrow tracks, believing that 'tanks fitted with wider tracks could have reached Thelus and beyond'.[6]

So swift had been the advance of the 2nd Canadian Division that the whole of the regimental staff and commander of the 3rd Bavarian

[5] Killed in action at Cambrai, 20 November 1917.
[6] PRO WO95/91.

Reserve Infantry Regiment had been captured before they knew what hit them. Many other Germans were trapped in their dugouts when the Canadians arrived, like one seventeen-year-old soldier from Kiel, Musketier Herman Kraft:

> We were lying on our bunks which were swaying with the concussion of the shells. Suddenly our electric lights went out and we lit candles. Our sergeant ordered us up the stairs, himself going first. Suddenly he yells, 'Tommies!' and fell back dead, tumbling down the steps. We all panicked and ran back into the cave and threw ourselves down with arms over our heads, fearing a bomb at any second. Then one of our 'old hands' (he was twenty-two) came down the steps and told us to abandon our weapons and come up the steps one at a time as the position was hopeless, the English were all over us. I walked up the steps behind a corporal who was very defiant and he spat on the floor when he reached the exit, but this did him no good for he was hit over the head by a huge Tommy who was brandishing a baseball bat. I covered my head with my hands and closed my eyes, expecting the same, but the blow did not come. Perhaps it was because I was so young. Looking at the soldiers, I noticed that they all had their faces blackened. I was prodded in the stomach by one with a bayonet and told to keep my hands on my head. One of the soldiers wore no helmet and had no hair apart from a small tuft on the top of his head. He also had white and red paint on his face and was very fearsome looking. I then realized that he was a Red Indian, and our captors were Canadians.

Swarming like ants over the German positions, the Canadians in the centre and right flank of the attack had seized all their objectives and walked on to the crest of the ridge.

To monitor the infantry's progress it had been decided to send up the RFC. At 7.55 that morning, Major Maltby and Corporal Morris of 16 Squadron duly took off in a rickety BE2.E to fly over Vimy Ridge. But the weather was atrocious: 'Sleet and rain were falling all the time, impossible to get above 700 feet,' Maltby reported. 'Ground invisible 800 feet away. Unsuitable for any form of work.'[7] Later in the day, however, the weather conditions began to improve and 16 Squadron was able to take off. But the RFC pilots now faced a deadlier danger than mere snow – they were flying into the British barrage. That day several planes were knocked out of the sky by their own side's shells. As Private Stanley Smart, of the 1st Canadian Mounted Rifles, recalled later:

[7] PRO AIR 1/1343/204/19/15.

One minute I saw one of our old two-seaters flying over the trenches, the next thing the engine stopped dead with an enormous crash, and I looked up and saw what looked like confetti falling out of the sky. It must have been like flying through a hailstorm, the amount of shells up there.

Private Smart's unit belonged to the 3rd Canadian Division, commanded by Major-General Lipsett. The 3rd's attack began with a dash straight into the enemy lines – thanks to two new 'bored mines', the work of 172 Tunnelling Company, Royal Engineers. In the weeks preceding the attack, the engineers had driven two long bores extending below the German defences, both of them packed with ammonal. At zero hour precisely, the ammonal charges were blown, leaving two massive trenches about fourteen feet deep, thirty-five feet wide and over 150 feet long. The explosions also served to nullify the German opposition, for the Germans were either blown sky-high or entombed in their collapsed dugouts.

Along these two new trenches, almost before the smoke had cleared, ran a company of the 1st Canadian Mounted Rifles, followed by the 5th Mounted Rifles in support, and with them went two assault teams from 172 Tunnelling Company. Their task was to locate, capture and make safe the main German tunnels under the ridge. The first team was led by Captain Dick Briscoe, MC, aged thirty-nine, who had earned a reputation for great daring in the winter of 1915, when he was at the forefront of the bitter underground fighting for the Bluff, near Ypres. Briscoe and his team soon found what they were looking for, Prince Arnulf Tunnel, but they also found a determined party of enemy defenders. Daring as ever, Briscoe rushed into the tunnel – but was instantly shot and killed.[8] There followed a sharp fire-fight, but the remainder of his team soon dispatched the opposition. Apart from the loss of their legendary captain, they suffered only temporary deafness caused by the concussion of exploding grenades, and soon proceeded to investigate the huge tunnel. A few terrified German soldiers were taken prisoner while a thorough search began for booby-traps and a start was made on clearing the tunnel for occupation by the Canadians.

Meanwhile the second assault team, led by Captain G. R. Cooper, had located the largest German tunnel under the ridge, the Volker Tunnel, which stretched from the steep eastern slope of the ridge to the enemy second line of defence and was capable of housing several thousand troops. After a few well-placed grenades had subdued a

[8] Captain Richard Brown Briscoe, MC. Buried Ecoivres Military Cemetery, Mont-St-Eloi.

1. Alberich: 'There was no doubt about it: the Germans had gone'.

2. *Siegfried Stellung*: 'The whole system was to be protected by dense thickets of barbed wire up to fifty feet in depth'.

3. Allenby: 'The responsibility for the Arras offensive rested on his broad shoulders'.

4. Haig: 'Expected to attack, whether he is ready or not'.

5. Captain 'Pat' Blair, 9th Royal Scots: 'Much loved by the boys of "A" Company for his fatherly manner and the way he lent a sympathetic ear to their perpetual grousing'.

6. Sergeant Bill Hay, 9th Royal Scots: 'Knew the ropes'.

7. Corporal Alf Razzell, 8th Royal Fusiliers: 'The most successful attack I took part in'.

8. (*above right*) Private Neville Tompkins, 26th Battalion C.E.F.: 'The other fellow might get it, but not me'.

9. (*left*) Private Arthur Betteridge, 4th South African Infantry Battalion: 'Bombardment was worse than any in Delville Wood'.

10. Livens Projectors Near Blangy: 'The Third Army had 2,340 projectors in all, ready to lob over 50 tons of gas into the enemy's positions'.

11. Easter Sunday. Fixing ladders ready for the Infantry assault.

12. Easter Sunday. 'Lusitania' moves up.

13. Easter Monday. 'Now came 4th Division advancing in artillery formation on the long walk from Arras over the captured ground'.

14. Easter Monday. German prisoners coming back:
'We no longer had any will to fight'.

15. 18-pounder Battery in action near the Arras-Cambrai Rd, west of
Monchy, 11 April, 1917.

16. Monchy: 'Look at that bloody cavalry up there'.

17. Monchy: 'Still patiently waiting'.

18. Monchy: 'The watching infantry cheered this magnificent and rare sight;
The cavalry was going in at last'.

19. Monchy: 'This was the cavalry'.

party of the enemy who had emerged from a tunnel entrance and were firing at the advancing Canadians, the engineers of 172 Tunnelling Company stormed into the main tunnel with the skill of the finest infantry, firing into the shadows, the noisy reports of their weapons echoing along the dank passages. The frightened defenders immediately threw down their arms. Working against time, Cooper frantically searched for any signs of a hidden mine which could destroy this important subway. He soon discovered a battery connected to a massive charge of explosive by electric leads which he quickly cut, thereby saving the tunnel. Throughout the morning these brave men continued to clear a further fifty mined dugouts and tunnels in the near vicinity. As General Currie later recorded, 'Sappers make good moppers up.'

For a brief period during the morning, there was chaos on the 3rd Division front as men from the 2nd Division lost their way and wandered into its sector. As the war diary of the 1st Canadian Mounted Rifles records:

> Trenches were unrecognizable, mud beyond belief. The whole of our battalion frontage was alive with men of the 2nd Division, consisting of 20th and 24th regiments who had swung right across our front. These men were sent back to their own areas. It was noted that only one officer of the 2nd Division was met with in our area and that their men were hopelessly lost and without idea of their flanks. Owing to 2nd Division coming across our front it is known that prisoners were headed off and taken care of by elements of that division.[9]

However, the general situation on Vimy Ridge by 11 a.m. that Easter Monday morning was better than expected. The 3rd Division had co-ordinated its battalions brilliantly, sweeping through Bonval Wood, knocking out strongpoints and rapidly surrounding the desperate defenders who bravely fought to the last. Only one battalion commander and six men were taken alive. Here, the Canadians were in total control of the ridge and thousands of demoralized German prisoners shambled back to the Canadian rear.

But any euphoria among the left-flanking battalions of the successful 3rd Division was to be short-lived. Just before 9 a.m. the 42nd Royal Highlanders of Canada, who had clawed their way forward against fierce resistance, were ordered to throw a defensive link to their left, right back to their original starting point. The 4th Division on their left were in deep trouble.

[9] PRO WO95/3870.

On the front of Major-General David Watson's 4th Canadian Division, the attack had got under way on time, with the explosion of two mines at zero hour on the 12th Brigade front greatly adding to the din. The capture of the heavily wired and stoutly defended Hill 145 – so called because it was 145 metres above sea-level, the highest point on the ridge – was vital to the Canadians' plans. Its sinister hump dominated the ridge. A thousand yards to the north stood 'Giessle Höhe' or 'The Pimple', which offered good protective fire against any attackers attempting to storm Hill 145. The only form of cover for attackers on the bare windswept slopes were shell-holes – of which there were plenty, though most were full of icy water.

The initial frontal attack on Hill 145 had been made by Brigadier-General V. W. Odlum's 11th Brigade, using two battalions of infantry, the 87th and 102nd. But soon the Canadians were deadlocked. Plumb ahead of the 87th Battalion lay a strong second line position known as Batter Trench, defended by men of No. 5 Company 261st Infantry Regiment. At the request of the CO of the 87th, who wanted to utilize the trench after capture, it was allowed to go unmolested by the British barrage – contrary to the wishes of the local artillery commander who deemed it more sensible to destroy it. Nevertheless, Major-General Watson had upheld the request. This was to prove a disastrous error.

Under the ghostly flickering light of golden rains and orange flares, the defenders of Batter Trench ruthlessly machine-gunned the ranks of the 87th as they emerged from the exit of Tottenham Tunnel at zero hour. Half the battalion fell in the first minute. Watson's most powerful strike force was broken and scattered, almost before the attack had got under way. Attention was then turned on the Canadians on the flanks, struggling to negotiate the dreadful shell-pocked terrain. Soon the whole 4th Division attack began to fade. To the north a smokescreen had been put down over The Pimple, giving the attackers on the left a chance to capture the northern flank; but the smoke cleared too quickly, posing an additional threat – that of enfiladed machine-gun fire. One nineteen-year-old soldier with the 72nd (Seaforth Highlanders) Battalion, which had gone over with the first wave to secure the northern flank of Hill 145, was Sergeant William Greggain from Richmond, British Columbia:

> There were thirty-eight of us in our platoon when we started and only three of us got to our objective; it was that hot. We took shelter in a shell hole, not daring to leave it as we were pinned down by two machine guns from the front and heavy

machine-gun fire from The Pimple. We had not been there long before we were put out of action by a large shell burst. Sergeant Meikle was wounded in the head, so was I. The other man, Machell, was blinded by the shell. That was my part in the capture of Vimy Ridge!

The German position now formed a deep salient from the crest of Hill 145 to Batter Trench. It was impossible for the German garrison to hold this position for long. But Watson feared they would hold out long enough to bring up their reserves and launch a heavy counter-attack, thereby driving his division off the ridge.

At 3.15 p.m., in a desperate effort to gain results before dark, Watson sent forward to 11th Brigade two companies of the green 85th (Nova Scotia Highlanders) Battalion, newly arrived in France and as yet untried in battle. Brigadier-General Odlum, at his HQ in the Tottenham Tunnel, was at a total loss as to what was happening. All runners sent forward to ascertain the situation had failed to return. All he had at his disposal were the two companies of fresh infantry. They were hurriedly ordered to capture the powerful position which had practically held up the whole division throughout the day. Lying in freezing mud in front of the tunnel, the two companies waited for the promised twelve-minute bombardment which would subdue the trench. It never came. The minutes ticked closer to zero, which was 5.45 p.m. The war diary of the 85th records:

> At zero hour, just as the last men of 'D' Company were emerging from the tunnel, a staff officer . . . arrived with a message from 11th C.I. Brigade, stating that it had now been decided to have no barrage and that the attack should be modified accordingly. The C.O. decided it was folly to attempt at zero hour to alter the plan. He feared that it might result in disconcerted action as it was impossible to communicate any order to everyone concerned before zero hour. He waited to see whether the companies would advance without a barrage. A half-minute after zero, 'C' Company on the left moved calmly and deliberately out of the trenches – the advance was taken up by 'D' Company.[10]

In the watery light of the setting sun which had broken through behind them, the single line of men advanced as fast as the mud would permit. Crossing the German front trench, now in Canadian hands, they pressed on for Batter Trench.

[10] PRO WO95/3909.

Astounded at the effrontery of this little group attempting to dislodge them, the weary Prussian defenders automatically clattered back the cocking handles of the heavy Maxims and methodically began to tac-tac along the line of khaki stumbling towards them. Watchers in the wings could clearly see the steam rising from the overworked weapons, and hear the shouts of the two company commanders as they urged their boys forward.

It looked a hopeless task. Men were falling into the mud as the bullets found them. The line grew pathetically thin. Suddenly a rifle bomber from 'C' Company, Corporal Milton Curll, fired off a bomb from the hip as he advanced. It was a lucky shot. The grenade exploded a few feet in front of the most dangerous machine gun, killing the crew. With a hundred yards to go, other bombers followed suit. With fifty yards to go, an incredible five machine guns were still blazing away from the top of undemolished dugout entrances. Suddenly the gunners turned and ran for the crest. The brave remnants of the Nova-Scotians let out a great cheer that must have been heard by Odlum in the Tottenham Tunnel. They gave pursuit – right to the crest of Hill 145.

Breathing an almighty sigh of relief, General Watson now decided that complete consolidation of Hill 145 could wait until the following day. The *Hangstellung*, the line of German defences at the bottom of the reverse slope, would be taken by two relatively fresh battalions, the 44th and the 50th. When that was secure he could turn his attention to The Pimple.

Over the years much confusion has arisen as to who actually captured Hill 145 and when it was captured. The soldiers themselves often confused it with The Pimple. But Watson, the 4th Division Commander, was in possession of better information than any historian will ever be. He acknowledges that there was no more fighting for Hill 145 after the evening of 9 April. In his short book, *The Story of the 4th Canadian Division, 1916–1919*, which he published himself, he states:

> On the first day, a certain portion of Hill 145 held out against us by virtue of its very commanding position and the extremely stubborn resistance of large groups of the enemy. However, the situation was completely cleared up that night.

From this it is quite clear that Hill 145 was captured on the evening of 9 April. An examination of the war diaries of all units of the 4th Division engaged in the vicinity produces no evidence that there was any further fighting for Hill 145 that day.

The massive weight of artillery fire brought to bear on Vimy Ridge and the meticulous planning by the First Army staff had paved the way for a great Canadian victory. However, it had been impossible for the Germans to implement their new defensive tactics here, due to the severe reverse slope of the ridge. Had they stuck to the 1915–16 'rigid' system of defence, which meant cramming the forward trenches with defenders, instead of leaving them in isolated 'islands' behind the first line, then the story might have been different. Either way, they would have still had to brave the artillery storm. The majority of Canadian soldiers were under no illusion as to what had won the day for them:

> We went over supported by the Lahore Divisional Artillery, and were they Crackerjack! Why, the Germans had been beaten before we got there, it was a walkover! (*Private Bill Tapper, 38th Battalion*)
> We didn't fight the Germans off Vimy Ridge. We *blew* him off; what with the weight of our artillery and the mines, we simply *blew* him off. (*Corporal P. G. Pinneo, 8th Battalion*)
> I have always felt that the Canadian success was overrated. We had more than enough artillery to do the job. This is not an official view. (*Bugler Bernard Ward, 24th Battalion*)
> Going over was like taking candy from a kid, it was so easy. You should have seen our artillery fire. (*Lieutenant C. B. Hamm, MM, 7th Battalion*)

By nightfall on 9 April, 1917, apart from the *Hangstellung* and Pimple – both of which would fall in the following three days – the whole of Vimy Ridge was in Canadian hands and would remain so for the rest of the war. The German High Command, by its very decision not to launch a counter-offensive, had accepted the loss of the ridge as irretrievable. The only day a counter-attack would have been viable was 9 April – but at dawn that day the five counter-attack divisions allocated for the purpose were twenty miles behind the front; it would have been well after dark before they made their presence felt. By then it was all over.

In relinquishing Vimy Ridge, the two German Divisions, the 79th Reserve and the 1st Bavarian Reserve, had lost between them a total of 6,604 men (up until 11 April). It had cost the Canadians 9,033 in killed, wounded and missing by 11 April, and by the 14th the total casualties to the Canadian Corps had risen to 11,297.[11] By First World War standards, however, this was a small price to pay for the

[11] Figures taken from British Official History.

capture of such an important position. Indeed, even General Horne, the First Army Commander, thought so, for on 12 April he wired to the Canadian Corps:

> The Vimy Ridge has been regarded as a position of very great strength; the Germans have considered it to be impregnable. To have carried this position with so little loss testifies to soundness of plan, thoroughness of preparation, dash and determination in execution, and devotion to duty on the part of all concerned. The 9th April will be an historic day in the annals of the British Empire.[12]

The exuberance of a team victory seemed to abound. Arthur Currie recorded in his diary on the night of 9 April that the day had been 'a wonderful success . . .' The euphoria of it all even affected Lieutenant-Colonel John Kirkaldy, Commanding Officer of the 78th (Winnipeg Grenadiers), who that morning had witnessed the total massacre of his battalion by the machine guns on Hill 145. Describing the loss of twenty officers and 774 other ranks as 'regrettable', that night he wrote an optimistic account of the day's events, concluding that: 'All ranks were eager for the attack and I am satisfied that the sacrifices were cheerfully made.'[13]

[12] PRO WO95/169.
[13] PRO WO95/3909.

9

Harper's Duds

Further south, while the Canadians were fighting and dying and eventually capturing Vimy Ridge, the British infantry of the Third Army continued their part in the offensive. The most northerly sector of their ten-mile front, bordering the 1st Canadian Division's sector, was that of the 51st (Highland) Division.

Arthur Currie must have been pleased to have the 51st Highlanders as his neighbours. Not only did they have an excellent fighting reputation, but Currie enjoyed a jovial liaison with their experienced commander, George Harper. Before the offensive, however, Currie had been concerned about the 51st's complicated attack plan. For a start, his Canadians were due to cross the front of the 51st Division and press on for Thelus. This would be fine, providing the Highlanders could keep up and not leave his flank open. But Harper had decided to attack on a two-brigade front, using 154 Brigade on the left and 152 Brigade on the right, with one battalion from 153 Brigade being attached to each. The remaining two battalions of 153 Brigade were to leapfrog over the assault force later in the day and proceed to the final objective, the Green Line or Point du Jour Line, which was a line running at complete right-angles to the 51st Division's jumping-off trenches. This would require an enormous degree of skill at company-commander level, for the Highlanders would have to make a sudden right-handed swing at one point, while at the same time maintaining contact with the Canadians on the left, whose first objective was in advance of the 51st Division. The success of the day would depend not only on fighting skill, but on brains.

The plan was further complicated by the fact that the front line at the junction between the two armies took an acute swing to the north, thereby creating a well-defended salient – The Labyrinth – which jutted dangerously into the British lines. This would have to be knocked out separately if the attack was to go in on schedule. One company of the 4th Seaforth Highlanders was assigned to this task. On their right was the 9th Royal Scots. These two battalions, forming the left-hand prong of 154 Brigade's attack, would face the hard-fighting 2nd Bavarian Reserve Regiment from Munich, part of the 1st Bavarian Reserve Division.

The majority of 'A' Company, 9th Royal Scots, had not noticed that the first British salvo of shells at 5.30 a.m., intended for the Germans, had fallen behind them – their minds were firmly set on the task that lay ahead as they jostled at the foot of the ladders leading out of their jumping-off trenches. Sergeant Bill Hay remembered a bit of 'pushing and shoving, like queueing for a Rangers' home game', but also 'a fair sense of relief we were on our way'. He continued:

Above the din of the barrage you couldn't speak. It was Jimmy Adams who tapped me on the shoulder indicating 'Go!' Well, I was first up the ladder and once on top I turned about and put out my hand to assist him up; then there was a loud 'Clang!' and his steel helmet went spinning into the air. He was shot clean through the head and fell straight back into the trench. 'How bloody ridiculous!' I shouted, as if the Germans were listening. 'He was only a boy!' Well, no time to feel sad . . . we had a job to do and, besides, there was a fair bit of machine-gun fire whizzing about us. Most of the lads got out of the trench OK but the other platoon commander, Bill Ferguson, was killed in exactly the same manner and at the same time as Adams. The first problem was the British wire; no paths had been cut. I caught my bloody kilt on it and in trying to free myself I got my hands caught by my woolly mitts. Then I dropped my rifle . . . But good old Sandy [Walton] was there and he managed to unhook me. We soon caught the boys up who were jumping from shell hole to shell hole and then Jock Leishman caught us up – he had been caught in the wire too. Soon we got to the German front-line trench. It was smashed to bits but there were several dugout entrances. We dealt with these first. I pulled the pin from a Mills bomb and chucked it down the steps – 'Come out, you fuckers!' There was a crash followed by shouts and screams. Jock Leishman threw another one in for good measure – crash! – and another 'Come out, you bastards!' Up the steps came four Jerries with their hands up. '*Kamerad, kamerad,*' they wailed. 'Never mind the fuckin' "*kamerad*", let's have you bastards out now!' Prodding them in the bellies with our bayonets, 'Keep those hands up!' we shouted. They were terrified and grovelling. Two of them were youngsters who started to blubber. I suppose they thought we were going to do them in. We got them by the scruff of their necks and directed them back to our lines, giving them a boot up the arse each, to help them out of the trench. By this time their own counter-barrage had started and I doubt if they got through it. I got the lads together and we set off for the second line, but then we came to more bloody wire! I turned around. 'Where was Jack?' I thought. Sandy was with me and I could see Doey Campbell just to my right, blazing away with the Lewis. Slowly we picked our way through the wire; then quite a few of the boys started to fall forwards on their faces, and I thought at first they were taking cover but I realized it was machine-gun fire.

. . . Suddenly there was a blinding flash – no noise, no pain, just a whistling in the ears, then redness, I could only see red. I was blinded! Slowly I came around and could feel this warm body lying on top of me. 'Sandy, are you OK, son?' I felt his face; he didn't answer. I put my hand on his forehead and my fingers went into an enormous hole just above the eyebrows. I knew he was killed.

Hay lost consciousness and lay in the shell hole until picked up by stretcher bearers of the 7th Argylls. Walton, his batman, was dead. Lying nearby, the burial parties later found the bodies of Jock Leishman, the Campbell brothers and many other members of 4 Platoon.[1] Hay, with the vision in his left eye permanently impaired, returned to his battalion six weeks later.

The majority of 2 Platoon managed to get a little farther into the German trenches than 4 Platoon. Corporal Bob Graham later recalled:

I can vividly remember seeing the Germans popping at us as we went through their wire and I felt a numbing blow on my foot but carried on. The Germans who had been popping at us suddenly threw down their weapons and stood up with their hands up. We jumped into the trench and began to get ourselves organized. It was here that my good friend Bill Dickinson was killed . . . Suddenly we heard single shots fired repeatedly from our left. We knew it was a sniper shooting at our men as they advanced. CSM Jack Renwick and Corporal Fermie traced the location of the sniper, stalked him and killed him. For this Jack got the MC and Fermie the MM. The pain was getting worse in my foot, so I took off my boot and found that I had a hole right through it, so I went back to the dressing station and that was me out of this part of the war!

By 7.30 a.m. the soaked survivors of the 9th Royal Scots were crouched in a battered indentation in the ground. According to the maps, this was the Black Line. It was still sleeting down and their kilts were sodden weights around their hips. In spite of the discomfort,

---

[1] All buried in Roclincourt Valley Cemetery. The officers, Adams and Ferguson, are buried in Roclincourt Military Cemetery.

hard-boiled eggs were passed around, cracked open by filthy fingers and devoured. They had forgotten it was Easter. Contact was soon re-established with the 4th Seaforths on the left and the 6th Seaforths on the right. The captured trenches were quickly reorganized and carrying parties were detailed to take ammunition forward to the support waves, now attacking the Blue Line.

The 4th Seaforth Highlanders' objective was the Labyrinth salient, near the Lille road. Scrambling out of his trench, Private Fred Hollingworth heard one of the Canadians calling out to him: 'Good luck, Jock!' This tickled Hollingworth; although he was wearing a kilt, he certainly wasn't a 'Jock'. And, remembering that moment when they went 'over the top', Hollingworth pointed out that this was no sudden charge such as one sees in the old movies. 'You couldn't run two steps,' he went on:

> It was just one continuous mass of shell holes, and some were so big you could put a decent-sized house in them. The Jerry wire which was supposed to have been blown to smithereens by our bombardment was still in place and it was impossible to get through. It had just been blown up in the air and was in a worse tangle. Well, we were trying to see spaces where we could get through and one fellow was shot dead as he was caught by his kilt in the wire. I don't like to think of it. Also, to see those machine-gun bullets hitting the wire, it was a right November the Fifth show, sparks going in all directions. Then I saw a gap where I could get through and I was jolly glad to slip into Jerry's front line – and sure enough, just what I expected: instead of mud and slush, a nice dry sandy bottom and a nice wide trench.

Despite their losses, the 4th Seaforths had succeeded in capturing the Labyrinth salient, and had also managed to maintain contact with the Canadians on their left. A single platoon was now ordered forward under Lieutenant Edwin Leslie, to work with the Canadians as far as the third German line and then link up with the main body of the battalion.

To reach the German third line, however, Lieutenant Leslie and his men had to cross a small grassy knoll just to the right of the Lille road, behind the German first line, which was not entrenched but commanded a good view. The divisional artillery would not shell it, for fear of hitting the advancing Canadians on the other side of the road. Leslie had no time to dawdle. The urgency of his orders compelled him to take one course of action; he would go straight over the top of the knoll. Foolishly he ordered his men to 'Dress Ranks' – a manoeuvre best left to the parade ground – and form up in two lines.

Jock (*in captured trench*): Coom awa' up here, Donal'; it's drier.

The platoon then advanced at the double in two straight lines. As soon as they topped the crest they were ambushed, a shower of stick grenades falling amongst them. Leslie was killed instantly and the whole platoon wiped out. Captain Andrew Fraser of the Seaforths, anxiously watching this catastrophe from a nearby tunnel exit, now collected together a storming party and, with the assistance of Canadians working around to the rear of the knoll, surrounded the fifty or so German defenders and rushed them with the bayonet. In the fierce hand-to-hand fight that followed, the Germans fought to the bitter end, dying where they stood, in a rough circle facing their enemies.

Next, it was the turn of the two support battalions, the 4th Gordons and 7th Argylls on the right. These battalions made a successful advance to the Blue Line, the left platoon of Gordons sticking with the Canadians who indicated their positions by waving blue and yellow flags. The advance of this platoon was fast – faster than the rest of their division, who had come up against some very stubborn Bavarians. But by mid-morning most of the 51st Division's battalion officers had been either killed or wounded – and it was these very officers who knew what direction the 51st Division was supposed to be taking. Consequently, when it was time to make the planned right-hand swing, the turn was too acute. The 7th Argylls veered straight across the front of 152 Brigade, which had been held up by heavy machine-gun fire, and then, having crossed two communication trenches and entered a third, believed themselves to have reached their objective: the Green Line or Point du Jour Line. In fact, however, they had merely found an insignificant communication cut called Tommy Trench. Here the Argylls spent the night digging in and clearing the trench, resisting all attempts to tell them that they were in the wrong place. It was not until the following morning that they realized their error.

Two companies of the 4th Gordons also lost their way but their battalion war diary puts the blame squarely on the 7th Argylls, who were 'responsible for direction'. The eager platoon of Gordons on the left had actually reached their objective, but finding 'no one on the right' decided that they had gone wrong and returned to their earlier position. As a result of this confusion a large gap now appeared in the centre of the 51st Division's front, which General Harper had to plug with his only remaining two fresh battalions. By nightfall on the 9th the gap was filled, but now there were no reserve battalions to relieve the badly mauled Jocks who had fought themselves to a standstill. 'Old 'Arper' had committed his whole division.

That night, with the 51st Division still several hundred yards off its final objective, Harper issued orders for 152 Brigade to press on under cover of darkness. Frantic messages from Arthur Currie had been arriving at the divisional HQ all day, asking where the 51st had got to; but Harper was adamant: his 'little fellers' were on their objectives. Fortunately, Harper's right flank was safe in the 34th Division's hands, although the 34th had faced heavy machine-gun fire. All Harper needed to do on the following day was to catch them up.

Arthur Currie had no reason to cross swords with George Harper. His own 1st Canadian Division had carried all its objectives. The 51st Division, in carrying out a far more difficult role had, as usual, attracted most of the enemy's firepower and absorbed much of the punishment meant for the Canadians. But if Currie's Canadians had failed, then Harper would have made the perfect whipping-boy.

For Fred Hollingworth of the 4th Seaforths, back in the safety of the tunnel and thanking the Almighty for his deliverance from the morning's perils, there was one more horrible task. Corporal George Tyler ordered the young private to join a search party for the men they had lost. 'They took a lot of finding,' Hollingworth later recalled; although three of his mates were recovered, 'we never did find the fourth.' One body was discovered in a huge water-filled crater:

Whether he had died from drowning or from this piece of shell, I don't know. I hope it was the shell but his head was under water and we only spotted him by the Mackenzie tartan kilt. We dragged him up the bank, to the top as it were, and aye, it were 'im all right. We trudged all three, one at a time, over them shell holes, what a trudge. It seemed rotten taking fellows that had walked themselves over it before. Now we were carrying 'em for the last time. But there was worse to come. We got to the Lille road by the instructions given us where to take bodies, and there was a great big notice high in the air with letters that must have been fifteen inches big. No notice must have been so big an' it were done in black paint: 'DEAD DUMP'.

10

Maxwell's Procession

The most critical battle of the day was the central attack by six divisions of Allenby's Third Army. With their backs to the town of Arras their task was to strike the Germans a massive initial blow, which would immediately be followed by two leapfrogging divisions thrusting through the enemy lines, so that three cavalry divisions could burst out towards Cambrai and roll up the enemy rear. All exciting stuff, but surely none of the British planners was *that* confident?

To the north of the River Scarpe and forming the left-hand flank of this mighty punch was the 34th Division, much recovered after its hammering on the first day of the Battle of the Somme and led by an efficient and popular officer, Major-General C. L. Nicholson. Attacking with three brigades up and with a far less complex plan than the 51st Division on their left, the lead battalions got off very quickly at zero hour. Their ultimate objective was the Green Line on the bare crest of Point du Jour Ridge, 2,000 yards ahead; but at the second objective, the Blue Line, there was to be a four-hour halt to enable the support battalions time to mop up and for the artillery to soften up the enemy defences for the final blow. In short, the initial advance of the 34th Division became a race – the 16th Royal Scots taking the tape by capturing three lines of enemy trenches in just *ten minutes*.

The 103rd Brigade on the left was to keep in touch with the 51st Division, but the lead battalions, the 24th (1st Tyneside Irish) and 25th (2nd Tyneside Irish) Northumberland Fusiliers, soon ran into trouble after crossing the enemy front trench, being held up by heavy machine-gun fire. In crossing with his headquarters to the first trench to sort out this problem, the Colonel of the 24th, Lieutenant-Colonel Edwin Hermon, DSO, was killed.[1] The 25th Battalion lost all but two

---

[1] Colonel Hermon, who had transferred from the cavalry in search of more action, is buried in Roclincourt Military Cemetery.

of their officers in the space of a few minutes, and to add to their problems, troops of 152 Brigade, 51st Division, after being lashed by this fire, crossed their front and came streaming back through their lines. Yet more confusion was produced when troops of the 26th (3rd Tyneside Irish) Northumberland Fusiliers came up in support, only to find themselves pinned down.

The sole cause of this setback was a single machine gun, the crew of which had survived the barrage and were now creating mayhem. One twenty-year-old Geordie from Riding Mill, Northumberland, Private John Herdman of the 26th Northumberland Fusiliers, had just returned to his battalion after being machine-gunned in the legs on the Somme and now he found himself facing the same menace:

> It were murder! . . . You seemed to be in a mixture of exploding shells, clouds of dirt and bullets flying. When we got to the second or third line, I noticed that blokes were going down all along our line, a single machine gun to our left was playing havoc with us. Then suddenly I felt a stinging blow on my left leg (again), and down I went. A bullet had gone clean through the shin, just above the ankle. Tom Bryan, our corporal, who had been advancing next to me, swore and ducked down. Then he went for the gun crew. He was mad! . . . But he knocked it out. Meanwhile, I had put iodine on my wound and tried to stop the bleeding, but I was really cold and began shaking and shivering. Our losses in men were terrible and I'll never forget that scene of horror; dead and wounded piled everywhere. It was awful.

Lance-Corporal Bryan, a Worcestershire man of thirty-five, had indeed knocked out the machine gun that had been holding up the whole advance, despite himself being wounded. As Major T. Reay of the 26th Northumberland Fusiliers later wrote to Lieutenant-Colonel J. Shakespear, the historian of the 34th Division:

> Captain Huntley and Bryan had gone forward up a communication trench to see what they could do. Huntley was killed on the way up . . . Bryan went on alone and killed the two gunners, so that the Blue Line was made safe for the other people who were to push on later in the day. The two witnesses said they saw Bryan stab the two gunners – they saw his bayonet flashing. I saw the ground afterwards and examined the machine-gun position. It had a wonderful field of fire . . . It had caught our people as they came over the ridge, about 300 yards in front of the machine-gun position. Our men and men of the Scottish Division (on our left) were lying dead in almost a line,

just on the ridge. But for Bryan,[2] the division would never have reached its objective that day.[3]

Similarly engaged in the rush to the Blue Line, on the front of the 101st Brigade, were the 11th Suffolks (the Cambridge Battalion). They had gone off so fast that their moppers-up failed to clear the Black Line properly and raced off after the leading waves. Their war diary records:

> Twenty German prisoners were captured by the five runners and orderly room sergeant, who together with the pigeon man and an RE signaller comprised the eight other ranks with Battalion HQ. The prisoners showed no desire to fight in spite of the fact that they were more than two to one – and there was an abundance of German hand grenades and rifles lying about.[4]

A private with the 11th Suffolks, Reg Gray, later described the pell-mell advance in more detail:

> Some of our men wanted to get on faster than the barrage moved, which resulted in several of them being hit by our own shells. About forty Germans came out of one dugout nearby and it was rather amusing to see our men shaking hands with them. Each German had an electric torch fastened to his tunic and some were carrying clean washing by way of a shirt or something under their arms. Then we had a fairly long wait as ordered. At last we set off again and for the first time in the battle, my section got the Lewis gun going, firing at several Germans who were retiring and several fell as the result. Next we came to a valley which was nothing but a mass of barbed wire; but our people had put thousands of 9.2 shells into it which had broken it up a good deal, enabling us to get through. Then we came to a deep railway cutting where we took hundreds of prisoners. There were lovely dugouts here and I had to smile to see the Germans come running out of these dugouts with their hands up, for it seemed they had just received a cigarette ration, for as they ran to the collecting place they were handing them out to all who were looking on.

All along the front of the 34th Division, General von Rauchenberger's proud 14th Bavarian Division, the left-hand prop of *Gruppe*

---

[2] Bryan was awarded the Victoria Cross.
[3] John Shakespear, *The 34th Division* 1915–1919, p. 101.
[4] PRO WO95/2458.

Vimy, had disintegrated before the oncoming khaki waves. Here and there little knots of men came forward under a white flag, some stupefied by the ferocious shell fire, others suffering from the effects of gas. The total collapse of this particular division opened the way for a further British advance – the German reserves were too far back to be of any immediate assistance. When the news reached Ludendorff at Kreuznach, where he happened to be celebrating his birthday, he was furious; the Bavarians had 'failed' him, he later wrote, yet this Division 'had previously enjoyed a high reputation'. But as August Beerman from Krumbach near Munich, a soldier in the 25th Bavarian Infantry Regiment, later wrote to his wife from Étaples where he was working as a prisoner of war: 'We were sick of gas, sick of shells, sick of the cold and sick of having no food. We no longer had the will to fight. Our spirit had been broken.'

The men of the 34th Division were ordered to dig in. Although frozen to the marrow by the biting winds on the featureless plateau, they felt they had done well. They had avenged their defeat on the Somme. In front of them lay open countryside, seemingly untouched by war. There was no sign of any Germans. They eagerly awaited the order to press on.

Brigadier-General Frank Maxwell, VC, DSO, had sharpened his 27th Infantry Brigade of the 9th (Scottish) Division to a fine edge, and he had every confidence that his Jocks would not fail him in the capture of the Green Line. Their prime objective was Point du Jour Farm, a large concrete blockhouse protected by deep trenches and thick hedges of barbed wire, which stood on the highest point of the ridge and gave complete observation over the Scarpe Valley and right down into Arras itself. The 27th Brigade consisted of the 6th King's Own Scottish Borderers, the 9th Cameronians (Scottish Rifles) and the 11th and 12th Royal Scots. The troops were equally confident and raring to go. They also knew that General Maxwell would be closely marking their progress on the 2,000-yard climb to their objective. He would be going with them.

The 9th Division Commander, Major-General Henry Timson Lukin, was a fifty-six-year-old Londoner who had seen much service in South Africa, having been seriously wounded in the Zulu War at the Battle of Ulundi. From there, he had risen to command the Union Defence Force of South Africa, and when the war broke out he had gone to German South-West Africa to fight as commander of the South African Mounted Rifle Brigade. In May, 1916, the South Africans in France were formed into a complete Infantry Brigade,

101

with 'Tim' Lukin in charge, and attached to the 9th Scottish Division. At first there was some resentment within the division, as the South Africans had replaced the established and Loos-bloodied 28th Brigade, but the South Africans earned the respect and admiration of the 'Jocks' by their distinguished and determined fight at Delville Wood in July, 1916, when they had suffered terrible casualties. In December, 1916, Lukin had succeeded to the command of the division, the South Africans being still under his wing. On the Arras battlefront the 9th Division had been in position since the previous December, on a four-mile sector astride the River Scarpe, and was therefore very familiar with the lie of the land and the enemy defences. Maxwell's brigade was to attack on the left, the South Africans in the centre and the 26th Brigade on the right. Two enemy-held villages, St Laurent Blangy and Athies, stood in the 26th's path; but it was hoped that saturation with gas would have subdued the defenders by Z-Day. Four tanks were also allocated to this division to assist in the capture of the villages, although three were hit by shellfire almost immediately and the fourth soon broke down.

The 9th Division was in possession of 4,000 smoke shells (no one else wanted them), which were due to be fired in the barrage at a ratio of one-in-four, with high-explosive shells, by eighteen-pounders. A dense curtain of fire was promised, behind which the troops could advance in safety. By zero hour the whole of the 27th Brigade, including General Maxwell – dressed in a private's uniform – had completely cleared out of their trenches in order to avoid the enemy's expected counter-barrage, each unit carefully adjusting formation in no-man's-land during the four-minute bombardment of the enemy front-line trench. At zero the assault units went forward – but no one could see the enemy front line. It had been smashed to obscurity; even the moppers-up over-ran it. Fortunately, this resulted in no major mishap, although one private in the Divisional Pioneers, Joseph Dobie of the 9th Seaforths, remembers:

> We strung out behind the first and second waves and followed a white tape laid by the engineers. Our job was to dig a communication trench between the (old) front line and the German front line. We were still under shell fire but the attack was going well. Prisoners were passing by and we told them to keep moving, ushering them along. Some were very bombastic and others would want to give us watches and other things. There were no more prisoners coming back so we guessed the advance was going well. We had got to about a foot deep with our trench, when rifle shots rang out; one of our officers was

killed and the other fell wounded. They had been standing there encouraging us to dig faster. We quickly grabbed our rifles and organized one party to the left and the other to the right and set off to cover from where the shots had come from. We found that three Germans had come up from a deep dugout. They tried to surrender but we shot one and bayonetted the other two. Then we went back to our digging . . .

This incident serves to illustrate the difficulties of mopping-up – the process of clearing the deep dugouts after the attack had passed through. The war diaries of all the units thus engaged on 9 April are profuse with reports of a similar nature – of groups of Germans emerging from deep dugouts and shooting into the backs of the advancing infantry.

In accordance with the timetable, the 27th Brigade surged on. The Black Line soon fell and at 9 a.m. word got back to Divisional HQ and the other brigades that Maxwell was on the Blue Line with the final objective, Point du Jour, in sight. Maxwell later wrote:

The attack was a procession, and happily so, for the heavy wire protecting the Brown Line was untouched. Passage through it was either cut or effected through gaps of the enemy's making. Our barrage, considering the range, was firstly effective but one gun fired consistently short, as it did while the stationary barrage remained east of the railway. Few enemy were seen and these surrendered. At the Point du Jour, a party of the 6th K.O.S.B. filling a gap between our left and the 34th Division right, rushed a machine gun, destroyed the garrison and demolished its breakfast.[5]

The signallers of 'C' Company, 4th South African (Scottish) Infantry, were due to go over at 5.47 a.m. with the support troops and so were in position just south of the St Nicholas–Bailleul road. Crouching at the bottom of a new mine crater which had been blown in no-man's-land two days previously to assist the assembly, Private Arthur Betteridge and his pal 'Stockie' Stockholm did not relish the prospect of carrying a heavy ground wireless across 400 yards of broken ground to the enemy trenches. Betteridge had recently returned to the battalion after Delville Wood where he had been seriously wounded in the thigh and now the bitter cold was stirring up the pain again. As the last of the fighting platoons got clear of the crater, it was now the signallers' turn to go:

[5] PRO WO95/1770.

Stockie and I got to some barbed wire. I pushed my rifle under the straps of the two-foot square instrument and left Stockie to pick up the butt-end of the rifle with his right hand. I grabbed the muzzle with my left hand and we staggered with all our other equipment through a gap in the wire. It was a most uncomfortable lift, but Stockie had the easiest part of it. He was a married man about twenty-eight years old and always grumbling about things. We hardly got through the wire gap when Stockie demanded to change hands and swop around with the wireless. No sooner had we lifted the heavy instrument again when a shrapnel shell burst right in front of us. Stockie collected two holes in the neck and a large one in the stomach. I saw that he had no hope.

Another of Betteridge's comrades with the 4th South Africans 'copped it before we even got to our objective'; but Private Don Ogilvie was luckier than Stockie Stockhom:

A shell landed on our Lewis-gun team of six, killing two and wounding me. The other three moved on and I crawled into the nearest shell hole and must have passed out. To save time, the stretcher bearers' practice was to stick your rifle in the ground with your helmet on top of it if you had been killed, thereby marking your place for the burial parties. I came around at about 4 p.m. and was shocked to see that this had been done with me, thinking I was dead! Eventually I was helped by a soldier in the Black Watch who was escorting Jerries back to the cages. I was carried to the dressing station on the back of a German prisoner. As we passed a crowd of our chaps, one of them called out 'Do you want some spurs, mate?'

Apart from a slight delay caused by machine-gun fire from a concrete strongpoint called 'the Parrot's Beak', the South Africans kept up with the dash of Maxwell's brigade. Brigadier-General Dawson, commanding the brigade, recorded: 'Throughout the day the men were in the highest spirits and had the utmost confidence.' In fact, he added, 'In many cases the wounded remained in the ranks until ordered to go back to the dressing station.'[6]

On the right flank, the 26th Brigade had in its path not only the village of St Laurent Blangy, but also the nearby fortress known as Railway Triangle. Formed by two high embankments carrying the Arras–Douai and Arras–Lens railways, with a branch track connecting the two before they merged, the Triangle stood out conspicuously like an ancient earthwork. If the 15th (Scottish) Division, attacking

[6]PRO WO95/1777.

on the right of the 9th Division, failed to capture the Triangle, then the 26th Brigade's flank would be in jeopardy.

Initial resistance among the ruined houses and cellars of St Laurent Blangy was soon overcome. However, the men of the 8th Black Watch got lost twice in the smoke and some of them ran into more serious opposition – like Lance-Corporal Alex Fisher, MM:

I had lost track of my chums but seeing one of them I lifted up my left arm to wave to him, rifle and bayonet wedged in my right hand, when a piece of shrapnel hit me right in the armpit. It burned and I felt sick but it didn't seem so bad, so I soon caught up with my chums. Suddenly some Jerries began firing at our backs. One who wouldn't come out of his dugout kept throwing potato-masher bombs out as far as he could. I put a bomb onto my rifle at a decent distance and it wasn't long before he was buried in his dugout. At this time we began to suffer quite a lot of casualties. I remember one fellow walking along with the fingers of his left hand touching the ground. It looked odd that, his arm was just a mass of skin and bone. It was cut off with a jack knife. We then rushed our objective, a railway embankment, firing for all we were worth, from the hip as ordered beforehand. The Jerries came running out crying 'Kamerad, no kill – wife and family at home!' One of our fellows, Bert Hamilton, was waiting at the entrance to a dugout to take his prisoners, when he was shot through the neck by a Jerry officer who came up the steps, after which he came running over to us with his hands up. He got a Mills bomb all to himself. We had just finished clearing out some dugouts when one of our shells landed. I got some mud from it but it killed my mate, Clark from Fife. It lifted him fifty yards and he fell on his hands and knees and not a mark on him but he was as soft as butter. I remember getting the letters out of his pockets and he had one from his kiddies telling him all about their birthday and hoping it wouldn't be long before he came home.

11

Centrepunch

South of Railway Triangle the land rose in a gentle slope and curved towards the Arras–Cambrai road. This was Observation Ridge and here the German defenders from the 51st Prussian Infantry Regiment, frustrated by the awesome British bombardment, had submitted a request to their Brigade Commander to attack Arras itself – anything was better than enduring the torture of the bombardment. But their request was turned down. Now, in accordance with the new defensive tactics, they had concentrated their weary but far from demoralized companies into 'islands' of defence: small egg-shaped redoubts, 200–300 yards apart, heavily wired and deeply trenched, and each of them held by one officer or senior NCO and thirty to forty determined men. Their presence was known to the British, however, having been photographed from the air and marked on the latest trench maps – Heron Work, Hamel Work, Harte Work, Holte Work and so on – and they would be tackled by Major-General F. W. N. McCracken's 15th (Scottish) Division on the left and Major-General A. B. Scott's 12th (Eastern) Division on the right, in their joint advance to the Brown Line.

The main armament of these small forts was usually a single heavy machine gun, which was to be brought up into position from the command dugout at the moment of attack. The Prussians had affectionately given their machine guns individual names, as one would name a pet dog – 'Rossbach', 'Hobick', 'Moritz', 'Kurt' and 'Wallenstein' to mention but a few. Each gun gave covering fire to its neighbour, so if the British infantry could get through the first trench lines – which was expected – then the machine guns in the small forts could do untold damage. This string of earthworks was built to defend one especially important position, Battery Valley, the northern entrance to which was protected by the railway embankment and the Feuchy switch trench. Here General von Scholer, commander of the 11th Infantry Division, had placed the bulk of his field artillery. The guns were 2,500 yards from the British front line and considered safe.

But if the forts on Observation Ridge should fail, then his batteries were doomed.

The men of the 12th and 15th Divisions were lucky. They had been selected to spend five days prior to the attack in the dry safety of the tunnels under Arras, although Corporal Tom Bracey of the 9th Royal Fusiliers groused, 'I spent much of the time in the tunnel wearing a waterproof groundsheet around me shoulders because of the water drips. A bloody nuisance that was.' The respective divisional commanders, working closely together, had decided to attack with their brigades similarly disposed, two in line up front, with one to follow through and seize the final objective. Two tanks were allocated to the 15th Division, anticipating trouble at the Railway Triangle. Another four were allocated to the 12th Division, two to assist in knocking out the island redoubts and two to advance up the Arras–Cambrai road – but these four never turned up.

At zero hour the 15th Division's two brigades, the 44th and 45th, went over. The first objective for the 13th Royal Scots was the village of Blangy – protected by three lines of enemy trenches and a strongpoint defended by machine guns. Because of their closeness to the British lines, these German positions had not been subjected to the bombardment; instead, a mine was placed beneath the strongpoint and at exactly 5.30 a.m. the mine was sprung. Unfortunately, too much explosive had been used. The blast not only destroyed the strongpoint but stunned the first wave of Royal Scots forming up in no-man's-land, and some were buried by falling debris. Quickly recovering, however, they reassembled and set off for the enemy-held village. By 8.45 they had seized Blangy and cleared it, taking thirty-eight prisoners.

The 15th Division ran into far greater trouble – as expected – at the Railway Triangle. The assault force was stopped in its tracks by lethal bursts of gunfire from the eastern embankment. On top of the embankment, almost forty feet high, the Germans had dug a deep trench, strengthened by concrete and steel embrasures with the railway lines providing further excellent reinforcement. At 11.30 a.m., seeing his division held up by this hail of fire, General McCracken made an important decision; he telephoned his artillery commander and requested the barrage to return to the eastern side of the Triangle. This was not the done thing when an artillery unit was limited to a strict timetable, but in this case it was the right thing. The gunners complied, concentrating their fire on the eastern defences. Carnage ensued as high explosive and shrapnel shells fell on the exposed machine-gun crews. As the barrage lifted, the 9th Black

Watch bombed, shot and stabbed their way into the Triangle, the garrison of which either died quickly or surrendered. But there was still danger. Some nests of machine-gunners, dug in at intervals under the southern railway embankment, had not been harmed by the plunging artillery fire. Thus an acute threat persisted right along the embankment to Feuchy Bridge. It was time to deploy the tanks.

Clattering ponderously along a half-sunken track alongside the Triangle came Tank 788, or 'Lusitania', commanded by Second-Lieutenant Chas Weber. He had managed to get the tank to the deployment point by 4 a.m. in spite of getting stuck in the mud on the way up, but had then discovered that he had lost four bolts from the back axle connecting shaft; this meant that the shaft would shear off unless replacement bolts were found. He immediately dispatched a crewman, fleet of foot, back to the Arras Citadel. At 8.30 the sweating man returned with the necessary bolts. The tank finally coughed into life at 9.30 a.m., crossing the British and German front lines without incident, and reached the support troops of 44 Brigade. After a couple of halts to let the engine cool down and clear water from a faulty magneto, Lieutenant Weber was informed about noon that the infantry needed assistance to clear the machine-gun posts on the railway embankment. He directed his driver to mount the railway at the flattened end of the Triangle and, driving east along the railway, began to fire his six-pounders at a machine-gun post in Fred's Wood just to the north of the railway. Then the tank ran out of petrol. Weber wrote soon afterwards:

> Received message from Brigade Major, 44th Brigade,
> requesting reason for stoppage. Informed him that we were
> filling up and would start in two minutes. Started engine and
> proceeded towards the Blue Line. Halfway over, Sergeant
> Latham informed me that all our infantry were following. They
> arrived almost simultaneously with us, in fact too close to allow
> me to use my guns, and found the Germans with their hands
> up.[1]

'Lusitania' continued her slow crawl along the railway, lashing Feuchy Redoubt with six-pounder shots and long bursts from her crew's Lewis guns; the defenders soon fled, to a dugout near Spider Corner. The tank now left the railway by another flat part of the line and continued along a sunken track, blazing away and squashing anything that resembled a machine-gun nest, with the infantry following joyously behind to round up the terrified defenders. By late

[1] PRO WO95/91.

108

afternoon and with shells falling dangerously close, Weber took 'Lusitania' up a steep slope in the direction of Arras but the tank would not have it and stopped. Having not slept for almost two days, the exhausted crew fell asleep. When the engine had cooled down, 'Lusitania' resumed the sport of German-chasing for as long as the daylight lasted. Then the distributor gave out. At 9.30 p.m., having fired fifty drums of Lewis gun ammunition and all but three of their six-pounder rounds, the crew abandoned the tank, deciding to return for it in the morning. By then, however, 'Lusitania' had succumbed to friendly shellfire.

Following behind 'Lusitania' as she rampaged along the embankment, the troops found a trail of havoc. Private Carson Stewart, 6th Cameron Highlanders, later recalled the scene at some smoking machine-gun pits which had just suffered a direct hit from one of the tank's six-pounders:

> There was one survivor lying in this stone shelter. He was about sixteen years old and looked very badly wounded but I took no chances. I had to make sure he was not out to get me by pretending he was wounded. I went through the motions of pulling out a pin from a Mills bomb and threw it into the shelter with him. If he had tried to throw the bomb back at me I would have shot him, but he didn't, he just went mad and the poor devil frantically tried to wriggle away from the bomb. But I had not taken the pin out. I then knew he was badly wounded. Now when I got word that my younger brother had been killed on the Somme, I vowed I would do in the first German I met, even if it was in cold blood, to level up the score. But here was a young lad in desperate need of pity and the better part of me prevailed. He begged me for water and so I gave him a drink from my precious supply. I told him in French that the stretcher bearers would come . . . I got some German black bread from the shelter and shared some with one of our young officers who had been watching this. He promptly told me off for being sympathetic to the young German and said, 'No more of that, Stewart.' But now, in the winter of my life, I am glad that I had pity on that young lad. I just hope he made it.

The Railway Triangle was now a gathering place for stragglers and other small groups of 15th Division men who had lost their units. Slowly they were sorted out – as were the German prisoners who had been rounded up for dispatch to the rear. One prisoner seemed to be hiding something, remembered Private Bill Good of the 9th Black Watch. 'It turned out to be a commemorative stein of Field-Marshal von Hindenburg,' he said. 'It was a good souvenir and is now in the Black Watch Museum.' Private Good also remembered one wounded German in particular, lying in a shell hole with 'an album in his hands, looking at his family photographs. That touched me up a bit. When I saw him later, he was dead.'

Among some of the units laying claim to dugouts in the Railway Triangle was a company of 13th Royal Scots who had captured Blangy that morning. Second-Lieutenant Eric Baker reported that the dugouts had been 'well furnished' by their previous occupants, who had even enjoyed the comfort of armchairs. But now the dugouts were in a state of devastation:

> There were dead Germans everywhere, lying down steps and
> scattered all over the place. We were ordered to tidy the place
> up, so we collected the bodies together and dug a large
> rectangular pit about twenty yards from the embankment. The
> burial of about twenty-four Germans was conducted by the CO,
> Medical Officer and Padre. When I returned to this spot on a
> visit to the old battlefields in 1979, the outline of the mass grave
> was still visible.

Advancing behind the creeping barrage at zero hour were the 11th Middlesex and 7th Sussex of 36th Brigade, 12th Division, with the 8th and 9th Royal Fusiliers in support. The Fusiliers' task was to leave the front line at 7.50 a.m. and leapfrog through the ranks of the Sussex and Middlesex battalions, picking up the moving barrage in front of the Black Line and pushing on to the Blue Line. The German historian of the 51st Regiment later described how the English troops came 'pouring out of the catacombs of Arras, shoulder to shoulder, in waves eight deep'. It must have been a terrifying sight to the defenders of the first line, who were quickly overcome. 'Only a few groups managed to defend themselves with rifle and hand grenades but it was soon all over for them,' reported the regimental historian.

Passing through the lead battalions, as they plodded up the slope towards Observation Ridge, the Royal Fusiliers now came under fire from the machine-gun posts in the island redoubts and began to take casualties. Diving to the ground, little bodies of men started worming their way forwards on elbows and knees to get to grips with the enemy machine-gunners, who seemed to open up from everywhere as the barrage passed over them. Some of the 8th Royal Fusiliers were stuck in front of 'Hamel Work' but their officer, Second-Lieutenant Maude, led them on. 'He was shot through the stomach almost immediately,' remembered Private Tim Collior, who added, 'I believe he was a brother of Cyril Maude, the actor.' Lieutenant Maude died shortly afterwards,[2] having given his revolver and cigarette case to Private Collior, but in an attempt to save the Lieutenant one of the stretcher bearers, 'the one who had conducted the church service the day before', said Collior, 'ran over to him but was shot through the head and killed.'

Slowly, little groups worked away at the machine-gun redoubts, some managing to outflank them and knock them out from the rear. One young fusilier, Corporal Alf Razzell, had seen his battalion destroyed by machine guns on the Somme and thus accorded them particular respect. 'As we advanced I could hear "Rat-tat-tat-tat" and I thought "This is it, now we're for it,"' Corporal Razzell remembered later. His company was held up for half an hour by a single machine-gunner:

> He was positioned in a shallow trench and was traversing his gun in a 180° arc. In short rushes, as the traverse passed us by, we gradually formed a semicircle around him until he was within rifle grenade distance. Inevitably, he and the gun were silenced – a brave man. We rushed his position and I jumped in first. I noticed that he was an officer[3] and was lying dead on piles of empty cartridge cases. The machine gun was mounted on a post driven into the floor of the pit with the barrel just above ground level. Hanging on the post was a leather holster containing a lovely Mauser pistol – I got that! – and I sold it to the Quarter-Master Sergeant for 75 francs. That was beer-money for me and the survivors of our section.

Apart from this hold-up, however, Corporal Razzell commented:

> This was the most successful attack I took part in – and I had been 'over the top' five times. Our casualties were not heavy in comparison and this was the first time we had seen a travelling barrage. What a brainwave that was! . . . I remember thinking at the time, 'Cor, we're getting on top of them at last!'

One by one the small redoubts were surrounded and overwhelmed by the waves of khaki, although one, manned by Sergeant Schwerk of No. 2 Machine Gun Company, allowed the British infantry to get within fifteen feet before mowing them down with his gun 'Wallenstein', before he too was bombed to death. It was during this 'Battle of the Redoubts' on the morning of 9 April that one young sergeant in

---

[2] Second-Lieutenant Gervase H. F. Maude is buried at Duisans British cemetery.
[3] Probably Leutant R. L. Heinrich, 2nd Machine Gun company, 51st Infantry Regiment (no known grave). The machine gun was 'Rossbach'.

the 7th East Surreys, twenty-three-year-old Harry Cator from Norwich, rushed one of the machine-gun redoubts single-handed and killed the crew. For this he was awarded a Victoria Cross.

Although the history of the 51st Prussian Infantry Regiment gives the reason for the capitulation of the redoubts as 'running out of ammunition', the simple truth is that they were outflanked and outgunned. Nevertheless, one German officer at least was unbowed in defeat; as Leutnant R. Schlensog of the 51st later wrote:

> This Easter Monday 1917 would go down in the history of the regiment as a glorious day. We felt we had been undefeated but as we no longer had any ammunition left, further opposition was futile. Any possibility of a breakout with the bayonet was hopeless as we were surrounded by the enemy. Such an attack would only have resulted in the deaths of the remainder of my men. As soon as we stopped firing we were overrun by the enemy who were not interested in us as individuals, but for what possessions we had. Watches, rings iron crosses and whatever else was worth taking they took from us as if it was their God-given right. As if robbery was their major line of work . . .

By 10.50 a.m. the 8th Royal Fusiliers were digging in on their objective, Houdain Lane, 200 yards from the crest of Observation Ridge. Elated by their success, pockets bulging with souvenirs, they awaited further orders. In the fight for the redoubts, they had lost forty-two men killed and 119 wounded, which was considered 'light'. The rain had stopped and the sun broke through. The day was looking good. Corporal Alf Razzell fired a green Very light to notify an overhead RFC spotter plane that the Fusiliers were in position and ready to proceed to their next objective.

The 5th Royal Berks were due to pass through the 8th Royal Fusiliers at 12.10 p.m. and capture the Brown Line, the final objective for the 12th Division. After some minor delays on the way up, the Berkshires soon crossed the ragged trenches crammed with cheering and clapping Fusiliers, deployed in line and advanced boldly towards the crest of Observation Ridge. Meanwhile, General Scott had sensibly ordered his artillery to bombard the crest of the ridge and the far side of Battery Valley where the strong Wancourt–Feuchy switch trench could seriously hamper any attempt by the Berkshires to cross the skyline. The 7th Norfolks, working to the right, had already captured Maison Rouge on the Cambrai road and the 9th Essex, pushing through them, had seized Feuchy Chapel Redoubt, which covered the southern exit of Battery Valley. At 12.45 p.m. the two lead companies of Berkshires duly crossed the ridge into Battery Valley – only to find themselves facing four enemy artillery batteries, which immediately opened fire at point-blank range. A score of men were cut down but, facing such a prize – the capture of the enemy's artillery, a rare event in any war – the surviving Berkshires charged down the slope, ably covered by the Lewis guns of the 35th Machine Gun Company which had somehow kept up with them.

Frantically attempting to reload, the enemy gunners were slaughtered by the Lewis gunners. Some of the batteries had already hitched up to their horse teams and were attempting to make off, but the 10th Scottish Rifles and the 7/8 Scottish Borderers of 15th Division now rushed into the valley from the northern end. There was no escape. Within seconds the Jocks and the Berks County men were on them with the bayonet. Few survived. Adding insult to injury, some of the 9th Essex men, who had seized nine guns at the southern end of the valley, now turned two of the pieces around and fired them at the Germans fleeing away up the eastern ridge of the valley. The rout was total. The capture of the German guns in Battery Valley was a great triumph for the British infantry; they had finally taken their revenge on the very gunners who had for so long made their lives a misery.

Eventually the 8th Royal Fusiliers received the order to move forward into Battery Valley. By the time they got there, however, the action was all over. Enviously the Fusiliers inspected the newly captured guns. Corporal Razzell describes the scene:

> Some of the guns had been caught by our machine-gunners as
> the crews hitched up the horses preparing to withdraw and
> there were gunners and horses still forever. I noticed that
> someone had written on one of the gun-barrels in yellow chalk,
> 'Captured by 5th Berks' and alongside was written 'Liar' . . . I
> thought, 'Who the hell carries chalk around with them in this
> war?'

The right-hand spike of the trident wielded by General Haldane, the VI Corps commander, was his old division, the 3rd 'Iron' Division. His central division, the 12th, had done well to overcome the string of redoubts barring their path; but they had failed to reach the Wancourt–Feuchy switch line and although Feuchy Chapel Redoubt had been captured, the powerful line beyond could cause trouble to his old favourites who had attacked directly to the right of the Arras–Cambrai road. The 3rd Division's frontage of attack was narrow – only half a mile – but the objective, the Wancourt–Feuchy switch, was

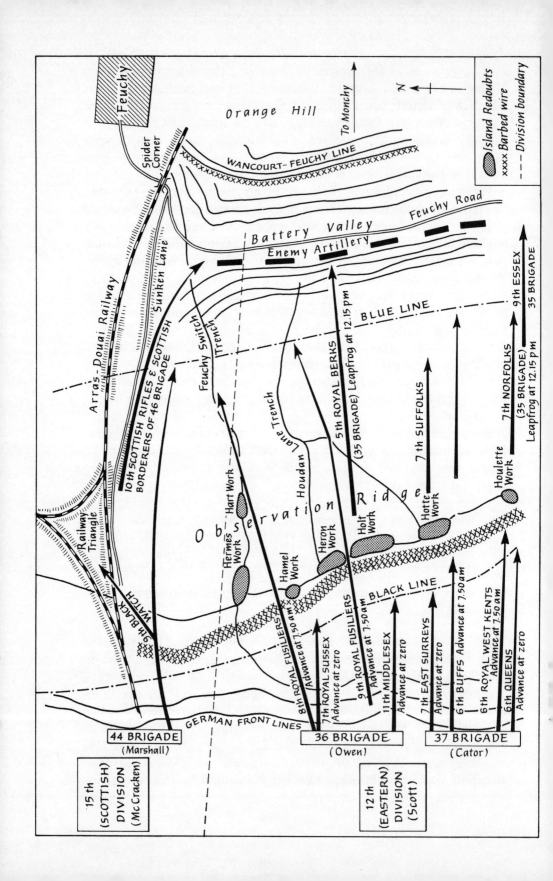

over twice as wide; because of this the 3rd Division Commander, Major-General C. J. Deverell, decided to attack with only one brigade up, using the others to follow through and capture the successive lines: the 76th Brigade would thus take the Black Line, 9th Brigade the Blue and 8th Brigade the Brown. In the 3rd Division's path, however, stood a fortified village, Tilloy-les-Mofflaines, defended by soldiers of the 76th (Reserve) Regiment who had suffered heavily from the British shelling, and further on was the heavily wired Chapel Hill, which in fact caused more problems than Tilloy.

The attack started brilliantly, with the well-rehearsed 1st Gordon Highlanders reaching their objective only minutes after zero hour, closely followed by the 10th Royal Welsh Fusiliers, who secured the Black Line. At 7.30 a.m. the 9th Brigade advanced to assault the ruins of Tilloy, while fanning out to attack a formidable position known as 'the Harp' from the north. Behind a creeping barrage, the 9th Brigade, reinforced by the 2nd Suffolks, advanced with great determination, bombing and shooting out nests of enemy defenders. Pockets of resistance held out in Tilloy for a time, but capitulated when waves of support troops arrived from the 8th Brigade, on their way to the final objective. The capture of Tilloy might have been accomplished earlier if six of the ten tanks of 9 Company, designated to assist, had not got bogged down in the Crinchon Valley before zero hour. However, despite this mishap, one tank did assist in the final capture of Tilloy and two tanks of 8 Company managed to get into the Harp.

Corporal Alf Sillitoe of the 7th King's Shropshire Light Infantry took part in the 8th Brigade attack on Tilloy. As he later recalled, 'We suddenly came under severe sniper fire from the trees along the edge of a wood and several of my section were killed.' But the rest of the men dived for cover and soon took their revenge, blasting their way into the shattered village and capturing droves of defenders. That task achieved, Sillitoe's section next pressed on for Chapel Hill, 2,000 yards ahead. It was now mid-afternoon and, although a bitterly cold wind was licking across the plain, the Shropshires raised a sweat as they stepped out towards the trenches of the Wancourt-Feuchy switch line, where they saw what looked like a copper-beech hedge. It was uncut rusty wire. Was the enemy still there? Or had the 12th Division driven them out? By now the barrage had been lost. With just over 400 yards to go, the questions were answered as machine-gun bullets ripped into them.

At 5.30 p.m. on hearing that the advance was held up, General Deverell hurriedly issued fresh orders for a renewed attack by two battalions from 76 Brigade: the 1st Gordon Highlanders, who had attacked that morning but were still comparatively fresh, having suffered only sixty casualties, and the 8th King's Own, who had hardly seen any action that day. The attack was to go in at 6.45 that evening, following a bombardment of the enemy positions. The Gordons duly gathered at the start point, but the King's Own were nowhere to be seen. They had not received the order. Undeterred, the Gordons went ahead, attacking in four-company waves from a sunken track running between Feuchy Chapel and Neuville Vitasse. From shell holes, the surviving 7th KSLI men watched the Gordons go in. Almost immediately, the enemy machine guns started chattering. The Gordons closed ranks and pushed on. They made a hundred yards before it was all over. What was left of them crawled back to the sunken track.

General Deverell had been misinformed. Feuchy Chapel had been taken by the 9th Essex of the 12th Division, but the strong fortifications behind it, Church Work and the Wancourt–Feuchy switch line, were still occupied by the enemy. Due to a total lack of liaison between the two divisional commanders, the 3rd Division had been unable to reach their final objective. They would have to try again the following day.

12

The Hindenburg Line

The divisions to the right of the 3rd were the 14th, 56th, 30th and 21st. This right-flank supporting operation was intended to assist the central attack by preventing the Germans from reinforcing the gap – but it was the hardest task of the day. Directly facing these divisions was a new section of the Hindenburg Line, which began at the Harp just north of Neuville Vitasse, cut through the village, then swung south-east in front of Heninel and Fontaine-les-Croisilles. If any success was to be achieved at all, the enemy line had to be broken here.

The 14th (Light) Division had been promised the assistance of fourteen tanks from 'C' and 'D' Battalions. It would need them – the wire defences were formidable. Captain T. C. Tanner, of the 5th King's Shropshire Light Infantry had spent the morning of Easter Sunday in an observation tower with General Dudgeon, scanning the ground over which his company was to attack the following day. 'It was a beautiful day,' he wrote later, and through his binoculars he could clearly see 'a dense mass of German wire. It must have been over fifty yards thick and my heart sank. I thought to myself, "My God, they've got an impossible task." '

The local Corps Commander, General Sir Thomas D'Oyley Snow, probably thought the same. Yet the 14th Division's task was the easiest of the four, as their jumping-off point was nearest to the Hindenburg Line. To compensate for the gradually increasing distance each division had to cover, Snow decided to stagger the start times. The 14th Division would start at 7.30 a.m.; the 56th at 7.45; the 30th Division would send in one brigade at 12.55 and the other two brigades at 4.15, while the 21st Division, on the far right, would also attack at 4.15 p.m. with a brigade on their right standing fast. All this depended, however, on the 14th and 56th Divisions breaking through at the Harp, Telegraph Hill and Neuville Vitasse and 'rolling up' the Hindenburg Line from the rear. If they failed, then these later attacks would be sheer suicide.

What happened surprised Captain Tanner. According to schedule, his company of the 5th KSLI, which had spent the previous night in the Arras caves, broke into the Harp defences and had seized their objective by 8.45 a.m. Although the German defenders from the 162nd Regiment fought well, they were jumped by the Shropshires who, keeping close to the barrage, killed or captured most of them before they could gather their wits. The tanks greatly assisted here, by rolling down the wire, and it was probably their presence that forced such a quick capitulation from the remaining defenders of the Harp and Telegraph Hill.

The bulk of Allenby's twenty-four tanks had gone into action on this sector but few survived the day. An extract from the tank report of No. 8 Company, 'C' Battalion, for 9 April shows dismal progress:

No. 790　Ditched on String trench.
No. 582　Track broken by being bombed.
No. 597　Went to assistance of 582 and became ditched and
　　　　　heavily shelled.
No. 599　Hit by direct hit.
No. 787　Ditched.
No. 588　Ditched on String trench.
No. 777　Hit by Trench Mortar and set on fire.
No. 578　Ditched on String trench.
No. 776　Ditched on the Harp.[1]

The report concluded that the tanks' chief weakness was their 'liability of ditching', but it is possible that at least one of them drove into a tank-trap, for the Germans had covered some old gun-pits with wooden frames and turfs, especially around the Harp position, with this very end in mind.

Just north of Neuville Vitasse, Jim Luxon from Hoddesdon in Hertfordshire was sweating in the uncomfortable driving seat of a 'D' Battalion tank, 'D.4' which the crew called 'Diana' in honour of their officer's fiancée. Delayed by a broken fan belt, 'Diana' was racing to make up lost time, bumping and rearing over rough ground and debris, and the crew were cursing Luxon. 'We got well toddied up with whisky beforehand,' he explained later, 'otherwise we would never have had the nerve.' And he went on:

> We had snow that day, but inside that tank it was too bloody
> warm. It was like hell in there, the engine was flamin' and the
> noise . . . Well, we hadn't gone far when we came in for some

[1] PRO WO95/91.

118

stick. 'Bang! Clang!' Bullets kept hitting the tank. Well, I kept my flap up quarter of an inch so as I could see where I was going. The bullets kept on coming at us, and my face and the backs of my hands were all little pin-pricks of blood – bullet splash, you see, where they come through the little hole. Suddenly in front of me I saw some of our boys, either dead or wounded, in a shell hole . . . I told the officer . . . 'Drive on, Luxon, drive on, there's a war on,' he said. I didn't like that. Anyway, we got to our objective and waited there a little while to cool down, then we turned round and come back to our starting point. There was an observer there, he had been watching the battle. He said to our officer, 'How you got through that bloody lot I'll never know, he didn't half paste you!' and the officer said, 'My driver kept going!' That was his motto: 'When in action, keep going.' And that's my motto in life still!

Wearily, but pleased with their success, 'Diana's' crew finally clambered out amid a crowd of onlookers – who all started roaring with laughter. The crew were literally black from head to foot.

Another vivid account comes from Archie Richards. A Cornish tin miner in civvy street, this young private of eighteen was now in charge of a six-pounder gun in his 'C' Battalion tank. Richards and his fellow crew members 'led a charmed life that day', he recalled later. He had personally scored a direct hit on one enemy machine gun when suddenly the tables were turned:

There was a terrific bang on the sponson and a piece of metal struck me in the mouth, smashing my two front teeth. Spitting out the blood and bits, I carried on firing the gun. Suddenly, bullets came flying into the tank and we all threw ourselves on to the deck. They whizzed around like bees for several seconds . . . Then we hit his main trench. As we went into the parapet we all hung on, and then down came the tank on the other side . . . What a bang! It almost jarred my head off. Well, I shot straight down the trench and skittled the Jerries who were running like hell. Then we stopped to let the bus cool down and got out to have a look around and cool down ourselves . . . Our officer was a gentleman; he said, 'Well done, boys, we've done our bit. We've got them on the run. Now let's get the hell out of it!'

The most worried man in the whole of the 56th (London) Division that morning was 'B' Company's Sergeant-Major Eddie Warren of the 12th Londons (The Rangers). Knee-deep in icy mud in their jumping-off trench, known as Deodar Lane, they were waiting to

119

attack the village of Neuville Vitasse which lay just over a half a mile ahead. It was not the daylight zero hour of 7.45 a.m. that worried him; the Rangers had gone over in daylight before, at Gommecourt on 1 July, 1916. What nagged at him was that the barbed wire in front of Pine Lane, a strongly-held German trench, had not been cut. During the night, while the Rangers assembled for the attack, he had met his old pal Charlie Clark, the Sergeant-Major of 'A' Company in the trench to their right; it was Charlie who had told him that the wire was completely uncut.

Pine Lane lay between the Rangers and the northern end of Neuville Vitasse and 'A' and 'B' companies were going in first. Colonel Baycliffe knew the wire wasn't cut, as did General Hull, who had even told Snow, the Corps Commander. The artillery was supposed to cut it but they hadn't. During the night a patrol had gone out under Second-Lieutenant Baron, who reported:

> The wire was found to consist of two belts of very thick wire about breast high with iron stakes, and had been practically untouched by our shell fire, except in one or two places where shells had burst in the wire without damaging it sufficiently to make it less of an obstacle.[2]

Sergeant-Major Warren knew in advance what would happen:

> At 7.45 a.m. we went over and executed our attack in perfect order – like a drill in Hyde Park. Our lads were mostly from Paddington and Kilburn and they were smoking and chattering away to each other in great spirits. I expect they thought it was the beginning of the end. Well, we got right up to the wire and everyone went quiet . . . The machine gun opened up from point-blank range and a dozen or so went down in the first burst. We all got down in the grass and a few of the boys ran along the wire looking for the gap, but they were shot down. 'A' Company on the right copped it the worst. Some of the boys threw themselves flat into the wire to act as a human bridge, but they were shot to bits – it was heartbreaking. I'd like to know why that attack was not cancelled when the General *knew* the wire was uncut.

Meanwhile, Second-Lieutenant Cunningham of 'B' Company had found a small gap in the wire, which he and his platoon were able to crawl through. Creeping along the enemy trench, they managed to bomb out and kill the machine-gun team that had been exacting such

[2] PRO WO95/2954.

slaughter. The attack was finally saved by the arrival of a solitary tank, which chugged up to the wire and flattened a large gap; whereupon the Londoners rushed through and killed or captured the remaining defenders of 163 Infantry Regiment.

The Rangers then pushed on to the north-east edge of the village. In the centre the 8th Middlesex also ran into uncut wire but managed to force their way into the village and when they reached the site of the destroyed church they found a strong pocket of Germans who had emerged from deep caverns, into a final redoubt of sandbags, well protected with rolls of wire. They were the survivors of 163 Infantry Regiment and were determined to sell their lives dearly. They were soon surrounded and mercilessly showered with bombs. Just before 11 a.m. sixty-eight survivors with four machine guns from this redoubt surrendered. Neuville Vitasse was in British hands.

Neuville Mill, a concrete emplacement on the Mercatel road, had promised to be a problem; all previous attempts by the 1/3rd Londons to knock it out had been thwarted. But at zero hour on 9 April a tank had driven straight up to the strongpoint and fired its six-pounder gun directly through the embrasure, killing nine of the defenders and destroying the machine gun. 'B' Company of the 1/3rd Londons captured the four stunned survivors.

In spite of the hold-up to the Rangers in the morning, the London Division advanced 2,000 yards, capturing 612 prisoners and meeting varying fortunes. 'No man's war was the same,' said Bill Partridge of the 7th Middlesex, and for him and his inseparable chum, Alf Davies, the advance of the London Division on 9 April afforded them both 'a nice day out':

> Our officer said, 'Come on, Diehards' as we went over the top . . . All very warlike – but the only bravado we got was from our rum! Oh, it was lovely stuff! It was a very successful advance for we went quite a long way and our section got off very lightly, keeping close to the barrage – it was much more concentrated than the Somme and no back-bursts. My next worry was the wire, having been held up by wire at Gommecourt where I was wounded. But no, the wire was all flattened and blown to bits, so we just stepped over it. And lo and behold! There was happy Jerry all ready with his hands up and smiling faces: 'Hullo Tommy,' which meant 'We've got it good now, you haven't!' The lucky sods. A German officer was wounded and he'd got these lovely field glasses. I took them off him – he spoke English, by the way. I said, 'I'm to take these, you're only allowed your gas mask.' I gave him some cigarettes, as a matter of fact . . . and they were lovely Zeiss glasses. When

our Colonel saw them, he said, 'Really I ought to impound these, Partridge; you're not supposed to have them. But I won't, you lucky young devil!' And what happened to the field glasses? Why, some bastard pinched them!

And Alf Davies added:

Speaking for myself, I never took any prisoners. It was quite unnecessary – they all gave up the ghost. They were quite pleased to come quickly. That day was the best attack of the war, we just walked into Jerry's lines smoking Bill Partridge's fags. He always had *plenty*.

As for Sergeant-Major Eddie Warren of the Rangers, he got through the day without a scratch, but he had found his pal Charlie Clark lying dead in a bloody tangle of young bodies in the German wire. The following day Brigadier-General Loch gave his permission for one officer and fifty-seven other ranks of the Rangers, all killed on the wire at Pine Lane, to be buried side by side in their old jumping-off trench, just to the right of the Beaurains–Neuville road.[3] Charlie Clark was placed at the head of his men.

Meanwhile, the advance on the right flank by the 21st and 30th Divisions had gone in as planned; but with the 56th Division delayed at Neuville Vitasse, the enemy were given ample warning to step up manning levels on the Hindenburg Line. Although a small sector of the line was captured in the late afternoon, it was by then impossible to complete the plan and 'roll up' the line as hoped. The supporting attack here was, as General Snow half-expected, a failure.

[3] London Cemetery, Neuville Vitasse. The Rangers killed on 9 April are buried in a trench grave, row 'A'.

13

Forcing the Gap

Scanning the green plain ahead through his binoculars, Frank Maxwell could not see a single German soldier. Buffeted by the bitter
wind on Point du Jour ridge, he stepped back into the old German
trench and was handed the field telephone that had been reeled out
to him. Miraculously, the line was still intact. Division wanted a
situation report.

Although it was only lunchtime, the great day seemed to be over
for the troops of 27th Brigade, 9th (Scottish) Division. They were
itching to press on, but a two-hour protective barrage had now been
put down 200 yards in front of their positions. This was in accordance
with Allenby's plan – to give protection from counter-attack and
enable the leapfrogging 4th Division to catch up and push on to the
Green Line. But in effect the barrage had boxed them in. Maxwell
could not see any point in hanging around waiting for the 4th Division
when the way ahead was clear. His 27th Brigade were still relatively
fresh and in great spirit. But he was merely a Brigadier-General. He
later wrote:

> Protective barrages kill initiative and exploitation. I confess to a
> very strong inclination, almost amounting to decision, to push
> my Brigade through the Brown Line protective barrage in order
> to seize the Green Line, thereby denying the enemy the two
> hours' respite allowed by the programme.[1]

At 2.10 p.m. the 'regulars' of Major-General 'Billy' Lambton's 4th
Division began to arrive. They had walked up from Arras across the
captured ground in artillery formation. As they passed through the
watching Jocks, they deployed professionally into waves, fixed
bayonets and advanced into the unknown. Although Captain Robert
Monypenny, a company commander of one of the lead battalions, the
2nd Essex, saw only what went on under his own nose and probably

[1] PRO WO95/1770.

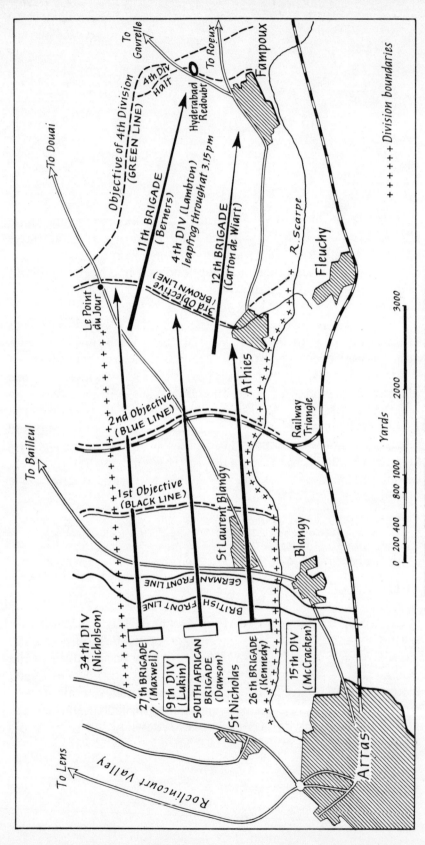

5. THE ATTACK OF THE 9th AND 4th DIVISIONS, 9 APRIL, 1917.

did not grasp the full significance until long after, his dramatic description of the 4th Division's advance on the afternoon of that historical day is quoted here in full:

The barrage kept a wonderfully even line, a curtain of continuous fire about a hundred yards ahead of us, creeping forward at a walking pace. The smoke and the fountains of earth helped to conceal our advance a little as well as tending to diminish any fire from snipers, machine guns or any entrenched infantry that might be in front of us. We had gone about 500 yards, when two field guns of the German artillery, hidden in a dip across our front, suddenly opened fire point-blank at us. We took them in one concerted rush after they had bowled over a few of our men. A few of the Germans who resisted with small arms were bayonetted, the rest had their hands up in surrender.

We presently came to the northern outskirts of a village called Athies and two lines of defence facing us. The wire was pretty well cut and defences pretty well battered. We found considerable resistance; however, we rushed the defences in which the few remaining Germans gave only a half-hearted attempt to resist with cold steel. There was some chasing in and out of a few battered buildings in Athies and clearing up of the two lines of trenches of any of the enemy still resisting. So far our casualties had been fairly light and we sent back a further batch of prisoners.

Our final objective of the day had yet to be overcome and so we set out on another half-mile advance. The first few hundred yards we were scarcely fired at, except by artillery, and we managed to get our lines into a parade-like order again. By this time, our own artillery had either ceased to function or we were so far ahead as to be useless to us until they had moved forward. Then, within sight of our last objective, the Green Line, we came under really heavy fire. Undaunted, we pressed on, men were dropping faster here and the gaps were filled up from behind. We moved steadily on with casualties continually increasing. When within charging distance we rushed at the barbed wire, which to our dismay we found almost untouched by our artillery and at least thirty yards deep. It was terrible stuff, with barbs an inch or more long and so close together as to be almost continuous. The enemy was blazing away at us at point-blank range. I could hear the swish of machine-gun bullets as they swept up and down our line. Feeling utterly non-plussed for a moment, I dived down to earth and the men followed suit. I then got them firing through the wire at the German parapets and got my nearest Lewis gun sweeping at the Germans to check their fire. Under cover of our fire, a party on my right discovered a gap in the wire and dashed through. On seeing this, we all got up and made a dash straight ahead across the wire. Men were getting caught and falling into the wire, I tore my hand and knees on the barbs, but kept going.

The machine-gunner opposite me was getting more frantic as he swung his gun to and fro and it is no exaggeration to say that as he traversed his gun, one bullet clipped my right ear and another my left ear. Has anyone ever had a narrower shave?! One of the bullets got my sergeant, who was just behind me, right through the head and he slumped over the wire dead. This was the first and last time I saw red. I lunged forward, revolver in hand (I still carried one although some officers took to carrying rifles and bayonets), and blazed at this German machine-gunner and his crew; how they never got me I don't know. I was in a tearing rage, shooting fast and bowling them over. I suppose the man on the gun actually went down first and the others were too dazed to act quickly enough to get me. The next thing I remember was all the hands stuck up in surrender.

By this time, my men were also seeing red but I had come to my senses and stopped the shooting and bayonetting of surrendered enemy. We sent the prisoners back, reformed and went on to the enemy support line, a hundred yards farther on, which we found deserted. So our objective was reached. Somebody asked me where I was hit as my face was pouring blood on both sides. I put my hands up and found the tips of the lobes of both ears bleeding where the machine-gun bullets had nicked the edges. I had forgotten about it in the earlier mêlée. We got ourselves organized and called the roll to find out who was missing. The casualties were fairly light, considering the nature of the final assault. Then we snatched a meal from our haversacks and prepared to consolidate the final position.

Other people across the River Scarpe not far from us on our right had advanced a little ahead of us, so apparently it was decided that we should go on ahead and keep up with them. To our right was the village of Fampoux and to our left the Hyderabad Redoubt.

We were ordered once more to launch our weary selves onto these objectives and the line joining them. So the Brigade once more pushed ahead. The enemy fire was very heavy now, especially machine-gun fire at long range from Greenland Hill, beyond the Hyderabad Redoubt. Our right flank, after a desperate assault, captured Fampoux but our centre and left got a heavy mauling and were held up until further reinforcements reached the line and pushed on. The German shelling was now becoming very heavy and in our last dash towards Hyderabad Redoubt, what felt like a thunderbolt struck me in the region of the heart and I went down in an agony of pain. A piece of shell from a high explosive had struck me in the chest. It was now getting dark and there I lay, breathing in great gasps. I never lost consciousness and lay there for what seemed a long time. Eventually, I heard somebody moving about and a pair of

126

stretcher bearers found me. A jagged piece of shell had smashed my chestbone and lodged beside my heart, cutting the pericardus.[2]

But Hyderabad Redoubt, the big triangular earthwork that meant so much to Captain Monypenny, was captured shortly afterwards by the 1st Rifle Brigade of 11th Brigade, 4th Division, one platoon of which drop-kicked a football into the middle of the redoubt and followed it up with a determined rush. Here, a German general was captured, having been abandoned by his chauffeur. The 4th Division's advance was over.

The experiences of Captain Monypenny were typical of the long walk taken by the Division on the afternoon of 9 April. The British Official History simply records that this feat marked 'the longest advance made in a single day by any belligerent on the Western Front since trench warfare had set in. It was a distance of three and a half miles'.[3]

Frank Maxwell, although an infantry commander, was a cavalryman by profession, and a brilliant one at that. By early afternoon on 9 April he had recognized a golden opportunity for the cavalry, as he urgently impressed on his divisional commander over the telephone. The Germans were on the run, Maxwell reported; it was time to bring in the cavalry, to pursue them through the gap. 'But it must be done now,' he stressed. 'Too late tomorrow.'[4] But the cavalry was twelve miles back. It would be impossible for them to reach the front before nightfall.

It is not difficult for armchair historians to criticize the decision to keep three powerful cavalry divisions so far behind British lines that they were unable to exploit the infantry's success – and just as easy, nowadays, to question the very involvement of cavalry in a war that had seen technological advances such as the tank. But the fact is that one small cavalry unit did prove its value on 9 April. The 1/1 Northamptonshire Yeomanry of VI Corps, based at Habarq, had arrived just west of Arras that morning, joining the Cyclist Battalion to form the VI Corps Mounted Troops. This oddball assortment of cyclists and horsemen was put at the disposal of the 37th Division, whose task was to leapfrog through the 12th and 15th Divisions and

---

[2] Robert Monypenny, after a long period in hospital, eventually returned to active service in the Far East. He did not serve in France again. He left the Army in 1922.
[3] Official History, France and Belgium, 1917, p. 231.
[4] Lieutenant-Colonel W. D. Croft, *Three Years with the 9th (Scottish) Division*, p. 117.

seize a line from Guémappe north to Roeux, beside the River Scarpe. The particular task of the Mounted Troops was to follow up the 37th and secure all road and railway bridges across the river.

After waiting patiently all morning, at 1.30 p.m. the Northants Yeomanry received orders to enter Arras and advance to Blangy. By 2.45, joined by two companies of cyclists, they were pushing on eastwards along the southern bank of the Scarpe. Progress was slow at first, particularly for the cyclists who were forced to dismount and carry their cumbersome machines over shell holes and marshy ground, but by 5 p.m. they had passed through the leading infantry at Feuchy. Just east of here the cavalry now split into two, 'B' Squadron under Major Benyon and 'C' Squadron under Major Nickalls. While the latter secured their right flank across the Arras–Douai railway – capturing two field guns, two howitzers and several prisoners in the process – 'B' Squadron galloped off towards Fampoux.

'The excitement was just incredible,' recalled Sergeant Bertie Taylor, riding with 'B' Squadron. Before the war he had worked on a large estate near Towcester in Northamptonshire, and horses were his first love. This was the day that he and his pals had trained for – 'to see some mounted action':

> The shells were dropping fast and thick, then we came to some
> slit trenches and we just jumped these with the horses squealing
> – just like a hunt! Then we passed through our leading troops
> and I remember seeing a lot of Scottish soldiers just lying there,
> machine-gunned. Hell of a do they had. Soon we got into
> Fampoux and the first thing we did was water our horses in the
> Scarpe. After we had mounted up again we came under shellfire
> and one of our officers, Captain Jack Lowther – who had an
> enormous nose – had the end of it sliced off by a piece of
> shrapnel. Well, we laughed, didn't we, but he got off his horse,
> picked up the end of his nose and wrapped it in his
> handkerchief! Sixty-five years later, I was talking to his son,
> who was the Lord Lieutenant of Northamptonshire, and he told
> me that he still had the piece of nose – it was a family heirloom!

So 'B' Squadron had ably assisted 4th Division's capture of Fampoux, despite the shell fire and snipers hiding in the houses, and captured two more field guns.

At 9 p.m. the troopers of the Northants Yeomanry went into bivouac in the Feuchy marshes, although they remained 'saddled up' ready for action. They had fulfilled their role as Corps Cavalry and taken their objectives, harassing the enemy along the Scarpe valley – and they were the last British unit in action that day.

128

If two mere squadrons could achieve so much, posterity is left to wonder how much more could have been done by a full brigade of cavalry. Sadly, none had been allotted to XVII Corps because Allenby did not consider operations on the north bank of the Scarpe to be as important as those on the south bank. However, during the afternoon of the 9th, he changed his mind. With such excellent progress reports flooding into Third Army HQ at St Pol, and with the agreement of Sir Douglas Haig, Allenby requested that one brigade of cavalry should be made available for action on the north bank of the river. It seemed that a breakthrough was possible between Bailleul and Fampoux, where the German line was defended by a couple of ragged companies of pioneer and transport men. It might be possible to capture Roeux, even to cut off that key to the enemy's line of defence, the village of Monchy . . .

The 1st Cavalry Division at Frévin, six or seven miles north-west of Arras, received word of Allenby's decision at 4.15 p.m. and one brigade was instantly placed on alert. But the final order to move out did not come that day. By the following day it was too late; the enemy had sent in reinforcements and the opportunity was lost forever. The capture of Monchy would have to wait.

Responsibility for this lost opportunity must be laid ultimately at Allenby's door. By late afternoon several companies of infantry from the 12th, 15th and 37th Divisions had advanced as far as Battery Valley and thus were in position to launch the all-important attack on Monchy. Although leading brigades of the 37th had lost direction and drifted too far south, becoming embroiled in the 12th and 3rd Divisions' fight for the Brown Line, even they had reached Orange Hill by nightfall and dug in on the northern side facing Monchy. But the battalion and brigade commanders were more immediately responsible for the delay. Gathered in Battery Valley, they demonstrated a sad lack of initiative. 'There was a good deal of talk and consultation as to what should be done,' General Sir Edward Spears has written. 'The general consensus of opinion was that it was rather late to push on. No effort was made to advance to Monchy as ordered.'[5]

To dwell on such lost opportunities, however, would be to paint a totally false picture of the British Army's achievements that day. As Captain Cyril Falls has asserted:

[5] Spears, *Prelude to Victory*, p. 594.

Easter Monday of the year 1917 must be accounted, from the
British point of view, one of the great days of the war. It
witnessed the most formidable and at the same time most
successful British offensive hitherto launched.[6]

And General Ludendorff would have agreed. Studying the reports
reaching him at Kreuznach, he concluded that the battle was almost
lost. As he later wrote:

The situation was extremely critical and might have had
far-reaching and serious consequences if the enemy had pushed
further forward. But the British contented themselves with
their great success and did not continue the attack, at least not
on April 9th.[7]

It is a trait peculiar to the British to revel in 'glorious defeats'. The
tragedies of the Somme and Passchendaele are etched on our national
consciousness, yet the achievements of our great amateur army
of 1914–18 are somehow forgotten. Perhaps one explanation for
this neglect is to be found in the words of that great Australian
commander, General Sir John Monash:

In a well planned battle nothing happens, nothing can happen,
except the regular progress of the advance according to the plan
arranged. The whole battle sweeps relentlessly and
methodically across the ground until it reaches the line laid
down as the final objective . . . It is for this reason that no
stirring accounts exist of the more intimate details of such great
set pieces as Messines, Vimy, Hamel and many others. They
will never be written, for there is no material on which to base
them. The story of what did take place on the day of battle
would be a mere paraphrase of the battle orders prescribing all
that was to take place.[8]

And, on the whole, the Battle of Easter Monday, 9 April, 1917, was
indeed a well-planned battle – although it is also true that the planners
had luck on their side. On 9 April the German counter-attack
divisions of Colonel-General von Falkenhausen were so far behind
their lines to avoid the risk of being shelled that they were unable to
retaliate when the front-line defenders succumbed.

In spite of some instances of uncut wire and artillery rounds falling

[6] Falls, Official History, France and Belgium 1917, p. 201.
[7] Ludendorff, My War Memories, p. 436.
[8] Monash, The Australian Victories in France, p. 291.

short, the 'creeping barrage' was a resounding success, especially when it is remembered that those unsung heroes, the forward observation officers, did not have any of the modern technological aids for accurate range-finding.[9] The new gas shells had also helped to paralyse the enemy's defence. But above all the day's successes belonged to the infantry. Despite all that a determined adversary could throw at him, the British infantryman had pressed steadily on, creating a sizeable gap in the Germans' lines of defence and capturing both men and artillery pieces. By 5 p.m. that day Third Army HQ estimated that 5,600 prisoners and 36 guns had been captured; but these were conservative figures, amended by 9 p.m. to over 8,000 prisoners and 152 guns.[10]

With the coming of night, however, the infantry faced a renewed onslaught from the weather. The temperature dropped below freezing and a savage blizzard lashed the troops in their shallow, hastily dug trenches. And there could be no sleep; at any moment the enemy might launch a counter-attack. It was worst for the men of Major-General C. L. Nicholson's 34th Division, up on the exposed crest of Point du Jour Ridge. Nicholson had ignored Allenby's order and allowed his soldiers to keep their greatcoats, but the icy squalls soon chilled them to the bone. As Nicholson himself later wrote, 'Some poor beggars actually died of exhaustion and exposure.'[11]

According to Private Tom Easton, a hardy miner serving with the 21st Northumberland Fusiliers, he and his companions had no cover at all: 'The next morning, many had frostbitten feet and had to be evacuated from the line.' Reg Gray, a private in the 11th Suffolks, remembered that night as being 'the worst I ever experienced'. Cold, hungry and exhausted, he reported:

> I didn't care what happened to me and as I walked along the top
> of the trench in the dark of the night, my eyes caught two of our
> men lying in a shell hole who had been killed that day. There
> they lay, silent, partly covered in a thin layer of snow. My
> thoughts travelled to their home, perhaps a mother or a wife or
> some loved one thinking of them . . .

Alive or dead, the snow covered them all – and the Highlanders suffered an additional discomfort, for their sodden kilts now froze solid.

[9] The most famous of FOOs to die on 9 April was the poet, Second-Lieutenant Edward Thomas, 244th Siege Battery RGA. Killed in a forward observation post, he is buried at Agny Military Cemetery.
[10] PRO WO95/362.
[11] Nicholson papers, Imperial War Museum.

It was the same for the cavalry behind the lines. The 1st Life Guards had 'pegged the horses down' on a racecourse near Arras, recalled Trooper Sam Bailey, and spent the night in the open, wrapped only in straw. But the following morning they awoke to 'a pitiful sight':

> The horses had pulled up their heel pegs and were huddled together. Some were dead through exposure, others had chewed their saddle blankets to pieces. It was impossible to release the head chains as they were completely frozen, and so were our fingers. Eventually we managed to get them moving and get some circulation going. After a while came the order to saddle up and mount. What with the freezing night which had weakened the horses and our combined weight, many of them just collapsed and died.

Back in England, the following morning's edition of *The Times* carried this comment on the Bank Holiday's atrocious weather:

> So far as London was concerned, yesterday was as bleak a day as could well be imagined. A bitter wind brought a dreary, desultory fall of snow, sleet and hail. The hailstones were in some cases as big as children's marbles. Many people spent the day at home.

Part III

A VICTORY WASTED

14

The Day of Delay

At 10.30 a.m. on Tuesday 10 April, an elated Sir Douglas Haig met his army commanders, Allenby and Horne, at Third Army HQ at St Pol. After an exchange of congratulations for the success of the previous day, Allenby and Horne briefed Haig on their respective gains and formally discussed plans for the continuation of the great offensive.

Allenby had placed his cavalry on standby from 7 a.m. and ordered the infantry to capture the remainder of the Brown Line. The attack was due to start at 8 but there was a delay on the 56th Division's front, caused by a prolonged bomb-fight in a section of the Hindenburg Line. Haig knew that the enemy would be rushing up strong formations of reserve troops, their commanders no doubt expecting another British onslaught. Consequently he urged on Allenby the importance of attacking the enemy as quickly as possible and seizing Monchy-le-Preux. As far as Horne's First Army was concerned, Vimy Ridge was in the Canadians' hands, apart from the *Hangstellung* and the Pimple which were due to be secured that morning. Throughout the senior command of the army, there was a euphoria not experienced before. 'Great goings on here,' Lieutenant-General Snow wrote to his wife on the 10th. 'Certainly this offensive has started well and no mistake. I am very glad for Allenby's sake as well as for everyone else.'[1]

The biggest nuisance was the weather. The next three days were to see the heaviest snowfalls of the winter, and the shell-churned ground was so sodden that it was difficult to get forward any heavy artillery to lend support to the infantry. Totally unruffled by this and with typical flair, Allenby issued an order for circulation to all ranks:

> The Army Commander wishes all troops to understand that
> Third Army is now pursuing a defeated enemy and that risks
> must be freely taken. Isolated enemy detachments in farms and

[1] Snow papers, Imperial War Museum.

135

villages must not be allowed to delay the general progress. Such points must be masked and passed by. They can be dealt with by troops in rear.[2]

But Allenby was wrong; the enemy was not defeated. True, they had suffered a very bad Easter Monday, but were tenaciously hanging on to a defensive line into which their reserves were now beginning to arrive. The yawning gap between Bailleul and Fampoux had been blocked overnight by battalions of boy-soldiers, some of whom had marched solidly for twelve hours to find nothing between them and the British. Ludendorff would have been proud of their face-saving efforts.

Typical of many young Germans rushed to the front was Otto Noack, a seventeen-year-old soldier from Altona, of 10 Company, 31st Infantry Regiment, who had carefully kept a diary of his war experiences:

> *8.4.17.* Easter Sunday. Swimming in an indoor pool, Douai. Marvellous!
> *9.4.17.* Alert! Marched to railway station. Travelled by train as far as Biache. On leaving the station shells from distant artillery whistled by. We are ordered to leave our big packs and webbing behind and prepare battle packs. We are issued with hand grenades from the nearby Pioneer Park. It looks like we are going to strike back, tit-for-tat. We advance towards Roeux. Level with Roeux we are met with rifle and machine-gun fire. Here we dig in and at dusk advance halfway to Fampoux where we dig a fresh trench with our short spades. We cannot counter-attack yet because of lack of manpower and the fact that our artillery is not ready. The night was extremely cold, although very quiet.
> *10.4.17.* Daybreak and English fighter planes appear. German fighters race overhead and shoot down three of the English. Now it seems the English artillery have advanced because they are beginning to register shells on us, although the majority land in the rear. All day we could see the enemy building up his strength in front of us. They tried to work forward during the afternoon but failed. In the meantime, it begins to snow.

No. 10 Company had dug in to the west of the Roeux–Gavrelle road. The left flank was protected by the railway embankment of the Arras–Douai railway and throughout the day the station buildings and the Chemical Works were reinforced by other companies of the 31st Infantry Regiment, complete with heavy machine-gun units. In

[2] PRO WO95/362.

136

front of them was the victorious British 4th Division and the German soldiers were thankful that this division had not pressed its advantage on the evening of the previous day. Now, expecting an attack at any moment, the Germans dug in and waited – but, to their surprise and relief, the British did not attack in any strength here during 10 April.

During the morning, General Lambton had issued orders for two of his brigades, the 11th and 12th, to secure the Roeux–Gavrelle road from Roeux station to an inn on the road, 1,300 yards to the north. The attack was due to go in at 3 p.m. However, this order was countermanded at 1.25 p.m. by the Corps Commander, Lieutenant-General Fergusson, who had persuaded General Allenby that it was feasible for cavalry to capture Greenland Hill which lay behind the Chemical Works and dominated the Scarpe valley. Consequently, the 1st Cavalry Division were presented with this somewhat ambitious task, the 4th Division lending support. What followed was a typical lack of liaison which regularly seemed to beggar the efforts of the British Army in the Great War. The brigades failed to get the new orders in time and Brigadier-General Carton de Wiart, commanding the 12th Brigade, had already sent forward the 1st King's Own, which had immediately fallen foul of heavy machine-gun fire from the Chemical Works. Likewise, the 1st Somerset Light Infantry had set off from Hyderabad Redoubt and were making for the Roeux–Gavrelle road when they came under intense small-arms fire from the enemy forward trenches, the first two platoons being wiped out. Needless to say, struggling up to Fampoux, the advance party of the cavalry, the 5th Dragoon Guards, arrived at 4.30 p.m. By then, with leaden skies and continuous snow falls, it was again too late. They turned around and went back.

In front of Monchy, the 37th Division had been under fire all day from the newly-arrived defenders of the 3rd Bavarian Division who had loop-holed the walls of the houses and cottages of the village. Heavy-calibre shells from the British guns sited around Arras now began to smash into Monchy, sending up a huge cloud of red dust from the pulverized roof tiles. The defenders were unimpressed, however, and continued to pour fire from every window and cellar at the British soldiers scraping for cover on the bare plain in front of the village.

Frustrated at its long wait in the freezing wind on the western slopes of Orange Hill, the 8th Cavalry Brigade edged forward. Uncertain as to whether the British infantry had got into Monchy but also eager for action, a squadron of Essex Yeomanry galloped forward in a probing effort towards Lone Copse on the north-western edge of the village.

137

In support, Captain R. Gordon-Canning led a detatchment of 10th Hussars towards the village, whereupon several machine guns among the houses and two enemy artillery batteries behind Monchy opened fire on them, many of the shells landing in the closely packed ranks of the 8th Cavalry Brigade behind the crest of Orange Hill. Fortunately, cover for the units heading towards Monchy came in the form of a blinding snowstorm and they made good their escape. Now it was confirmed to all and sundry that there were no British units in Monchy. The war diary of the 10th Hussars recorded only eight men and ten horses lost, very light casualties due to high-explosive and not shrapnel being used. The drama was witnessed by Corporal W. B. Walker, crouching with other infantrymen of the 6th Beds in nearby shell holes:

> One of our blokes said, 'Look at that bloody cavalry up there!'
> On our left the land sloped upwards and right on the skyline we
> saw a great mass of cavalry apparently waiting to charge
> Monchy. Then we saw great holes appear where the German
> artillery were dropping their shells into them, then several
> riderless horses, terribly wounded – some with their insides
> hanging out – came galloping through our front.

After the success of the previous day, which had gone better than expected, nobody had been prepared for the disappointments of 10 April. The British staff had been unable to capitalize on the previous day's success; in simple terms, they had not been sufficiently educated in the art of dealing with positive situations, the likes of which they now found themselves in. They possessed every ace card apart from the weather but were ignorant of the game.

15

The Crucial Day

Late into the night of 10 April the typewriters of Third Army HQ rattled furiously with the issue of fresh attack orders for the morning. In Allenby's opinion the 11th would be 'the crucial day' because, 'if the enemy could not be kept on the move now, stagnation might ensue'.[1] The most important objectives for the day were to be Greenland Hill, Roeux and the Chemical Works, the high ground south-west of Wancourt and Monchy-le-Preux.

On the evening of the 10th, the 13th Royal Fusiliers of the 37th Division had made an abortive attempt to get into Monchy, but after taking a bad mauling from the defenders, their CO, Colonel Layton, had withdrawn them to the shelter of a small wood to the west of the village. Here, with the assistance of a party of Royal Engineers, they set about digging a new trench. They were cold, wet and tired; it was their second night of exposure to sub-zero temperatures, and they had no hot food. But they soon began to warm up. With enemy shells pounding the wood, they needed no persuading to dig. By 4 a.m. the trench was deep enough, apart from some impossible tree roots, and the men crawled in and instantly fell asleep. But then Colonel Layton received word from Brigade HQ that his battalion was to capture Monchy at 5 a.m. He immediately sent his only three unwounded officers to rouse the weary men. Snow was falling heavily and the ground was now covered in a thick white carpet. The fusiliers had no time for even a warming drink of tea or a tot of rum – just time to get their equipment buckled up and help each other out of the trench.

In an all-out gamble to capture Monchy, Major-General H. Bruce Williams had decided to throw all three brigades of his 37th Division into the attack, supported by the 15th (Scottish) Division on his left flank and the 3rd Division on the right. The divisional HQs had received their attack orders at 11 p.m. the previous night – but

---

[1] *Official History, France and Belgium 1917*, p. 259.

shamefully, the majority of the assault battalions, like the 13th Royal Fusiliers, did not receive their orders until five hours later.

In the pitch darkness, made worse by a howling blizzard, the infantry silently found their assault positions by compass bearing and at 5 a.m. went forward, crunching through the fresh snow towards Monchy. Suddenly a red flare rose into the night sky above Monchy. The British infantry had been seen. This was followed by sheaves of white flares which lit up the snow-covered battlefield almost as brightly as daylight. Shouted on by the officers and NCOs, the British line broke into a trot, but immediately a storm of small-arms fire crackled forth from the houses in Monchy. The British soldiers had 200 yards to cover to reach the village. A tank was rapidly left behind in the rush, although its Lewis gunners engaged the machine-gun positions, firing in long bursts at the orange stabs of light. But the hail of enemy fire was accurate and intense. The attack faded. The whole line went down and scratched for cover, while some of the more determined crawled forwards on their elbows, pushing their rifles in front of them.

The 6th Cameron Highlanders had been ordered to advance north of Monchy to the Scarpe but in the darkness and confusion, compounded by bursts of machine-gun fire from north of the river, the battalion wheeled to the right and found themselves facing Monchy. Private Carson Stewart takes up the story:

> The Cameron lads were advancing in very heavy snow and as we advanced over the white surface we were easily spotted. Once we got near the village, Jerry opened up with several heavy machine guns and my chums began to fall. I wondered how long I would escape. We all threw ourselves down. Suddenly above the noise of the bullets and shells, I heard a voice shouting, 'Follow me, Camerons! Follow me, Camerons!' I often wondered who that brave lad was and whether he came home again. Well, we got up and made a final rush and my thoughts were not of a cheery nature. Then I was hit in the right leg – a bad one which broke the thigh and rendered my leg useless. I fell into a shell hole and set about dressing my wound with my emergency bandage. I then painfully began to crawl back to the rear and I remember passing my dead pals and seeing them being covered in their last shroud of snow.

If it had been left to Private Jim Beeston, a Lewis gunner in the 13th Royal Fusiliers, he would have settled for a pair of fried eggs on toast and half-a-dozen rashers of crispy bacon for his breakfast, washed down with a large whisky in his coffee. As it happened, he was lying

140

face down in the snow, with nothing in his stomach but air. He was cold, wet, shivering uncontrollably and at that very moment didn't give a toss whether he lived or died. Then he lost his temper. About a hundred yards from the nearest house in Monchy, he stood up and walked purposely forward, swearing out loud, firing the Lewis in short bursts from the hip, at the flickering flame of a machine gun firing from an upstairs bedroom window. The machine gun stopped. His mates stood up and followed suit:

> I reached the large house which was at the entrance to the village and, kicking open the door, went inside. I fired a few rounds down the hall and then another burst up the stairs. I ran up and entered the main bedroom which had a huge window right across the room. On a large table with six chairs around it was a map covered with small flags. I could smell cigar smoke. I had obviously just missed the previous occupants who had cleared out. By now it was daylight, and from this bedroom you could see right back to Arras. My gun crew shouted for me to come down where I saw Lieutenant Jerome who said, 'We must get forward into the village.' I said, 'Have you ever done any street fighting sir? . . . We won't get ten yards.' He said to me, 'Well, just try and do your best.' I told the lads to follow me and to keep close to the walls of the houses and take shelter in the doorways. I put a new drum of ammunition on the gun and we set off. We hadn't gone far up the street when a dozen or so Germans came running out of a house about twenty yards away . . . I let them get clear into the street and then let them have the whole drum, aiming at their thighs so that as they fell the bullets caught them again. Down they all went – and there wasn't another movement out of them.

Street fighting – a new form of warfare to the British troops – now erupted in Monchy, with an assortment of 37th and 15th Division men fighting tooth and nail to dislodge the enemy garrison. *Unteroffizier* Alfons Bernardini of the 23rd Bavarian Regiment was already a veteran at the age of twenty-one and held the Iron Cross 1st and 2nd class. Holding out with a few of his men in a house on the main street of Monchy, he wrote:

> We had arrived in Monchy during the night. The village was very badly damaged and we were ordered to occupy the western part of it, so we hurriedly set about fortifying the houses. Early in the morning we came under heavy artillery fire and the English attacked the village. As dawn broke a tank came rattling across the cobbles of the main street, closely followed by the English infantry who obviously felt quite safe. Hidden in

141

this house, I ordered my men to hold their fire until I gave the word. I waited until the tank had got past and then we opened up with everything we had. The English were totally caught by surprise and many were shot down by our hail of fire. The rest scattered. Then we found out that the English had broken through at both ends of the village. Afraid that we would be cut off, we fought our way back to the east side and made good our escape.

In fact, two tanks of 9 Company, 'C' Battalion, had managed to get into Monchy that morning, climbing over piles of rubble in the streets and firing at any sign of opposition. Throughout the morning the street battle raged, with ricocheting bullets sparking and whining off the cobbles, but the most useful weapon was the hand grenade or Mills bomb, tossed into any house or cellar where the Germans lingered. Gradually the British began to get the upper hand, and some of the troops began to remember their empty bellies. In one house Private Edgar Crane, of the 6th Beds, found 'bread, sausage and tinned chicken' which he and his companions seized upon eagerly:

> We all went down the cellar to get stuck into some grub, while our Lance-Corporal, a nice chap who was due to go on leave the next day, kept watch at the top of the steps. Suddenly he came rolling down the steps into the cellar. He had been shot dead. That spoiled our appetites.

Despite rumours that the food had been poisoned, Edgar Crane suffered no ill-effects, although he was to be badly wounded later in the morning.

Ernie Wilford from St Albans, Herts, a private in the 11th Royal Warwicks, well remembered his part in the south-flank attack on Monchy:

> It was so cold that morning that we took our boots off, stuffed them with straw and set fire to it, then we put our feet in 'em. That was the only warmth we got. Well, the attack went in, and we got no briefing at all. I hadn't got a clue where I was going. That was the trouble, you never knew what you were supposed to be doing. I seemed to be harnessed in a mob. Where the mob went, I went – just follow the crowd . . . like sheep really. Well, right from the start I threw my pack away. It was too heavy and what with slipping in the slush, I didn't care less. Then I saw it – you wouldn't believe it, just on the left of the Arras–Cambrai road, long lines of men just mowed down, lying flat where they went forward.

142

Facing the attack of the 6th Beds and 11th Warwicks were two companies of the 84th Reserve Regiment, among them *Musketier* Herman Keyser:

> It was dawn when the call came, 'The Tommies are coming!' and without any covering fire, they advanced in lines up the Arras–Cambrai road. We were lying about 150 metres to the left of it, and there was a tank supporting their attack and when it was directly opposite our trench the thing started shooting at us with eight machine guns. Our rifle fire was useless against it and we had to withdraw. It would take too long to describe the ensuing fight, but later we saw the tank burning on the hill.

Also meeting a British tank for the first time was *Feldwebel* Wilhelm Speck, of the 84th Reserve Regiment:

> The advancing Tommies were 600–800 metres away, the 17th Bavarians had run back and left our right flank open. Orders were issued to fill the gap to prevent a breakthrough. The hedges of the Route Nationale gave us good cover. Suddenly we heard a shout from 3rd Company: 'A tank is on the right of the road!' We stared aghast as slowly a tank crept towards us. At fifty metres range we opened fire with rifles and machine guns but as it got within thirty metres of us, it suddenly turned off to the right towards the Bavarians. We clapped and cheered! And standing up we shot from the hip at the tank – but our celebrations were a bit premature! . . . Suddenly the tank turned back towards us and advanced. We hoped the wide ditch at the side of the road would stop it. Little did we know of the capabilities of a tank! It entered the ditch and tipped acutely to the left and remained there for one or two minutes but he straightened himself out and crossed the road towards us, repeating the ditch-crossing manoeuvre on the other side. Then the tank moved to within five metres of the right section of 1st Company and stopped without firing. Now a concentrated fire from 1st and 3rd Companies was directed at the tank, hand grenades were thrown and some brave men got up and advanced from their positions. At this moment the tank tracks began to move and the tank crew opened up with a murderous machine-gun fire which was slowly directed along 1st Company trench. Those that were not killed instantly, screamed as they lay there wounded. Leutnant Hardow gave orders to clear the trench to the left towards 3 Company but the tank was already on them too. Then the panic started, everyone from 1st and 3rd Companies jumped out of the trench and ran the fastest race of his life, pursued by the merciless tank machine-gun fire which cut down many men as if it were a rabbit-shoot. The troops that ran wildly from the enemy were experienced soldiers and they

143

only stopped running when they reached the lane from Boiry to Guémappe about one kilometre away.[2]

The battle for Monchy was being anxiously watched from the slopes of Orange Hill. By now it was daylight; the snow had stopped and a watery sun had broken through the grey clouds, glinting on the burnished leather of the cavalry. But although Brigadier-General Charles Bulkeley-Johnson could clearly hear the din of heavy fighting, the tiny khaki specks of infantry dashing between houses were half obscured by the great pall of smoke rising over the village.

Bulkeley-Johnson – old Harrovian, former big-game hunter and now commander of the 8th Cavalry Brigade – was uncertain which way the battle was going. He told his squadron commanders to take the Essex Yeomanry and 10th Hussars round the north of Monchy; but, if they faced the same heavy machine-gun fire that they had met the previous day, then they should veer into the village to support their comrades in the infantry. And so, at 8.30 a.m., a squadron of the Essex Yeomanry under Lieutenant Chaplin, followed by a squadron of the 10th Hussars under Captain Gordon-Canning, each with a section of machine-gunners, cantered smartly round the southern slope of Orange Hill. They made a magnificent sight, and the watching infantry cheered them on their way. The cavalry was going in at last.

Towards the northern edge of Monchy they did indeed come under fire; several saddles were suddenly emptied. The other riders duly swerved to the right, galloping headlong for the village while German shells exploded all around them. And there was worse to come, as Trooper Clarence Garnett, of the 8th Machine-Gun Squadron (Essex Yeomanry), later recorded:

> I was riding a little horse called Nimrod and leading another
> with a pack saddle on his back loaded with boxes of
> machine-gun ammunition. We had not gone far when a huge
> shell burst to my right. Someone yelled, 'Garnett's pack-horse
> has broken its leg!' Our corporal, Harold Mugford,[3] shouted at
> me to keep going but the pack-horse fell, and as I was holding
> on to him so tightly, he pulled me out of the saddle. I let go and
> managed to stay on Nimrod, regaining my balance, but then my
> saddle slipped under his stomach. I rode on, hanging on for
> dear life, on his bare back. All the rest of the column had left
> me and seeing a huge hawthorn tree, I got behind it and

[2] Speck, *History of Reserve Regiment 84*, p. 190.
[3] Lance Corporal Harold Mugford, 8th Machine-Gun Squadron. Awarded the VC at Monchy 11 April 1917 for keeping his machine gun in action when severely wounded in both legs.

144

adjusted the saddle. I remounted and rode on alone to where the others had gone and quickly entered the village where I saw a dead pack-horse with ammunition on his back, so I dismounted and took a box. Galloping along the street I soon reached the building marked 'Château' on my map, where I was stopped by our officer who demanded my box of ammunition and told me to follow him. By now there were a few of us and the shelling had become very heavy, so the officer ordered us to lie down under the shelter of a wall. As I was lying in a gap between two cottages, I immediately got up, still holding my horse, and lay down under the wall of a cottage opposite. I had not been there long when a light shell came through the gap in the cottages and cut down the officer and most of the others. Nimrod was terrified and he reared up violently, dragging me along the street for some yards until I was forced to let go. I never saw him again after that. As it was pointless staying in that spot, I wandered along the street and into the main square which was simply covered with dead horses and men. To my horror, I saw one of our blokes cut in two at the waist. One half of him was on one side of the street. the other on the other side. Later that morning it started to rain and I swear the streets of Monchy ran red with blood.

Clarence Garnett's description is echoed by another cavalry trooper, Bertie Taylor of the Northants Yeomanry. Following their exciting ride to Fampoux on the evening of 9 April, the Northants Yeomanry had spent two freezing nights in the Scarpe marshes. At dawn on the 11th they had received orders to proceed to the west of Orange Hill and follow up the attack of the 37th Division. Seeing the Essex Yeomanry ride pell-mell at Monchy, they joined the charge, heading for the south-east end of the village. In Taylor's own words:

We got over the top of the rise and there it stood, red bricks showing – Monchy! The snow was laying thick and I remember at this point some of our horses collapsed, buckling the swords of their riders. We extended into one long line, a bugle sounded and we charged! Over open ground, jumping trenches, men swearing, horses squealing – a proper old commotion! The bugle sounded three times – and we had come under quite heavy shell fire and some of the saddles had been emptied. But the horses knew what to do better than we did, and galloping by me came these riderless horses. Mine, poor devil, had been wounded badly in the coronet so I pulled him up and dismounted and had a look at him. Well, he looked at me, there were tears in his eyes. Poor devils, they know you know. Another one came flying past me with half his guts hanging out, I'd never seen anything like that. Well, my horse perked up, so we galloped off after the others. The riderless horses were still leading the charge. Eventually I caught up with our officer, Mr Humphriss, who was riding a few yards ahead when a shell exploded just beneath his horse and split him like a side of beef hanging up in the butcher's shop. Both horse and rider were killed instantly. Next we got into the village and the streets were so narrow that tiles from the roofs were raining down on us – that's what caused a lot of injuries. The shell fire was so hot that the bugles sounded the retirement and back we went, led by the riderless horses!

Taylor and his chums in the Northants Yeomanry had escaped in the nick of time. Upon seeing the British cavalry enter Monchy, the German artillery laid down a severe box-barrage which gradually drew inwards, trapping the cavalry and infantry in the village. Lieutenant-Colonel Whitmore of the Essex Yeomanry, finding himself the only senior officer in the village, now took command and set about organizing the defence of Monchy amidst the havoc caused by the heavy shellfire. The enemy had by now been driven out or killed. Monchy was in British hands – but for how long?

At midday, concerned as to what was happening in the village and impatient for news, Bulkeley-Johnson had walked up to assess the situation. Meeting Captain D. W. J. Cuddeford of the Highland Light Infantry, he asked him to show him the enemy dispositions. Cuddeford later wrote:

> I told him it could be done, but that to reach a point of vantage on the low ridge in front, the snow having cleared just then, the greatest caution was required, and that if the German snipers spotted us it would be necessary to dodge them by sprinting from shell hole to shell hole, as we did. Nevertheless the General insisted on going on against my advice and perhaps being rather old for that sort of active dodging or, as it seemed to me at the time, too dignified to get well down at the sound of a bullet, he would persist in walking straight on. That of course was deadly, as I well knew.
>
> I led the little procession, and sure enough, as soon as we reached the ridge, a fusillade of bullets hummed around our ears. We had not gone far when one skimmed past me and struck the General full on the cheek bone. I shall never forget his piercing shriek as he tumbled down and rolled over on the ground.[4]

With Bulkeley-Johnson dead, the consolidation of Monchy now depended on Colonel Whitmore and the mish-mash of troops he found himself commanding. Frantically they prepared makeshift

[4] Cuddeford, *And All For What?*

146

barricades and trenches to meet the expected counter-attack – it never came. The cavalry troopers scraped shallow trenches for themselves, on the eastern edge of the village from where they could see the enemy massing in a small copse. Meanwhile a German spotter plane overhead had signalled the artillery and the box-barrage had descended, causing bloody mayhem among the tethered horses in the village. All horses of 'C' Squadron, 10th Hussars, were killed.[5]

Nightfall arrived and the enemy was observed to be digging in about 300 yards to the north-east of the village, having given up the idea of a concerted attempt to regain Monchy that day. Colonel Whitmore, in his hour of glory, handed over the defence of Monchy to the infantry of 37th Brigade, 12th Division, in the able shape of Lieutenant-Colonel William Dawson, DSO, of the 6th Royal West Kents. The full horror of the morning's street fighting in Monchy and the ghastly effects of the enemy box-barrage shocked the relieving infantrymen, as second Lieutenant Alan Thomas later wrote:

> As we turned the bend of the road to go up the hill I stopped. The sight that greeted me was so horrible that I almost lost my head. Heaped on top of one another and blocking up the roadway for as far as one could see, lay the mutilated bodies of our men and their horses. These bodies, torn and gaping, had stiffened into fantastic attitudes. All the hollows of the road were filled with blood. This was the cavalry.[6]

As the infantry dug deeper and improved the makeshift defences established by the cavalrymen that afternoon, the remnants of the Essex Yeomanry and 10th Hussars shambled out of Monchy in the darkness. 'The order rang out: "Cavalrymen line up in the road,"' wrote Lance-Corporal G. W. Davis. 'So goodbye and good luck. Captain Stokes led us away from Monchy-le-Preux past the place where the bodies of our horses lay. Dumb, dead heroes.'[7]

Hailed as one of the great British successes of the war, the capture of Monchy-le-Preux on 11 April, 1917, was also the turning point in the Battle of Arras. From now on fortune ceased to smile on the British. Indeed, the Monchy success was overshadowed by more sombre events which occurred during the grim fighting for two shoulders of high ground directly flanking Monchy – to the north at Roeux and to the south at Wancourt.

---

[5] The losses in horses to the 8th Cavalry Brigade are not recorded but after the action 600 remounts were drawn.
[6] Alan Thomas, *A Life Apart*, p. 97.
[7] From the 10th Royal Hussars Gazette, vol. 21, 1959.

A photograph taken by the Royal Flying Corps on that cloudless Easter Sunday, just a few hours before the start of the battle, had clearly indicated that the buildings of the old Chemical Works at Roeux, both to the north and south of the Arras–Douai railway, were completely intact and undamaged by artillery. Discernible by the long shadow cast over the ground by the late afternoon sunlight, one of the sixty-foot-high brick chimneys was still standing just north of the railway, and on top of this old smokestack the ever-resourceful Germans had established a precarious but useful observation post. Two volunteers from the 31st Regiment had climbed the sooty iron rungs on the interior of the chimney, dragging with them a heavy field telephone and cable in order to relay their observations to the company HQ set up in an old drying-shed below. The ant-like movements of the two figures on the chimney top and the occasional glint of sunlight from binoculars could clearly be seen by the British soldiers in and around Fampoux. It was also noticed that the enemy had hung a large Red Cross flag from a third-floor window of one of the factory buildings south of the railway, as if the building were being used as a hospital. But the British were not taken in by this ruse. They had also spotted, protruding from the windows, the sinister black snouts of Maxim machine guns.

By 11 April the British had still not been able to bring up anywhere near sufficient heavy guns across the morass of captured ground, in order to pound the Chemical Works and dislodge the strong detachments of defenders, now being solidly upgraded by troops of the newly-arrived 18th and 26th Divisions who had also brought their field artillery with them – one battery brazenly positioned in front of the Chemical Works on the south of the railway embankment. With the old cave system providing safe shelter for the defenders, what was there for the taking on the evening of 9 April was about to become a thorn in Allenby's side.

At 6 p.m. on 10 April, Brigadier-General Charles Gosling, commanding 10th Infantry Brigade, 4th Division, had received a message from division, ordering an attack on the Chemical Works and Greenland Hill the following morning; but it was not until 5.30 a.m. on the 11th that the 2nd Battalion Seaforth Highlanders, holding a ragged line of posts to the rear of Fampoux, were told that they would be attacking the Chemical Works at 12 noon. The attack orders had been meticulously written out in longhand by the bearer of the bad news, the Brigade Major, Captain Hedworth Fellowes, MC, and contained the following order: 'At 10 a.m. Seaforths will advance in fours down road to crossroads, then up sunken road to Hyderabad Redoubt . . .

148

To be in position by 11 a.m.'[8] But no one had told Fellowes[9] that the road from Fampoux to Hyderabad Redoubt was *not sunken* for fifty yards after passing the last house in Fampoux. The Seaforths, marching to their attack positions, would easily be seen by the enemy in the Chemical Works.

As ordered, the Seaforths marched into Fampoux, duly followed by the 1st Royal Irish Fusiliers, due to attack to the right of the Seaforths, the company commanders of both battalions hurriedly scribbling out attack orders on the march to give to their respective platoon commanders. No one had been forewarned that the Chemical Works were strongly defended. No one in either battalion had ever seen the Chemical Works or had a chance to survey the bare plain, devoid of cover, over which they were expected to advance. But the enemy was expecting them. A German plane had swooped low over the marching column of men on the road from Athies. As the Seaforths reached the crossroads in Fampoux and turned up the sunken road, indicated on the officers' trench-maps, they came under shell fire. Troops watching from the houses of the village were amazed at this flippant parade and repeatedly shouted warnings to the Seaforths' officers of the impossibility of venturing along the 'sunken' road without being seen by the enemy. The battalions carried on.

By 11 a.m. the Seaforths had crossed the fifty yards of open ground to the sunken road and had promptly come under long-range machine-gun fire from the Chemical Works. The presence of the Royal Irish Fusiliers, close on their heels, had made the sunken road a very congested place and as the enemy began to drop shells into it, some of the Seaforths worked their way along Huddle Trench where they waited for zero hour. At 11.57 a.m. came the order, 'Fix bayonets', and the last few seconds ticked away. At zero hour the Highlanders scrambled, swearing and slipping in the snow, up the steep bank and out into the open. A weak barrage had been put down 400 yards in front of them, and forming up in a single wave in company order, they advanced towards it. The barrage was useless. For a start there were no enemy soldiers under it and no shells fell near the Chemical Works 1,500 yards ahead. There was nothing to keep down the heads of the Germans who could see the thin line of Highlanders advancing across the white plain towards them.

[8] PRO WO95/1483.

[9] The following day Fellowes was shot dead by a sniper and his brigadier, Charles Gosling, killed by a shell. They are buried side by side at Hervin Farm Military Cemetery, St Laurent Blangy.

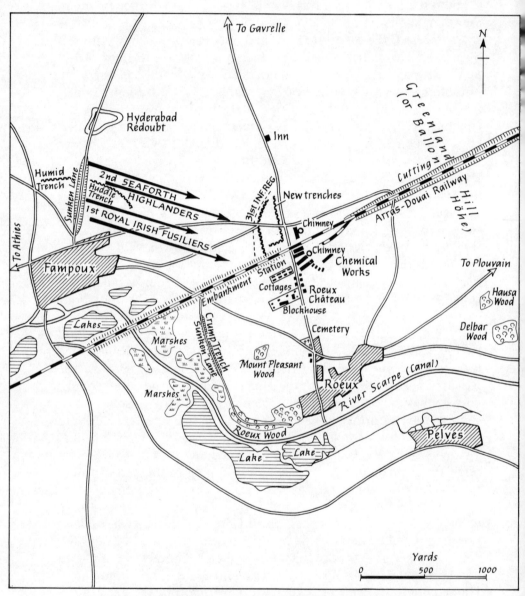

To Gavrelle

N

Hyderabad
Redoubt

Inn

Greenland
(or Ballon
Hill
Höhe)

Cutting

Humid
Trench

Sunken Lane

2nd SEAFORTH
HIGHLANDERS

Huddle
Trench

1st ROYAL IRISH FUSILIERS

31st INF REG

New trenches

Chimney

Arras-Douai Railway

To Arhies

Fampoux

Chimney
Chemical
Works

To Plouvain

Hausa
Wood

Embankment

Station

Cottages

Roeux
Château

Lakes

Blockhouse

Delbar
Wood

Marshes

Crump Trench

Sunken Lane

Cemetery

Mount Pleasant
Wood

Roeux

River Scarpe (Canal)

Marshes

Roeux Wood

Pelves

Lake

Lake

Yards

0   500   1000

6. THE ATTACK OF THE 10th INFANTRY BRIGADE ON THE CHEMICAL
WORKS, 11 APRIL, 1917.

There are recorded many gallant acts during the Great War but there are few as courageous as the now-forgotten advance of the 2nd Seaforth Highlanders and 1st Royal Irish Fusiliers on 11 April, 1917, at the Battle of Arras. The concentrated fire from no less than thirty machine guns in and around the Chemical Works was now directed as the meagre line of Celts. As the bullets found their mark and men pitched forward into the snow, so the ranks closed in. The reputation and discipline of these old regular army battalions held firm.

One Second-Lieutenant of the Seaforths, badly wounded in the attack, wrote and spoke to the author in 1981. Still exceedingly bitter at the memory of such a terrible day he did not want his name to be mentioned:

> Right from the start it was a dreadful affair. A fine battalion totally destroyed. It was a total disgrace that the powers that be could order such an attack in full daylight and against such defences. We had no chance at all and I lost many good friends that day, including Donald Mackintosh, who of course won the VC. I had only gone about 200 yards before I was shot through the chest. I am sorry, but I cannot talk about it any more . . .

Albert Ross, a Private with the Seaforths, was more fortunate. He remembered:

> As we advanced, one of the old heads remarked that Jerry was shooting high – you could feel the swish of the bullets passing way overhead. In the distance we could just hear the faint 'tac-tac' of machine guns, but as we got closer to the Chemical Works, Jerry found our range. The thing I vividly remember, which sickens me still, is the hollow thump that a bullet makes when it hits the human body – *thump! thump!* – and your mate next to you would fall flat. Well, someone shouted an order to double, which we did, but soon it seemed I was the only one left . . . So I went straight into the nearest shell-hole and stayed there. What a waste of good men, and most of 'em new lads. The regulars had copped it on the Somme.

Major N. C. Orr recorded in the Seaforths' war diary:

> This situation, the sighting of the enemy's machine guns beyond the barrage area in invisible and unknown positions, was responsible mainly for the failure of the attack as it had been responsible for the failure of many attacks during the later stages of the battle of the Somme. Until some system of dealing with this tactical problem is devised, the enemy will continue to cause heavy casualties among attacking infantry. The heavy

machine-gun fire maintained by the enemy made it impossible to obtain information regarding the course of the action but it required no report to realize that a single wave of 400 men who had to advance an average distance of 1,600 yards with a battalion front of 1,100 yards could not obtain their objective in face of such machine-gun and rifle fire. The total losses sustained by the battalion were 12 officers and 363 other ranks out of a total of 12 officers and 420 other ranks who took part in the attack. I leave these losses to speak for the gallantry of all ranks.[10]

And the war diary of the 10th Infantry Brigade forlornly records: 'From Hyderabad Redoubt, there is now a long row of dead Seaforth Highlanders visible where they were swept down by the enemy machine-gun fire.'[11]

Not all the Seaforths and Irish Fusiliers had been hit, however. Here and there, small parties of men had bombed the enemy out of their forward posts and pushed on. Some Irish Fusiliers, hugging the northern side of the railway embankment, got to within 200 yards of Roeux station before being forced back. On the left a group of Seaforths entered a freshly dug trench, just 150 yards west of the Roeux–Gavrelle road. Led by a twenty-one-year-old Glaswegian, Lieutenant Donald Mackintosh who had been shot through the right leg, there they organized the defences of the newly-won position and drove back several counter-attacks. Wounded for a second time and unable to stand, Mackintosh continued to control the situation; but with only fifteen men remaining and all ammunition expended, he ordered them to prepare for a final desperate bayonet charge. Making a supreme effort, he climbed from the trench and urged his men forward. This time he was hit for a third and final time.[12] Awarded a posthumous Victoria Cross for his bravery, Mackintosh's actions were paid further tribute in some German accounts, which also stated that 10th Brigade's attack on the Chemical Works was 'characterized by an exhibition of true British tenacity'.

The untried German youngsters of 11 company, 31st Regiment, in forward trenches opposite Hyderabad Redoubt, had initially run back from the determined advance of a company of the Seaforth Highlanders (probably that of Lieutenant Mackintosh). Later in the afternoon, seeing the remnants of this company fall back, the 31st Regiment restored its position by counter-attack. As Otto Noack recorded in his diary:

[10] PRO WO95/1483.
[11] PRO WO95/1479.
[12] Buried Brown's Copse Military Cemetery, Roeux.

The Battalion Commander Hauptmann Simonsen[13] formed up two companies from the survivors and drew us up in position. The dividing line was the Roeux–Fampoux road. At about 3 p.m. a bugle sounded and we advanced in counter-attack. Immediately the enemy opened up on us with a hail of fire and we suffered losses but we were lucky their artillery did not open on us. 'Perhaps they have gone for a tea-break,' we joked. We sought cover in trenches near the road on the left, but unfortunately they were not deep enough and we had to crouch down as low as possible. Nevertheless the English retreated back towards Fampoux, one by one, then more and more of them. This further inspired our counter-attack and we pushed on. Suddenly I found myself in front! So I increased my pace. To the left I could see some of our chaps keeping up with me. It looked good. I soon reached our old positions and so I stopped and glanced behind with an enquiring look on my face: 'Should we go straight on or take over our old trenches?' Those behind me were excitedly trying to draw my attention to something on my right. I turned around and found myself staring with fascination straight down the barrel of a revolver which was emitting small puffs of smoke. There were at least two puffs before I reacted to the danger and dodged out the way. It dawned on me that the man behind the revolver was wearing an English helmet and there were two others with him. He was only about five metres away. The next moment one of our chaps threw himself down next to me. I pressed a grenade into his hand and we both threw them over the small mound that was between us and the enemy. There were two muffled explosions. I jumped up and leapt through the clearing smoke into the enemy position, where I found the three men lying dead. I snatched up a weapon hitherto unknown to me – a Lewis gun which was out of ammunition. We held that position throughout the day and later that night were relieved by the 86th Fusilier Regiment.

The three British soldiers killed by seventeen-year-old Noack were probably the remnants of Mackintosh's gallant company, fighting to the last bullet.

The attack of the Seaforths and Irish Fusiliers had been supported by the Household Battalion and 1st Royal Warwicks, who left the sunken road at 12.10 p.m., but were unable to get as far as the first two battalions. The failure of Gosling's 10th Infantry Brigade resulted in the collapse of the whole 4th Division attack, the flanking brigades being unable to make any headway in the face of such fierce machine-gun fire. General Lambton was furious; in spite of the fact that the 10th Brigade had just lost 1,000 men out of the 1,600 who had

[13] Killed in action at Roeux, 23 April 1917. No known grave.

gone in to the attack, he ordered them to attack again immediately. Gosling, upon receipt of these orders at his HQ one mile behind Fampoux, and unaware that his brigade no longer existed, sent a message to the nearest field artillery requesting them to bombard the Chemical Works and Roeux Château. He also ordered the 2nd Seaforths and the 1st Royal Irish Fusiliers to attack again at 3.30 p.m. This message did not reach Battalion HQ in the Hyderabad Redoubt until half an hour later. But there were no 2nd Seaforths left to carry out any attack.

This was just one example of the apparent bull-headedness that unfortunately gave so much ammunition to post-war critics, politicians and the usual 'never-again' brigade. But it is all too easy to make judgements with the benefit of hindsight, and posterity must accept that the generals of both sides made the best decisions according to the facts available at the time. If the men who had to make these decisions possessed a modern telecommunication system, things might have been vastly different.

Roeux and the Chemical Works were to become Allenby's greatest stumbling block on this part of the Third Army front, for the 4th Division's ill-fated attempt on 11 April was only the first of many doomed to failure. Without the crushing might of artillery power that had been available on the 9th, and without sufficient reconnaissance of the ground to be attacked, the infantry were simply walking to their deaths. Yet their grit and determination in advancing against all the odds was proven time and time again – as typified by the heroic efforts of the 7th King's Royal Rifle Corps to capture Wancourt village, a few miles south-east of Monchy.

During the previous afternoon, the 7th Battalion of the KRRC, part of the 14th Division, had been moving up the Cojeul valley towards Wancourt when their advance was abruptly halted by heavy machine-gun fire from Hill 90, a prominent feature south of Monchy. For there the Germans were heavily entrenched behind thick entanglements of wire. Under cover of a snowstorm the KRRC men dug themselves into some recently abandoned enemy trenches and waited for further orders. Meanwhile, Captain George Williamson, MC – twenty-eight years old and a former teacher at Oundle – decided to make a preliminary foray that evening along the sunken road below Hill 90, where a small pocket of the enemy were holding out. 'A' and 'D' Companies, with Williamson in command, managed to capture the position after a sharp fight; but the snow had cleared and they came under renewed fire from the hill. In a desperate attempt to locate the enemy guns, Williamson now sent four men and an officer up to the German wire; the officer was none other than Williamson's kid brother, Kenneth, a second-lieutenant aged nineteen. They had not gone far when the deadly guns opened up again; all five men went down. But Kenneth Williamson, although mortally wounded, had located the machine-gun positions. Sadly, the information was too late to help his brother. George Williamson, while watching the little party's progress from the sunken road, had also been hit, and he died the following day. By midnight on 10 April the two companies had lost nine officers and sixty other ranks.

About one hour later, at 1 a.m. on the 11th, Lieutenant-Colonel C. H. Bury and the KRRC were visited in their freezing trenches by Brigadier-General Skinner, sent by General Snow to discover why the advance had halted. It was soon obvious to Skinner that 'any advance up the valley was sheer madness', as Bury later wrote; 'He agreed that it was quite impossible to push on until Hill 90 had been taken.' Skinner went back to General Snow's staff with his situation report – but was immediately overruled. General Snow was insistent that the attack on Wancourt should go ahead. The 56th Division, he said, would take Hill 90.

At 4.30 a.m. on 11 April the KRRC received the fateful news. As Colonel Bury wrote:

> The attack orders arrived and in spite of all protests we were ordered to carry them out. There was no time to copy them and the originals had to be sent up to the forward companies. 'B' and 'C' Companies, supported by the 8th Rifle Brigade, were to advance up the valley and try to push on to Wancourt. The 56th Division never left their trenches or made any attempt to take Hill 90. 'B' Company under [Captain Charles] Whitley made a most gallant attempt to push forward, but from the start it was an impossible task; and the staff who had ordered the attack, if they had ever come near enough to have looked at the ground, would have realized it too, and would never have ordered the attack. Whitley was alas killed,[14] gallant soldier that he was, and his body was found nearest to the German wire which was totally uncut . . . The whole show was a complete failure from want of preparation and organization on the part of the staff.[15]

In their valiant efforts to capture Wancourt village on 11 April the 7th King's Royal Rifle Corps had lost all twelve officers who went into the attack, and 174 other ranks. And the crowning irony is that the enemy cleared out that same night – abandoning both Wancourt and Hill 90.

[14] Captain Charles Whitley, MC; buried at Hibers Trench Military Cemetery, Wancourt.
[15] PRO WO95/1896.

16

The Defeated Enemy

As darkness fell on 11 April the exhausted British soldiers steeled themselves for another freezing night in the open, unaware that the Germans had recovered from their defeat of the 9th and that fresh reinforcements were continually arriving in the opposite trenches. All they thought about now was hot food and warm billets – like Lance-Corporal Alex Fisher of the 8th Black Watch, wounded in the armpit by shrapnel on the 9th, but still in the line:

> We were wondering when it would all end. We were dead beat from want of sleep and were starving. We had managed to get some water out of the River Scarpe but it only made us feel worse. We had only our hard biscuits to eat . . . thinking of how those at home would be coming home from work to a good meal. Our boots hadn't been off since Sunday morning and we were beginning to lose hope. We didn't know how far Jerry was away, or when he would counter-attack. We could hardly stand, let alone fight!

It would have been no consolation to Alex Fisher and the thousands of others who shared his predicament, but a few miles to the south, at Bullecourt, the Australians had joined the Battle of Arras.

It was on the morning of 11 April that the 4th Australian Division of General Sir Hubert Gough's Fifth Army had launched a converging assault against the Hindenburg Line, in an attempt to distract attention from the main Third Army front. The 4th Australian Division was a fine fighting formation and eager to join the fray, but their assault had already been postponed by twenty-four hours. The original plan had been for the Australians to go in at dawn on the 10th, without preliminary bombardment but following a cluster of tanks – which, the enthusiastic 'Thruster' Gough had been advised by a junior tank officer, would flatten the enemy wire and thus create a gap through which infantry and cavalry could rush. Unfortunately the tanks had got lost. The Australians spent the night of 9/10 April lying out in the open, lashed by a snow blizzard, waiting in vain for the tanks to turn up, and then had to be recalled. They were lucky to regain their own lines without being spotted by the enemy.

Undeterred, Gough decided they must try again on the 11th. At a midday conference on the 10th, General Birdwood, commander of the Australian and New Zealand Army Corps (Anzac), expressed deep misgivings about the plan, which he considered 'fraught with danger'. But Gough impressed on Birdwood that it was Sir Douglas Haig's wishes that the attack should go in as arranged – even though it is doubtful whether Haig ever knew quite how flimsy Gough's tactics would be. Birdwood gave in, and the Australians prepared for another uncomfortable night in their forward trenches.

Oliver Lyttelton, who had a special affection for Australians, stated that 'They are perhaps not the best of troops to handle when there is no one to fight, but let them get sight or scent of a battle and they are superb.'[1] And so they were. Although only three tanks arrived on time, the attack went in at 4.45 a.m. on the 11th. The first wave of infantry had 700 yards of a flat, snow-carpeted plain to cross before reaching the German trenches, and they were soon spotted by the vigilant enemy, who lit up the scene with flares. Quickly overtaking the tanks in their rush, the Australians approached the great wire belts of the Hindenburg Line, which seemed to 'swarm with fireflies' where bullets glanced off the metal. Braving the hurricane of fire and led by flamboyant officers like Major Percy Black of the 16th (Western Australia) Battalion, an old gold prospector who shouted 'Come on, boys – b— the tanks!',[2] the infantry found one of the few gaps in the wire and swarmed through. Leaping into the enemy's trenches they now faced the tough Wurttemburgers of the 124th Regiment, later described by the surviving Australians as 'the stubbornest opponents they ever encountered.'

While the vicious bomb and bayonet battle continued in the trenches, some of the Australians pressed on for the village of Riencourt, where the enemy could be seen crowded at the upper windows of the villagers' homes, firing into the advancing troops. But the Australians, much to their dismay, had been given no artillery support; they were on their own. And it was now that the German infantry chose to launch a counter-attack, effectively closing the gate behind the Australians by means of a murderous machine-gun barrage.

[1] Chandos, *Memoirs*, p. 98.
[2] C. E. W. Bean, *The Australian Imperial Force in France, 1917*, p. 295.

To observers in the rear, the scene was too distant and chaotic for any clear picture of the battle to emerge. As the daylight increased, the slug-like shapes of tanks were seen to creep slowly towards Riencourt, followed by the tiny figures of Australian infantry. Suddenly there was a flash, then another, and one tank lurched to the side. A German field gun, firing over open sights, was evidently concealed among some nearby trees. The tank seemed to have been hit, and the crew came scrambling out, but several khaki-clad figures lay sprawled in the tank's wake. What was less clear, however, was whether any actual progress had been made. Conflicting reports began to circulate – that the Australians had breached the Hindenburg Line, that they had taken Riencourt, that Bullecourt had fallen . . .

Ever the buoyant optimist, Gough close to believe the more encouraging reports. He ordered his cavalry forward; with Bullecourt in the infantry's hands, he reasoned, the cavalry could now advance to Fontaine-les-Croisilles and Chérisy. At 9.35 a.m. elements of the 4th Cavalry Division duly approached the front line – and immediately ran into enemy machine-gun fire. The 4th Cavalry now learned the ugly truth: Bullecourt was still in German hands.

Hopelessly caught in the enemy's defensive trap, the Australians fought on alone. The British 62nd Division had been intended to give support by attacking Bullecourt, along with four tanks; but the tanks failed to materialize and the dense wire hedges remained unpassable. The troops of the 62nd never even left their trenches. By early afternoon the Australians had run out of grenades and were being slowly forced back by a skilful foe. It had become painfully obvious that their only chance now was to retreat through the deadly curtain of machine-gun fire behind them. The order went out: every man for himself. Only a few managed to make it back to their lines.

The Australian losses were catastrophic. In all, the six and a half battalions and accompanying units of the 4th Australian Division had lost 3,000 officers and men, of which 28 officers and 1,142 men had been captured – the highest number of Australians taken prisoner in a single battle in the First World War. The heaviest burden had fallen on the 4th Brigade, with casualties amounting to 2,339 out of some 3,000 engaged. Of the eleven tanks that eventually went into action, ten had been destroyed by 11 a.m. and the tank crews had suffered accordingly; out of 103 officers and men, 52 had been killed or wounded or were missing. But it was the tank crews who now came in for some harsh criticism from the Australians. Many of the tanks had opened fire at the start line, thereby alerting the enemy, and the

Australian battalion commanders who had witnessed the ensuing massacre of their men were especially bitter. Lieutenant-Colonel E. Drake-Brockman, of the 16th Australian Infantry Battalion, later wrote:

> The tank crews seemed to know little or nothing of an attack by infantry and nothing whatsoever about the particular operation they were to participate in. For instance, in the case of No. 2 Tank, the tank commander had not even synchronized his watch, his time being five minutes behind true time as given to infantry. Further, tank crews did not even know the direction of the enemy. This is verified by the fact that they opened fire on our own troops, thereby causing many casualties. One tank in particular opened fire on our men in the jumping-off place, killing four and wounding others.[3]

Another Lieutenant-Colonel, J. H. Peck of the 14th Battalion, reported that one crew left their tank, claiming that it had caught fire, but were later seen returning to it with two sandbags, 'one containing enamel ware and the other food':

> Personal safety and comfort seemed their sole ambition. The whole outfit showed rank inefficiency and in some cases seemed to lack British tenacity and pluck and that determination to go forward at all costs which is naturally looked for in Britishers.[4]

In another incident, Lieutenant-Colonel R. L. Leane of the 48th Battalion watched one tank returning to the start line after advancing for a mere 300 yards. It stopped near Leane's HQ and he went to ask the tank's NCO what had happened:

> He said they had a direct hit, and I believe one man was slightly wounded by the door blowing in. He said it was going all right and could be driven away, but declined to try. The crew left for the rear. The enemy put a heavy fire onto the tank and about 7.30 a.m. it caught fire. I believe this tank could have been salved, had the crew possessed the necessary pluck. They were absolutely panic-stricken.[5]

And further criticism came from Brigadier-General Robertson of the 12th Brigade, who expressly blamed the tanks for 'the heavy casualties occasioned in my brigade and finally our inability to hold the

[3] PRO WO95/3488.
[4] Ibid.
[5] PRO WO95/3506.

positions taken', and confirmed that this experience had 'resulted in a loss of confidence in the tanks by all ranks'.[6]

Whatever the tank crews' failings, however, it was General Gough who bore ultimate responsibility for the well intentioned but disastrous attack that day. As Sir Edward Spears wrote in *Prelude to Victory*, it was 'a costly failure well calculated to lower the morale of all but the very finest troops and certain to shake the participants' confidence in both staff and leadership, for the plan turned out to be as unrealizable as the arrangements were inadequate'. And in a harrowing account of the battle, the Australian Official Historian justifiably criticizes Gough's tactics and plan:

> Gough's general conception of assisting the Third Army by a stroke at the enemy's exposed flank and rear was indeed sound, provided a tactical means of delivering that stroke could be discovered. But with almost boyish eagerness to deliver a death blow, the army commander broke at every stage through rules recognized even by platoon commanders.[7]

Gough, who made other costly errors in 1917, nevertheless retained his command until March, 1918, when he was sacked – ironically, after he had displayed fine leadership during the great German offensive. But there was no enquiry into the reasons for the Bullecourt and Riencourt fiasco; it was conveniently obscured by jubilation for the Easter Monday success. If there had been such an inquiry, it would undoubtedly have considered that Sir Douglas Haig also bore some responsibility, for his over-confidence in Gough had led him to give the Fifth Army commander a free rein in the attack; but it was Gough alone who had implemented the plan and devised the hollow tactics. As for Gough himself, he blamed Allenby and the Third Army for letting him down by failing to advance as planned, beyond Fontaine-les-Croisilles on the right flank and beyond Monchy in the centre. Shrugging off his own failure as 'a tactical defeat', he claimed that it 'would be justified if it helped to secure the strategical success of the higher command'.[8]

A few of the reserves who hadn't gone into action with the 9th Royal Scots, together with camp details and unfit men, shuffled into small groups to watch the ragged remnants of the battalion come in to Larasset huts. Colonel Green – who had already been reported as

[6] Ibid.
[7] C. E. W. Bean, *The Australian Imperial Force in France*, p. 351.
[8] Gough, *The Fifth Army*, p. 284.

killed in the Edinburgh *Evening News* – led the men in. Captain Blair halted his company by the cookhouse and dismissed them. The smell of frying bacon in the cold early morning air almost sent the men wild and a long barging queue formed as sympathetic cooks dished out eggs, bacon, fried bread and hot sweet tea. Between 9 April and relief by 2nd Division troops on the night of the 11th–12th the 'Dandy Ninth' had lost twelve officers and 234 other ranks, killed, wounded or missing. Now the survivors rejoiced in their hearts that they were through with the Battle of Arras.

Not so lucky were Arthur Betteridge and his mates of the 4th South African Scottish, who had suffered another miserable night under persistent falls of snow in old gun pits behind Fampoux. On the morning of the 12th many of the South Africans found their kilts frozen as stiff as plywood, as they stretched their weary limbs and hoped for news of relief and perhaps a hot breakfast. But the news when it came was far from pleasant. They were to attack the Chemical Works, with orders almost identical to those given to the ill-fated 2nd Seaforths on the previous day.

In order to expedite matters Major-General Lukin had decided against relieving the scattered survivors of 4th Division who were holding the forward positions. His South Africans would go straight through them. At 11.45 a.m., however, Brigadier-General Dawson telephoned Lukin to protest. The men were in no condition to launch any attack – they were exhausted. Lukin, ever sympathetic towards his old brigade, telephoned his Corps Commander, Lieutenant-General Fergusson, who replied that 'if the attack was delayed we would not have such a heavy concentration of artillery to support our attack on a subsequent day'.[9] The South Africans had no choice. They were also informed that their ultimate objective was Greenland Hill – way beyond the Chemical Works. If they failed to take it, they were informed that they would have to attack again the following day. In spite of the disaster which befell the 2nd Seaforths on the previous day, the operation order directed the South African Brigade to form up *on the main street in Fampoux*. They could not fail to be observed.

Similar orders had been handed to Frank Maxwell. His brigade was to attack from the same sunken road that the Seaforths had gone over from the day before. In an effort to view the ground over which his brigade was to advance, Maxwell rode his horse up to Fampoux, but his small party was spotted and shelled. Realizing the danger of following these thoughtless orders to the letter, he decided to form up

[9] PRO WO95/1738.

161

his brigade well to the north of the shell-trap village and attack from there. That, however, entailed a long advance of 1,800 yards down the slope in full view of the enemy. Maxwell rode urgently back to his HQ and telephoned Divisional HQ at St Nicholas. He asked that there should be no protective barrage once the objective had been reached and requested a small barrage to cover the attack of his brigade down the long slope – but just as the message was being relayed the line was cut.

The bombardment of the Chemical Works by heavy artillery, promised by General Fergusson, failed to materialize. Just a few shells landed, intermittent and inaccurate. As Maxwell later wrote, 'No heavy artillery FOOs were seen in the Green Line trenches, the best, if not the only position for observation. The large collection of buildings round Roeux Station remained quite intact and only one shell was seen to fall near the Chemical Works between 10 a.m. and 1 p.m.'[10]

In order to allow the heavy artillery to bombard the Chemical Works prior to the advance, General Lukin had delayed the attack until 5 p.m.; but, as Maxwell witnessed, there was no bombardment. The South Africans, as ordered, assembled in Fampoux in bright sunshine, the snow clouds having temporarily scattered. Betteridge recorded:

> Two companies of the Scottish and two of the 2nd Regiment marched into the main road of Fampoux, which consisted of about two hundred houses and a few shops. It was virtually intact owing to the quickness of our advance. There were a few hastily-dug trenches half a mile beyond the village, facing the railway embankment which was about twenty feet high and five hundred yards long. There was almost no activity as we all concentrated in the main road of Fampoux. It was 4 p.m. The first platoon had gone through the village to enter the communication trench when a Very light was fired from a house in the village. Instantly, the most incredible barrage of shells fell on the men massed in the main road. Within minutes, half of them were casualties. I must truthfully say that this brief bombardment was worse than any in Delville Wood while it lasted.

The South Africans were shelled so violently that the brigade was virtually annihilated. A few stunned survivors regrouped for the attack at zero hour, behind the field artillery barrage; but when it came the barrage moved too fast – twice as fast as on the 9th when the

[10] PRO WO95/1770.

troops had been fresh and fit. The South Africans began to deploy from the shelter of the houses at the eastern edge of the village, only to come under machine-gun fire from the Chemical Works. Already they had lost the barrage. Not only had it gone away too fast, it had started too far forwards – *behind* the first enemy trench, in fact, and thus proving no deterrent to the German riflemen and machine-gunners. The attack was another total failure, although, according to John Buchan, bodies of South African soldiers were later found in the ruins of Roeux station. The South African Brigade had been so badly decimated that there was grave concern that it would have to be disbanded altogether; but, although it took no further part in the Arras fighting, the brigade did manage to preserve its identity.

At the same time as the remnants of the South African Brigade went forward from Fampoux, Maxwell's 27th Brigade set off on their long walk down the slope towards the Roeux–Gavrelle road. Watching their advance from the Hyderabad Redoubt was a young artillery subaltern, Richard Talbot-Kelly, who later wrote:

> From where I was sitting in a half-dug German reserve trench, the noise of the German machine guns was completely inaudible and, as I watched, the ranks of the Highlanders were thinned out and torn apart by an inaudible death that seem to strike them from nowhere. It was peculiarly horrible to watch: the bright day, the little scudding clouds and these frightened men dying in clumps in a noiseless battle.[11]

As Talbot-Kelly added, 'The attack failed completely.' And Maxwell wrote, after watching the destruction of his proud brigade:

> The attack was checked almost at once, and the artillery barrage moving at 100 yards in two minutes soon left the assault behind. A new enemy trench, some 200 yards west of the objective road, was not known to exist, so was passed over more or less untouched by the artillery, and by the time the barrage had reached and passed the objective, the attack had hardly progressed 300 yards on the extreme left and less than that on the right . . . I regret the failure of my brigade to take the objective.[12]

On the evening of 12 April, seemingly oblivious to the mounting catalogue of disasters to the north and south of his sector, Lieutenant-General Snow wrote to his wife saying, 'Things have gone very well

[11] Richard Talbot-Kelly, *A Subaltern's Odyssey*, p. 158.
[12] PRO WO95/1770.

since yesterday and we got over the petty annoyances. Commander-in-Chief and Allenby most awfully jolly – latter too pleased for words. I am glad for his sake.'[13] But Allenby's joviality of 12 April did little to quell the fears that rattled his staff. There was now a definite reversal of fortune. His shattered divisions could do no more. Permission was sought from GHQ for fresh divisions to relieve them. Subsequently, the 17th replaced the 15th between Monchy and the Scarpe; the relief of the 37th by the 29th had already taken place; the 63rd (Royal Naval) Division was ordered to replace the 34th; the 2nd Division had replaced the 51st, and the 33rd and 50th Divisions had gone into the line further south to replace the 14th and 30th. Little time had been given to these fresh divisions to familiarize themselves with their new sectors, plans already being issued for the 29th Division to break out from Monchy and capture Vis-en-Artois on the Cambrai road – an optimistic target. Farther south the 50th Division had been sent in against Wancourt Tower. The bedraggled 9th Division with its shattered contingent of South Africans was still in the line and a division would have to be conjured up for its relief.

News of the fighting of 12 April as it trickled into GHQ was not all bad, however. On the First Army front, north of Vimy Ridge, the 50th and 44th Canadian Battalions had captured The Pimple – sealing the capture of Vimy Ridge and reducing the likelihood of an enemy counter-attack from the north – and the 30th Division, on the Third Army's southern flank, had seized 1,000 yards of the Hindenburg Line after the enemy had given up this particular sector. But, despite these and other optimistic reports, the wasteful actions of 11 and 12 April had seen the last flicker of British hopes at Arras dwindle and expire. The great victory won on 9 April, proclaimed as such by the Allied powers and acknowledged by the enemy, had terminated at nightfall on that day. By 13 April the lethargy among British generals and staff – symptoms of which had first become noticeable on the evening of the 9th – was now spreading dangerously.

On the 13th, a Friday, Sir Douglas Haig motored to Beaumetz where he was informed of a telephone message from French Headquarters: the French Army Group Commander desired to postpone the French offensive for a further twenty-four hours (having already postponed it once, due to bad weather on the 11th). But General Nivelle wanted Haig's approval – thus switching the onus of responsibility to the British Commander-in-Chief. Haig sensibly advised Nivelle to do as

[13] Snow papers, Imperial War Museum.

164

he thought fit, but this news must have been a bad blow to him; it meant that the British must hold out at Arras for another day. That night he wrote to his wife, expressing 'a tremendous affection for those fine fellows who are ready to give their lives for the old country at any moment. I feel quite sad at times when I see them march past me, knowing as I do how many must pay the full penalty before we can have peace.'[14]

The question was, who would pay the full penalty next?

As dawn broke on 14 April, the Royal Newfoundland Regiment, refurbished after its losses on the Somme, was in assembly trenches to the east of Monchy alongside the 1st Essex Regiment, part of 88th Brigade, 29th Division. Both battalions were under orders to advance eastwards from the village and capture the high point of Hill 100 or Infantry Hill which lay between two small woods, Bois-du-Vert and Bois-du-Sart, easily visible from Monchy, 1,500 yards ahead and defended by troops of the 23rd Bavarian Regiment who occupied a thin line of trenches on the forward slopes of the hill. The 4th Worcestershires and 2nd Hampshires were to be in support to cover the flanks; but at zero hour they had still not appeared. No unit had been detailed to occupy the positions vacated by the attacking force in front of Monchy. According to the war diary of the New-foundlanders, 'The result of this operation, if successful, would be a balloon-shaped position blown from Monchy-le-Preux which was already the apex of a salient.'[15] All the enemy needed to do was close the neck of the balloon and burst it.

At 5.30 a.m., following a weak and scrappy barrage, the little force advanced. It was just daylight. The morning was misty and the ground soggy with the recent snow and rain. Over the first 200 yards some casualties were caused by machine-gun fire, but the Newfoundlanders on the right flank quickly surrounded and captured a troublesome strongpoint at Monchy windmill. With that secured they advanced on the Bois-du-Vert, the Essex moving in on the other wood to the left. The Germans were seen running back from their first trench and both this and a second trench further on were found practically deserted. After a pause, the two battalions went on in high spirits, meeting little opposition. At 7.20 a.m. the Essex telephoned to Brigade HQ that the objective was taken. Observers in Monchy could see the Newfoundlanders digging in near some burning huts on the edge of a small copse – but that is the last that is known of them. The battalion never returned.

[14] Robert Blake (ed.), *The Private Papers of Douglas Haig*, p. 217.
[15] PRO WO95/2308.

The Germans, counter-attacking from the woods on both sides, simply surrounded both the Essex and the Newfoundlanders. They had walked into a trap. Some of them tried to run back but were shot down; the rest surrendered. The Newfoundland Regiment and the 1st Essex had ceased to exist as battalions. Just after 10 a.m. a wounded soldier of the Essex limped into Newfoundland HQ in Monchy and reported that all the Essex had been killed or captured. In this brief action the Newfoundlanders lost 17 officers and 468 other ranks, the Essex 17 officers and 585 other ranks. This was the first occasion on which the new German 'elastic defence in depth' was staged on a modern battlefield. Monchy-le-Preux, the village that had cost so many lives to capture, now stood wide open and defenceless.

Lieutenant-Colonel J. Forbes-Robertson, commanding the Royal Newfoundland Regiment, could hardly believe the news. He sent his signals officer, Lieutenant K. F. Keegan, to ascertain the situation. Twenty-five minutes later Keegan reported that Monchy was practically deserted and that no one was manning the trenches on the eastern edge; furthermore, hundreds of German soldiers were now advancing on the village. Colonel Forbes-Robertson quickly took his battalion HQ – about twenty men – through the village towards the assembly trenches. Climbing a ladder against the wall of the last big house in the village, he saw to his horror a line of Germans jumping into the empty assembly trenches just 100 yards away. Between Forbes-Robertson's party and the enemy was a small bank topped by a hedge, but as they rushed forward to the cover of the hedge, a machine gun opened up from the left and several of the party were killed. Only Forbes-Robertson, Keegan, the Provost Sergeant, Orderly Room Corporal and five other men were now left. Bravely pressing on, they reached the bank and found a good stretch of trench. For the next five hours, these nine men – and one other who had crawled into the trench later – kept the Germans under constant fire, killing over forty of them with the first few fusillades and driving the rest to cover. They and their excellent marksmanship were all that now stood between the enemy and Monchy-le-Preux.

At 1.55 p.m., seeing the enemy build up in strength and wondering where British reinforcements had got to, Forbes-Robertson sent a runner for help. Eventually a platoon of the 2nd Hampshires managed to work their way through the enemy blocking barrage to the west of Monchy, and at 2.45 arrived at the houses on the eastern edge of the village, adding the weight of their rifle-fire to that of Forbes-Robertson's little body of men who were almost out of ammunition. There now followed a severe artillery duel, with the Germans heavily

166

bombarding Monchy and the British putting down a barrage to the east of the village: 'This fire,' Lieutenant Keegan recorded in the war diary, 'must have killed a good many of our wounded lying out in the open and those collected in the assembly trench.'[16] The barrage worked, however. After being pinned down for several hours by the action of a few stout hearts, the enemy withdrew and Monchy was saved.

As the power of the British offensive at Arras began to fizzle out, the senior army bigwigs and politicians were becoming increasingly impatient. After all, was it not the French who were responsible for the launching of a British attack in the first place? So why hadn't they fulfilled their side of the bargain and launched their much-heralded offensive? Like a fish out of water, the British Army had been left high and dry and was now gasping for air. Spears, in his unenviable task of liaison, had already warned French High Command of the frustration at British GHQ:

> I had bluntly spoken of the disgrace of allowing the British
> success to peter out uselessly because the support which had
> been promised was not forthcoming. I had protested against the
> delay. But I felt sick at heart at the thought that the French
> attack might fail through haste, and that if it did fail the position
> in Artois would not be changed, however many thousands of
> lives were sacrificed on the Aisne. Now on the eve of the attack,
> I was dominated by a sense of impending disaster.[17]

Sir Douglas Haig had kept the French continually informed of the progress of his Arras offensive. On the evening of 11 April he had told General de Vallières, Chief of the French Military Mission, 'No change – objective Cambrai', which summed up his optimistic hopes. But on the 12th, when all reports of the previous day's fighting had been received and collated, Haig politely wrote to Nivelle:

> I regret that owing to the bad weather and the consequent state
> of the ground, my troops have not been able to follow up the
> success already gained as rapidly as would have been possible
> under better conditions. The enemy has therefore had time to
> bring up reinforcements and is offering strenuous opposition, to
> overcome which, without great sacrifice of life, it is necessary to
> bring forward artillery, a slow and difficult task.[18]

[16] PRO WO95/2308.
[17] Spears, *Prelude to Victory*, 482.
[18] PRO WO158/37.

Nivelle had set his sights high, and Haig quietly suspected that the French Army was not equal to the mammoth effort demanded by their Commander-in-Chief. He also knew that the French were playing their last card. The better weather hoped for by Nivelle had not arrived but the freezing rain which drenched the French infantry did not dampen their ardour. To the faithful *Poilus* of whom he expected so much, Nivelle made his final proclamation: 'The hour has come. Courage. Confidence.'

The hour had also come for the Germans. Forewarned and prepared by the capture of the attack plan, they waited to receive the French onslaught, many of them safe in deep *creutes* or caves on the thickly wooded slopes of the Aisne valley.

At 6 a.m. on 16 April, under a mighty but ineffectual artillery umbrella of 5,350 guns, the French infantry, with characteristic dash, attacked the German trenches on a front of forty kilometres. But in the majority of places the wire remained uncut and the defences intact. Where they did break through, the Germans emerged from the *creutes* and slaughtered them with machine guns – and if ever there was a heyday of the machine gun, it was on this day. Never before had so many of these weapons been in action at once. In one small wood appropriately named Petit Bois on the Vauclerc Plateau, no less than a hundred machine guns were captured. With Nivelle's stirring words ringing in their ears, the French infantry died in their thousands. In spite of grievous casualties, some early gains were made, with the first German position between Soissons and Craonne captured and over 10,000 prisoners taken. The good news was short-lived, however. By nightfall the French had been driven out.

News of the slaughter on the Chemin-des-Dames ridge was brought by the bitterly disillusioned and demoralized stragglers now streaming back through the fresh battalions waiting to enter the fray – and although casualties were often exaggerated, the soldiers of these advancing support battalions soon learned for themselves the appalling truth. The Aisne was little more than a slaughterhouse. Someone with a macabre sense of humour started baaing like a sheep as he shuffled forward, and soon the others took it up, bleating and baaing on their way to face the guns.

By the end of the first day, in spite of token footholds gained in the enemy lines, the spirit of the French soldiers had been broken. For many of them the final straw was the news that over 5,000 of their badly wounded countrymen had died unattended in forward ambulances whilst waiting to be evacuated. Nivelle's prediction of 10,000 wounded by the end of the first day fell tragically short of the 120,000 incurred by nightfall on the 17th. It soon became clear to even the more optimistic that the grand attack had failed – even though the French Army would struggle painfully on until the end of the month. Nivelle's vaunted breakthrough had failed. The only thing broken was his army.

At first the French tried to disguise the full horror of their losses from their Allies. Indeed, as Haig wrote in his diary on 17 April:

> I could get no details from the French Mission as to results of today's fighting. This is always a bad sign and I fear that things are going badly with the offensive.[19]

But if details were missing, the overall picture was clear enough. Spears sent a carefully worded telegram to the War Office on the 17th, warning that the French offensive 'did not apparently achieve results expected'.[20]

Lloyd George's confidence in Nivelle had been misplaced; he had no choice now but to rely on his own generals, however much he disapproved of their 'wearing out' tactics, and they were all agreed – they would have to proceed alone. As Sir William Robertson wrote to GHQ on the 19th, 'Our only chance is to continue, since to discontinue would mean defence against increasing strength for an indefinite period.'[21] The British pressure at Arras would have to be maintained.

[19] Robert Blake (ed.), *The Private Papers of Douglas Haig*, p. 218.
[20] PRO WO158/23.
[21] Ibid.

17

Comical Works

'There's too much fuckin' artillery in this bloody war!' These senti-
ments, so colourfully expressed by Manning's immortal character
Jakes,[1] were no doubt echoed by the survivors of 'A' Company, 9th
Royal Scots, as they cringed and scraped for cover in the half-sunken
track they called 'Crump Trench' that twisted from the railway at
Fampoux along the edge of the Scarpe. For the first time in the battle
the German artillery held the upper hand. Having learned the hard
lessons of 9 April, the majority of the artillery was safe in the rear and
out of reach of British heavies, which had still been unable to get
forward, due to the parlous state of the roads.

Now, as the continuous 'crumps' exploded with remarkable
accuracy on the chill dawn of Monday 23 April, the shaken Jocks
were bracing themselves for battle. It was their turn to attack Roeux
and its sinister Chemical Works. Doubtless, none of them knew it was
St George's Day – and none of them gave a damn that it was Allenby's
birthday. Their 'rest' had lasted a mere forty-eight hours before they
were back in the line, which was no time at all to recover from the
trauma and shock of battle. On 15 April, much to its general disgust,
the 51st (Highland) Division, as Third Army dogsbody, found itself
holding the front trenches at Fampoux. Someone had to relieve the
shattered 4th Division; but as Bill Partridge of the 7th Middlesex
claimed: 'We used to say, "If there's any shit to be shovelled, give it to
the 51st Highland Division" – and they always did!'

On 20 April, during one of the lulls in the fighting, 'A' Company
had been ordered to dislodge a pocket of the enemy from Mount
Pleasant and Roeux woods. The attack had hardly got under way
before the Company met sturdy enemy resistance which stopped the
attack dead. If anything was gained by this misadventure, then it was
the sure knowledge that the enemy was in Roeux in some force.
Before any headway could be made, the sunken track would have to

[1] Frederick Manning, *The Middle Parts of Fortune* (1929).

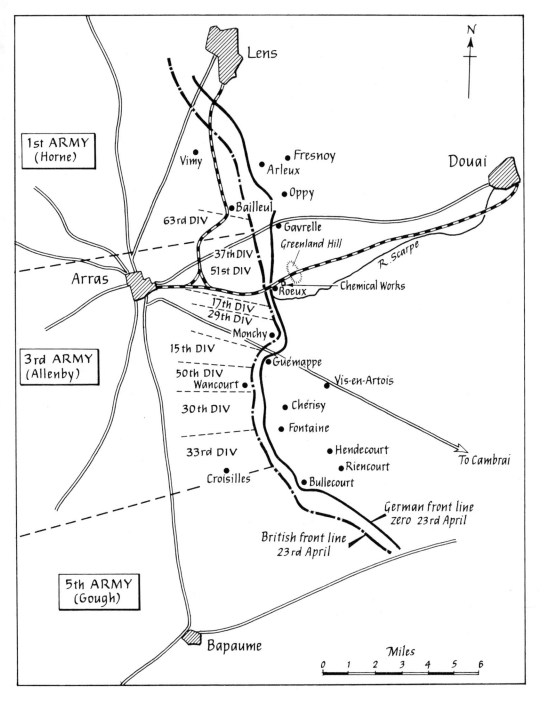

N

1st ARMY
(Horne)

Lens

Douai

Vimy

Fresnoy
Arleux

Oppy

Bailleul

63rd DIV

Gavrelle

Greenland Hill

37th DIV

51st DIV

R. Scarpe

Chemical Works

Roeux

Arras

17th DIV

29th DIV

Monchy

15th DIV

3rd ARMY
(Allenby)

Guémappe

50th DIV

Wancourt

Vis-en-Artois

30th DIV

Chérisy

Fontaine

33rd DIV

Hendecourt

Riencourt

To Cambrai

Croisilles

Bullecourt

German front line
zero 23rd April

British front line
23rd April

5th ARMY
(Gough)

Bapaume

Miles

0 1 2 3 4 5 6

7. THE INFANTRY ATTACK PLAN, 23 APRIL, 1917.

be lengthened to give the Royal Scots and other battalions more room. The problem was the Germans held the half of the track that disappeared into Roeux Wood. On the 21st, 'A' Company went into action again, this time attempting to push the enemy back into the wood; but again the advance had been stopped, 'A' Company suffering heavily at the hands of the Germans dug in on the wooded terraces which shelved steeply to the river.

Allenby's plan for his renewed offensive, due to start that day, incorporated a tough role for the 51st Division. This would primarily be a Third Army effort, although Horne's First Army was to break into the Oppy line and capture the village of Gavrelle, thereby protecting the left flank of Third Army – the main objectives of which were Roeux, Greenland Hill and the Chemical Works, now cynically renamed 'Comical Works' by the Jocks. South of the Scarpe, other objectives were Bois-du-Vert, St Rohart factory and the main road and, even farther south, the spur beyond the Sensée brook between Chérisy and Fontaine-les-Croisilles – the Hindenburg Line again. This affair was to become known as the Second Battle of the Scarpe.

Having lost the important element of artillery surprise, Allenby knew that he had little chance of success. There could be no deep penetration of the enemy defences, as there were no reserves to support any large breakthrough. The attack was to be largely carried out by tired troops, without the benefit of reconnaissance and the careful preparation need to ensure success like that of 9 April. Added to that gloomy outlook was the important factor of the losses in good officers and NCOs suffered in the opening days of the battle. This applied in particular to the 37th, 51st, 15th, 30th and 29th Divisions, destined to bear the brunt of the fighting. The relatively 'fresh' divisions which had not yet been fully engaged were the 63rd, 17th, 50th and 33rd.

The Blue Line, the first major objective of the day, Allenby directed 'must be gained at all points and *at all costs*'.[2] There were two more lines – brown and red – an optimistic 1,000 yards further on. Nine divisions would spearhead the attack along a nine-mile front (see map 8, p. 171) which was to be launched at 4.45 a.m. on 23 April. Major F. W. Bewsher, historian of the 51st Division, wrote that it 'developed into perhaps the most savage infantry battle that the division took part in'.[3]

In spite of the storming reputation of 51st Division, Lieutenant-

[2] PRO WO158/224.
[3] Bewsher, p. 164.

General Fergusson as Corps Commander doubted whether the tired Scots would be able to take the Blue Line – which straddled Greenland Hill and was also at the very limit of the range of his eighteen-pounders. Fergusson sensibly suggested that the Highlanders should halt at Roeux and the Chemical Works but this was dismissed by Allenby. Harper, as always, was totally confident of the fighting prowess of his 51st Division, which would be assisted in this attack by five tanks – a generous allocation from the mere twenty salvaged and repaired after 9 April.

Facing the British attack was a total of eleven enemy divisions of which nine would actually be deployed in defence. Only one division, the 220th, had been heavily engaged on 9 April. Five of these divisions were in immediate reserve, close to the action should they be called upon. In short the enemy was fully prepared for the British attack. In and around the buildings of the Chemical Works, the station and Roeux village and preparing to receive the 51st (Highland) Division were strong elements of no less than three enemy divisions.

As dawn broke on the 23rd the valleys and marshes of the battle front hung thick with a dense mist, intensified by smoke from the British barrage. Waiting nervously in a shallow assembly trench with just a few minutes to zero, Corporal Albert Smith of 'B' Company, the 7th Gordon Highlanders, made the last checks on his Lewis gun. Alongside him was his old friend Henry Gilmour. Both men were just twenty years old and hailed from Banchory, Deeside. The platoon commander was Second-Lieutenant Jim Stitt, dressed in a private's uniform and carrying a rifle and bayonet; the only signs distinguishing him as an officer were the single pips on each shoulder, now dulled with wet clay, and the single white line daubed in blanco on the rear of his tin hat. Studying his watch, he stood up and indicated by a wave of his arm for his men to leave the trench. They advanced and lay down behind the scrappy barrage. Their first objective was the Black Line, which they had to overcome before they could press on to the Blue and they were due to begin their advance at zero plus fifteen minutes. Already the din of battle was tremendous and from the station buildings and Chemical Works ahead could be heard the tac-tac-tac of the enemy machine guns. Pulling back the cocking handle of the Lewis, Bert Smith winked at Henry Gilmour. *Friends are good on the day of battle.*

> By now it was getting light and we could clearly see the big
> chimney of the Chemical Works directly ahead of us. Mr Stitt

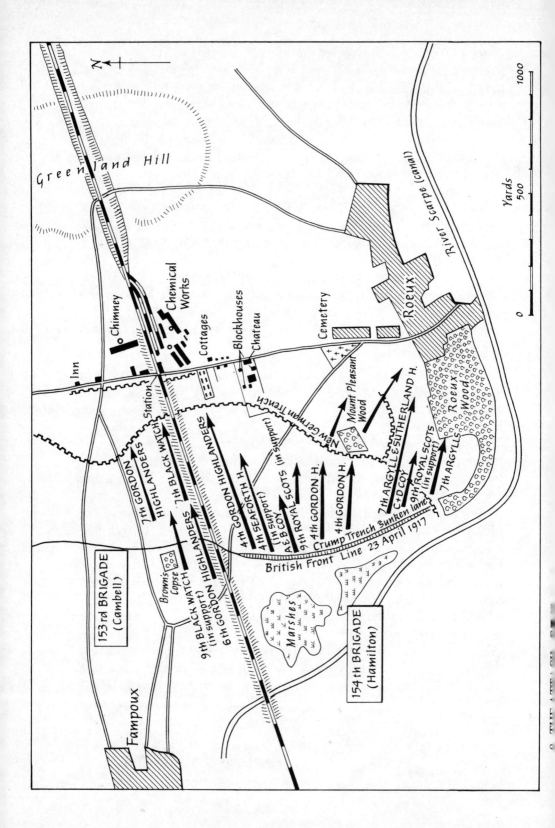

N

Greenland Hill

River Scarpe (canal)

1000

Yards

500

0

Chimney

Chemical Works

Cottages

Blockhouses

Chateau

Cemetery

Roeux

Inn

Station

7th GORDON HIGHLANDERS

7th BLACK WATCH

6th GORDON HIGHLANDERS

9th BLACK WATCH (in support)

Brown's Copse

153rd BRIGADE (Cambell)

Fampoux

4th GORDON HIGHLANDERS

4th SEAFORTH H.

A & B COY

9th ROYAL SCOTS (in support)

4th GORDON H.

4th GORDON H.

New German Trench

Mount Pleasant Wood

7th ARGYLL & SUTHERLAND H.

C + D COY

9th ROYAL SCOTS (in support)

7th ARGYLLS

Roeux Wood

Crump Trench Sunken lane

British Front Line 23 April 1917

Marshes

154th BRIGADE (Hamilton)

8. THE ATTACK ON

stood up and said, 'Head for the chimney, boys,' and motioned towards it with his arm. As he uttered the words a salvo of shells came whining overhead and down went the chimney in a great blast of smoke and rubble! Soon we lost the barrage and got cut up by the machine-gun fire. The boys were going down everywhere but we pressed on and I kept firing short bursts at the trench in front of us. When we reached this trench we killed all the enemy that had been holding up there – those of us that was left, that is. Henry was still with us and Mr Stitt – he was the only officer left by this time and he got us all together and took us past the station on to Greenland Hill. He was a good chap all right. We were up against damn good soldiers here.[4] They fought like tigers. Pretty soon we came to a Jerry dressing station where we captured fifty or so unwounded Jerries, but by this time there was so few of us left that Mr Stitt thought we should get back to the road. This we did and the Jerries we sent scooting off back towards our lines with their hands on their heads. We soon occupied this enemy trench and then something funny happened which I suppose always stands out in your memory. In the middle of the battle I could hear this voice from behind shouting 'A.W., A.W.,' which were my initials, usually called out at pay as there were three Smiths in our platoon. Turning around I saw a small figure running towards us through the smoke and dust. It was another pal of mine, little Harry Marr, an officer's batman who had brought up a parcel of 200 Players cigarettes which my father sent me every week – and I didn't smoke, so you can see how popular I was! Well, Harry knew the boys would be glad of a decent fag but he also knew that I would split them with him, so there he was risking his life to bring up the fags, the stupid bugger. So I gave him two tins and back he went running like a long-dog, swerving from side to side to dodge the bullets which were ringing all round him. 'Go on Harry, run!' we shouted and Jerry even exploded shrapnel over him but he got back OK.

Runner after runner had been sent forward by Battalion HQ to find out what had happened to the 7th Gordons as all contact during the morning had been lost – they had disappeared. 'D' Company in reserve had failed to follow the deep penetration made into the enemy lines by Stitt and his small party and the only runner to get through appeared to be Harry Marr although his business had been hardly warlike. Jim Stitt got his MC. His platoon had killed and captured over 200 Germans as well as knocking out two trench mortars and one machine-gun post.

[4] The 161st Regiment of 185th Division, who had just relieved the 86th Regiment of 18th Division the previous night. They were actually driven out of Roeux – only to counter-attack and recapture it.

Watching the progress of his brigade from his forward HQ in the infamous sunken road north-east of Fampoux, Brigadier-General Campbell could see the ant-like movements of his Highlanders as they disappeared beneath the huge pall of smoke and dust that marked the site of the Chemical Works. At 8.15 a.m. with the aid of field glasses he saw what he thought were kilted Highlanders, albeit a mere few, on Greenland Hill. He thought right. It was Stitt and the remains of 'B' Company. Campbell noted in his report, 'Only five men of this company eventually came back.'[5] On his left flank the position was uncertain and, desperate for more information, he sent for more runners. This time he decided to use two valuable and experienced officers: Captain Pat Blair, acting 154 Brigade Major, of the 9th Royal Scots, and his own 153 Brigade Major, Captain Lean. As Campbell later reported:

> During the whole of the 23rd I received no definite information from the 7th Black Watch or 7th Gordon Highlanders as all runners apparently failed to get through. At 1.30 p.m., being still without any more definite information from units, I sent Captain Blair, 9th Royal Scots, to ascertain how matters stood. He reported that the Black Line was held by us, that the 6th Black Watch were holding the Roeux–Gavrelle road and that the 6th Gordon Highlanders and 7th Black Watch were in the trench just west of the village and north of the railway. Both the reconnaissances made by Captain Lean and Captain Blair were carried out with difficulty, and under artillery, machine-gun and rifle fire from Greenland Hill.[6]

Pat Blair, the well-loved 'A' Company Commander of the 9th Royal Scots, was killed by a sniper in the Chemical Works during the afternoon of the 23rd, while carrying out yet another dangerous reconnaissance for General Campbell. Although his brave conduct was recommended for reward by Campbell, the matter came to nothing. Throughout the day Campbell had very little information to send back to General Harper who thought he was deliberately being kept in the dark. No wonder the battle for Roeux and the Chemical Works was called a soldiers' battle – the Generals from Brigadier upwards simply had no say. All Allenby could reiterate was 'At all costs' which he telephoned through to General Fergusson at 2 p.m. and there the order-passing stopped.

To the right of the railway embankment and attacking the Chemical Works and Roeux château and village was 154 Brigade, and on the

[5] PRO WO95/2872.
[6] PRO WO95/2872.

left were the 4th Gordon Highlanders who had spent a most uncomfortable night in 'Crump Trench'. Albert Anderson, 'A' Company's Sergeant-Major, later recalled:

> At zero plus ten, we went forward in two waves and we soon
> reached and entered Mount Pleasant Wood, with surprisingly
> little resistance. As we came out of the wood and made for
> Roeux I noticed that some of our men were being picked off by
> snipers in the tree-tops of the wood we had just come through
> and supposedly cleared. Four of us jumped into a shell hole and
> the lad in front of me turned around to talk to me when he was
> shot through the head, the bullet passing through his eye. We
> knew the fire was coming from the wood behind so I decided we
> would have to go back for the snipers. I told the other two lads
> to follow me and we made back for the wood, dodging from
> shell hole to shell hole, with bullets whizzing all around us.
> Soon we reached the wood and darted in among the
> undergrowth. 'Where were they?' we thought and we lay very
> still, trying to spot movement. Then we saw them! Right up in
> the tops of the trees, well camouflaged. Taking careful aim, we
> shot them down. Eventually we got into the village at the trench
> line where there were some deep dugouts, which we later found
> out to be the entrances to tunnels because throwing Mills
> bombs down them had no effect and Jerry appeared at every
> window and doorway of every cottage. If anyone tried to cross
> the road he would be cut down. Jerry was spraying the cobbles
> with machine-gun fire from a window of a house farther down
> the street, about fifty yards away. This caused the bullets to
> 'windmill', making a weird moaning noise, and I saw one lad
> decapitated as a result of being struck by one of these bullets.
> During the fighting, I noticed a curious thing; Jerry had his
> bayonets fixed. I had never seen that before, so I guess he
> meant business. No quarter was asked, and none was given.

Albert Anderson was one of a special breed of men, the British NCO, and as a sergeant-major often hated by the lead-swingers and dodgers in the company. If the battle of Roeux was a soldiers' battle, then 23 April was the NCOs' day. Almost all officers had been killed or wounded. Consequently the outcome of the desperate close-quarter fighting in Roeux village and the Chemical Works depended on the skill and tenacity of these men. Captain Cyril Falls describes them thus:

> When he really was a trained soldier, the British
> non-commissioned officer was unsurpassed in skill and
> initiative. His value was then very great, because even at his
> weakest he hardly knew the meaning of the word defeat. The

British rank and file drew upon an almost inexhaustible fund
of courage and endurance. Few factors contributed more
to the final victory than their doggedness, and, above all,
their resilience.[7]

Another young Sergeant-Major, twenty-two-year-old Jack Renwick of the 9th Royal Scots, had just learned of the award of the
Military Cross to add to that of his MM, for gallantry on 9 April. At
5.15 a.m., following on behind the 4th Gordons and 7th Argylls, he
led the remainder of 'A' Company forward from Crump Trench.
Immediately they were raked with machine-gun fire from the château
and Chemical Works but made their way forward in small sectional
rushes. 'B' Company, on their left, fought their way into the Chemical Works but walked into a defensive trap. They were surrounded
and fought to the last man. Sticking closely to Renwick, 'A' Company
managed to reach the road between the cemetery and the Chemical
Works, where they occupied some old German trenches. Suddenly,
they were subjected to murderous enfilade fire from the concealed
blockhouses among the château buildings. Renwick and the unwounded survivors of 'A' Company then set off in an apparent
attempt to assist the remainder of 'B' Company, fighting for their
lives in the Chemical Works. The small party was last seen going
forwards into the smoke and dust about 11 a.m. None of them was
seen again.

Sparse accounts have been left describing the fighting for Roeux
and the Chemical Works on 23 April but all, including the Official
History, are clear on one point: there was total confusion throughout
the day and a complete breakdown in all forms of communications.
With many units leaderless – the 1/7th Argylls, for instance, had lost
all fifteen officers in the first hour of the attack – it is small wonder that
Regimental Histories are thin on information as to what really
happened. Even Cyril Falls, the Official Historian, with all sources at
his disposal, is not clear on the order of events that day. A study of all
documents and diaries from Third Army down reveal nothing but
muddle.

A fact unknown to the officers who kept the daily war diaries was
that the Germans were largely hidden *under* Roeux in the maze of
tunnels that connected the village with the Chemical Works and
château. The diarist of the 7th Argylls came close to guessing the
truth when he recorded: 'In the village, bombing parties began to
clear the houses and considerable numbers were cleared, but the

[7] *Official History, France and Belgium 1917*, p. 554.

178

houses and gardens seemed to be connected as the Germans cleared out of one seemed to appear in the next, while the machine guns were well active from the upper storeys.'[8] And one British officer who witnessed the fighting wrote:

> At every hour it seemed a voice from division announced a further attack on the Chemical Works by the Highlanders. Each time they won it, and each time they were driven out. Our line lay waiting for them to finish. There was no finish. Each time they went in they killed everything that was on the ground and each time, like dragon's teeth, the enemy sprang up again.[9]

The Germans were also continually launching powerful counter-attacks, each time preluded by a hurricane bombardment, and as more than one witness remembers, 'The enemy bombarded the Chemical Works regardless as to whether his own troops were present.' Most diaries of the Highland Division units also praise the action of the tanks on that day, in particular two of the five allocated to the division which did much to assist the infantry. One of them, Tank C7, was commanded by Second-Lieutenant L. Victor-Smith, who arrived in Roeux to find the infantry being pinned down by enemy machine guns located in the surrounding houses. He later reported:

> Our barrage could only have been very slight to judge from the comparatively small amount of damage which was done to the buildings. Here I used 200 rounds of 6pdr ammunition. It is difficult to estimate with any accuracy the number of machine guns actually 'put out'. One of my best targets was a party of some thirty men whom we drove out of a house with 6pdrs and then sprayed them with Lewis gun fire. I am sure that at least one 6pdr shell dropped amongst them – this made a distinct impression. Another target that presented itself was a party of men coming towards us. I do not know whether they intended giving themselves up or whether they were a bombing party. I took them for the latter. Parties were frequently seen coming up from the rear through gaps in the buildings. Twice an enemy officer rallied some dozen or so men and rushed a house that we had already cleared. Here again a 6pdr through the window disposed of any of the enemy remaining in the buildings.[10]

Victor-Smith then turned his tank towards a troublesome machine-gun post under the railway embankment. But this was the end of C7's

[8] PRO WO95/2886.
[9] Guy Chapman, *A Passionate Prodigality*, p. 124.
[10] PRO WO95/91.

run of good luck; it shortly afterwards became stuck in the spongy ground. Much to the joy of the Scottish troops, however, the tank had also squashed several machine-gun nests in Roeux. As Brigadier-General Hamilton, commanding 154 Brigade, later wrote, 'The tank was certainly of assistance to the infantry and if it had gone on the village could have been cleared with comparative ease.' But Hamilton added: 'Unfortunately, on at least one occasion, the tank went over a shell hole in which wounded were lying. It would seem from this that the view of the driver must be very limited.'[11]

Lumbering slowly towards the mayhem of the Chemical Works, Tank C22, commanded by Second-Lieutenant Kann, was suddenly hit by a hail of armour-piercing bullets. The crew of a German machine gun had fired off a belt of the new 'K' ammunition at the metal monster that crawled towards them. Showers of sparks and scabs of hot metal flew off the tank's interior plating. Several of the steel bullets penetrated the thin metal skin and wounded the officer and a lance-corporal. Fortunately for the crew, the new ammunition was in short supply. Although the tank was forced to return to the British lines where the wounded were evacuated and shattered prisms replaced, Sergeant J. Noel then took over command of C22 and with great determination set off again for the Chemical Works. Crossing the first German line he scattered the terrified occupants and then straddled a communication trench, along which he drove. Upon reaching the Chemical Works, Noel noticed that 'a party of about thirty infantry put up a white flag and pretended to surrender, but immediately Lewis guns were switched off them they attempted to escape. Lewis guns were at once turned on them again and they became casualties.'[12]

Advancing straight into the Chemical Works the driver took C22 along the supply road, gingerly avoiding large heaps of rubble. The tank was followed by a party of Gordons and Seaforths who set off into the jumble of factory buildings, hurling Mills bombs through the shattered windows and down the steps leading to the cellars. For one eighteen-year-old private from Aberdeen, James Mackay of the 6th Gordons, this was his first action:

> Most of all I remember the noise – it was incredible! And I was fascinated to see our boys in action. They would all throw their Mills bombs in a salvo at a Jerry trench which would all explode together; then came back a shower of taddy-mashers – and

[11] PRO WO95/2884.
[12] PRO WO95/91.

180

20. Ditched British tank on the newly-captured Fampoux road:
'We hoped the wide ditch at the side of the road would stop it'.

21. Roeux Chemical Works. Before and after the Battle of Arras.

22. 'Onward, Joe Soap's Army'.

23. 'Dead Dump'.

24. Sunken Road. Fampoux, 1985: 'At 10am, Seaforths will advance in fours down road to crossroads, then up sunken road to Hyderabad'.

25. Battery Valley. 1985. On the horizon: Monchy-le-Preux.

26. Great blockhouse at Roeux. 1985. (When the author visited this site in 1989, the entrance had been bricked up, and the ruins of the Chemical Works bulldozed over.)

27. Arras 1989: 'By 1932, the spectacular Hotel-de-Ville had been restored
to its original Gothic splendour'.

28. 'The boys who really did the job are dead and in their graves'.

29. 9th (Scottish) Division Memorial on the windswept 'Point du Jour' ridge. The remains of the German blockhouse where 'a party of the 6th K.O.S.B. rushed a machine gun, destroyed the garrison and demolished its breakfast' can still be seen.

30. Sergeant Bill Hay, 9th Royal Scots. Back in the trenches, Vimy Ridge 1983: 'Last wish duly carried out'.

31. Corporal Alf Razzell. 8th Royal Fusiliers. Observation Ridge 1985: 'Putting my mind at rest'.

more than once I saw one of our chaps catch one of the bombs and throw it back! Quite hair-raising stuff.

Covered in red brick dust, Tank C22 emerged from the eastern side of the works, turned at the north-east corner of Roeux and trundled back along the main road, where it re-entered the Chemical Works at the request of the infantry, to deal with a remaining machine-gun crew who were causing casualties to the Highlanders now darting with unbounded fury among the broken buildings in an attempt to dislodge the enemy. Sergeant Noel dutifully destroyed this machine-gun nest, but, with his tank almost out of ammunition, turned back. Of the other three tanks assisting 51st Division, one failed to reach the start line and the other two got lost in the British smoke barrage, after emerging from which they were put out of action by armour-piercing ammunition, fired by machine guns in the Chemical Works.

Throughout the long day the Highlanders retained their precarious hold on Roeux. But the enemy, seemingly regardless of cruel losses inflicted on them by the British eighteen-pounder shrapnel shells, continued to advance in ranks over Greenland Hill. Without reinforcements, the Jocks were unable to hold out, many casualties being inflicted on them by the enemy in the château strongpoints. The only British officer left alive in the Chemical Works was Captain Hutcheson of the 6th Gordons, who in the initial advance had been amazed to see the elderly civilian gate-keeper of the level crossing standing bewildered by his hut as bullets flew all around him. It was Hutcheson who had organized the desperate defence of the Chemical Works following its temporary capture, using little parties of men which he threw into small outposts around the perimeter. Urgent messages for reinforcements were sent by pigeon and runner throughout the day, but none was forthcoming. Consequently Hutcheson was forced to abandon the Chemical Works at noon, even though several vicious fights were still taking place within the buildings.

During the afternoon the 6th Seaforth Highlanders, placed at the disposal of General Campbell's 153 Brigade, were sent forward in order to meet any hostile counter-attacks. Personally led by their able CO, Lieutenant-Colonel S. Macdonald, the battalion quickly occupied the trenches facing the Chemical Works. Macdonald decided to wait until dark before making any attempt at recapture; by then he would have the assistance of two battalions of the 34th Division which had been 'lent' to 51st Division and sent forward by General Harper

181

in the last-ditch attempt to win the day. But by 8 p.m. the 26th and 27th Battalions Northumberland Fusiliers, assigned for the task, had still not arrived and Macdonald decided to push his patrols forward into Roeux and the Chemical Works unsupported. At this critical moment, with Macdonald the only senior officer forward, he was recalled by the impatient General Campbell for a situation report. In the absence of their Colonel, the 6th Seaforths launched an uncoordinated advance into Roeux station, but were promptly driven out. The battalion was then ordered to dig a new trench on the north of the railway to form a flank guard to the 37th Division on the left.

This was the last action of the 51st Division on 23 April. By 10 p.m. the shattered Highlanders who had survived the gruelling day were back on their start line. They had given their all, leaving over 2,000 of their comrades dead, wounded or missing in the village of Roeux and the ruined Chemical Works. Harper's proud 51st Highland Division, although it would live to enhance its reputation in later battles, had been crippled by the day's fighting – and although the Jocks did not know it, they had not yet seen the back of the 'Comical Works'.

18

A Deuce of a Fight

The small village of Gavrelle lay on the northern flank of the area to be attacked on 23 April. Ordered to seize this important feature was First Army's 63rd (Royal Naval) Division – the 'sea soldiers' as they were known, with a jealously guarded and self-proclaimed reputation of being the best fighting unit in the army, not unlike the Royal Marines of today. The Royal Naval Division insisted on keeping naval ranks and traditions; even the battalions sported salty titles such as Anson, Drake, Hood and Nelson. Complementing the division were two battalions of Royal Marine Light Infantry. The third brigade in the division consisted merely of 'landlubbers' – 1st Hon. Artillery Company, 4th Beds, 10th Royal Dublin Fusiliers and the 7th Royal Fusiliers. The Division sported a unique esprit de corps, its ranks of landlocked sailors abounding with personalities such as Alan Herbert, the poet and wit, serving as an officer in Hawke Battalion.

Horne, the First Army Commander, was determined that the Royal Naval Division should capture Gavrelle. Five heavy artillery groups were ordered up to support the attack. Gavrelle promptly began to disintegrate. Taking up their assault positions at zero hour were Drake and Nelson on the right, with the 7th Royal Fusiliers and 4th Beds on the left. In close support was Hood Battalion, recently cheered by the news that its old CO, Commander Arthur Asquith, DSO, almost fully recovered from his wounds receive on the Somme, had been recalled in the previous twenty-four hours from a staff post to lead the battalion into the attack, Colonel Freyberg, VC, the outgoing CO having been promoted to the command of a brigade two days earlier.

Thirty-four-year-old Arthur Asquith, 'Oc' to his friends, was the third son of the late Prime Minister. (His eldest brother Raymond had been killed on the Somme the previous September.) Studying the ten pages of orders for the attack, Asquith was unhappy that Hood had not been selected to lead the assault. He was also worried by the fact that Hood had been ordered to follow on twenty minutes after the lead battalions. By then, as Asquith knew only too well from bitter experiences in the Ancre valley, the enemy would have put down a counter-barrage which would fall on Hood. Asquith was determined that Gavrelle would be *his* battle. He sent his second-in-command, Lieutenant-Commander Ellis, to try to persuade Brigadier Phillips to change his mind. But in vain. Later, however, when Asquith himself went to plead with the Brigadier, he discovered that 'It appeared from air photos that the wire was only indifferently cut, he did not wish Hood to be on the heels of Nelson and cut up with them if Nelson were held up by uncut wire.'

Brigadier-General Phillips was determined not to be hustled by this exuberant battalion commander, newly back on the scene. He was sure that his plan would not fail. By 2.30 a.m. all units reported to him that they were in position. Small patrols were out, including one from Howe Battalion, as Sub-Lieutenant Tom Lawrie later recalled:

> The password to safeguard the passage into our lines by those returning from the patrol was 'Blackhall' – the name of our company commander. By the time this information had come along the line the password had altered to a very clear 'Buggerall'.

Patrols sent out by Drake Battalion discovered that the wire on their right front was mostly uncut, and a message to Phillips reporting the fact ended with the bland enquiry: 'Is the attack cancelled?'[2] The reply is not recorded. Commander Bennet of Drake, however, took the matter seriously and issued amended orders to his battalion. They would attack on a one-company front only, the right flank being covered by a massive Stokes mortar bombardment.

As dawn began to break, Asquith took up a position in the centre of his leading wave. At 4.45 a.m. the lead battalions went in. Asquith waited just ten minutes, then, in his own words, 'decided it was not worthwhile hanging about in full blast of enemy barrage, so I led on, and sent back word for the rear companies to follow'.[3] Within five minutes, Hood had crossed the first enemy line where the wire was found to be well cut. Five minutes later, Asquith, at the head of his men, was in the second German line where he reorganized the advance into Gavrelle. Taking with him an assortment of men from Hood, Nelson and Drake, Asquith went right through the village,

[1] PRO WO95/3115.
[2] Ibid.
[3] PRO WO95/3115.

sending back droves of shell-dazed prisoners. At 5.40 a.m. Asquith was in the thick of the fighting and wrote: 'Enemy still sniping at and being fired at and rushed by our men, in cottages: a good deal of mixed fighting at twenty yards range.' He also noticed 'Some few of our guns still firing short and causing casualties among our men.'[4]

The lack of experience by the troops in the complicated and dangerous art of house-clearing was beginning to have repercussions. Many German soldiers of the 90th Fusilier Regiment defending the village put up a brave fight, as twenty-year-old Fusilier Hans Lutmer remembered:

> Due to the terrible bombardment we had hidden in the cellar of a large house. Sergeant Kloke shouted, 'Tommies are here!' so we took up positions by the shattered windows on the ground floor. Before we got the chance to open fire, a Tommy threw a grenade into the room which bounced along the floorboards. We all threw ourselves down but Kloke picked up the grenade and threw it back out of the window where it exploded. We began to shoot at the English but being on ground level made easy targets; two of my schoolchums from Warin were shot through the head. Resistance seemed useless as we were surrounded. Then another grenade was thrown into the room and Kloke picked it up to throw back but this time he was too late, it exploded in his hand. There was a terrific bang and then whistling in the ears and the next thing I know, I woke up in the street outside the house where I had been dragged. I had many shrapnel wounds from the British bomb but was later well treated by the English doctors. Everyone else including Kloke[5] had been killed by the bomb. In 1973 I had more shrapnel removed from my back while in hospital.

In house clearing, Mills bombs were a powerful and useful weapon – providing they were not thrown back at the thrower – but they soon became in short supply and casualties began to mount among the British bombers. Corporal Robert Willson, MM, of the 4th Beds reported that 'some of our men had dumped their bombs to lighten their load'; fortunately Willson was not one of them:

> Soon there came a call for 'Bombers forward' as they were badly needed and so as I was a bomber and had kept my bombs I went forward to do what I could. Soon I came to a point where Jerry was sniping from. There must have been at least thirty of our blokes lying there killed or wounded and to get through I had to crawl very carefully. When in their midst I came across

[4] Ibid.
[5] *Unteroffizier* P. E. Kloke: no known grave.

one of our men who was wounded and in great pain. He was lying on his back and had a dead man lying on top of him. He was in such pain that he implored me to kill him. This I could not do and begged him to hang on for a bit and relief would come. Anyhow, I crawled on along the street when I came to a trench where two tall Jerries were badly wounded and sitting up. I gave them both a tot of brandy which I always carried and one of them offered me his watch – which I declined to take. I pressed on but suddenly came under close small-arms fire and was forced back to where the Jerries were and found them both dead. (I took a small cap that one had been wearing which I still have.) I decided I would have to go forward again and deal with the resistance, so I did. I threw my bombs and obviously knocked out the enemy post but in doing so a bomb was thrown back at me and being on my hands and knees I felt an explosion and was hit in the neck, throat, right foot and both arms. I immediately collapsed and was dragged back by some of our chaps.

Halted by a hurricane of fire as he emerged from the east side of the village, Asquith decided that it was impossible to push on to the final objective which was a line of trenches due east. He made the consolidation of the village his number one task and set about neutralizing some troublesome sniper positions, in particular a trench 150 yards east of the building known to them as the mayor's house. Later Asquith reported:

The helmets of 20–30 Germans could be seen in this trench. Four of us went up the ditch A, Lt Asbury and one of the two were shot dead. It became obvious that the heads of the enemy occupants of this trench must be kept down if the trench were to be attacked by a flanking rush. I therefore went up the street and led some men into the Mayor's house and occupied it, taking 10 German prisoners, some of them NCOs sleeping or shamming sleep in the two cellars. I established snipers in the upper storey from which an excellent view could be obtained of the helmets of the enemy manning this trench due east of the house. These we sniped with good effect. I placed a Lewis gun and sniper in other parts of the house and handed its defence over to Sub-Lieut Cooke of the Hood, acting Brigade Intelligence Officer, with orders to harass the enemy as much as possible. He later in the morning led a Lewis gun team out into the open, to try to get at the enemy occupants of the trench from close quarters. He and all of the team except Charlton became casualties. Charlton maintained himself alone for five hours, causing the enemy considerable casualties; then, his ammunition running out, he withdrew.[6]

[6] PRO WO95/3115.

At 10.30 a.m., realizing that the village was lost, the enemy launched the first of many mass counter-attacks, which would continue for two days across the open plain towards Gavrelle. But Asquith had organized and reinforced the defences of the village well. As Sub-Lieutenant Basil B. Rackham of Hawke Battalion later wrote:

> We had expected the attack and we could clearly see them forming up in bright sunshine in the open country outside Gavrelle; long lines of men in field grey with steel helmets, they came on, wave after wave of them, but the forward observation officers for the artillery had done their work well and our gunners were marvellous, they absolutely cut them to pieces. The counter-attack was shattered, stopped dead. Our machine guns were also deadly. They suffered terrific casualties, some of them managed to reach Drake but were cut down. One had a feeling of immense relief. The leading light behind the defence of Gavrelle was Commander Asquith of course.

The capture of Gavrelle was complete, but not so the Windmill which stood on high ground to the north-east side of the village. This remained in enemy hands and, in spite of several gallant attempts by the Royal Marine Light Infantry to seize it, the strongpoint proved to be a stumbling block for any possible advance out from Gavrelle.

To the right of the 51st (Highland) Division and leading the assault of the 17th (Northern) Division on the open undulating slope between the River Scarpe and Monchy were the 7th Border Regiment and 8th South Staffords. Just prior to the attack, the Colonel of the Border Regiment had issued his final order: 'Bayonets will be fixed for dealing with the enemy at close quarters with the cold steel.'[7] Unfortunately for this battalion, it would not get anywhere near the enemy on 23 April, having been spotted as it moved to the jumping-off trench, just south of Lone Copse, by a concealed enemy outpost of the 125th Regiment, part of the hard-fighting 26th Division.

About to take part in his first attack at zero hour was seventeen-year-old Private Reg Eveling. As the only southerner in his company of the 7th Border Regiment, Eveling felt that he was regarded as something of a 'foreigner' at first. Fortunately this did not last:

> The vast majority of these men were either coal miners, dalesmen or farmers, but all from Kendal, Whitehaven, Cockermouth, Workington and the surrounding villages, as

[7] PRO WO95/2008.

grand a body of men as one could wish to meet, and once I had
learned to understand the dialect I was accepted as one of
themselves. Now this brings us to the day I shall never forget,
April 23rd 1917, St George's Day, the day when very few of my
pals came back. It was my first and last action. I remember
arriving in the trench and it was full of mud – the firestep was
broken down and so we had to scramble up over the parapet.
Well, I was totally terrified, but the lads tried to buck me up a
bit – but I suppose it felt like you were about to commit suicide.
'This is the end,' I thought. 'My last day . . .' and then came the
order: '*Over!*' And when you got an order in the army, it had to
be *done* and you *did it*. Well, as soon as we went over I kept
well back from the creeping barrage. I was very frightened, you
could see the shells bursting only fifty yards in front. Then we
came to the barbed wire and it wasn't properly cut . . . It was
sheer murder, that was. There were paths cut through the wire
and, like animals, we crowded into the paths. That's where
most of our casualties came from, machine guns were trained
on the gaps, blokes just fell in heaps. Somehow I got through
that OK and kept on going, but then I looked to my left and
right and couldn't see another soul. To my utter dismay, I was
on my own. I panicked and dived into the nearest shell hole and
stopped there till it was dark. That was one of the longest days
of my life. When I crawled back, a Scots Regiment had taken
over our bit of the line and were going to shoot me as they
thought I was a German. I never saw a single German that day,
yet the whole battalion was wiped out.

The destruction of the 7th Border Regiment could not be better told.
The battalion had lost 15 officers and 404 other ranks, out of the 19
officers and 505 men who had gone into action – 204 of the them listed
as 'Missing'.

The 8th South Staffords fared no better, their attack being a bloody
shambles, but even more tragic was the attack of the 7th Lincs. The
Lincs had been sent forward to the Lone Copse assembly trenches,
once again comfortably observed by the enemy. The GOC 51st
Brigade ordered the Lincs to attack the north end of Bayonet Trench
– the same objective as the Border Regiment – and a request had been
made for the barrage to be brought back to cover their advance. The
request was refused. Major-General P. R. Robertson, commanding
17th Division, realized that an attack without artillery support was
tantamount to suicide and cancelled it. But it was the same old
story;the message failed to reach the Lincs in time. At 8 a.m. they
scrambled from their trenches, jumping over the bodies of the Border
Regiment men and rushing forward; but the barrage was missing. Alf
Rossington, a private in the 7th Lincs, remembered later:

188

We went forward at the double with no artillery support, nothing, the only sound being that of our equipment rattling and chinking and blokes puffing. Then we reached the highest point and the machine guns started. Nothing could exist. We were ordered to get down, but we were pinned in front of the wire. Then Jerry started sending shrapnel over to finish us off, that's when I got mine – through the left foot, so I scrambled back on my stomach.

The Lincolns lost 200 men in five minutes, although many wounded, like Rossington, managed to scramble back. Later in the day the 17th Division made a brave effort to advance again but to no avail. On the left, and with the 51st Division driven out of Roeux, the German defenders added the weight of their fire-power across the Scarpe to that of the 26th Division who had scored another victory.

Of the divisions attacking farther south, the 29th, forcing its way out from Monchy, managed to establish a new line 200 yards short of the Blue Line, while the 15th (Scottish) Division fought a ding-dong battle for Guémappe from which they managed to drive the enemy, and, resisting several heavy counter-attacks, maintained a precarious hold on a line of shell holes east of the village. Any further advance was stopped by the determined defenders of Cavalry Farm – the insignificant ruin on the south side of the Arras–Cambrai highway, for which the 7th Cameron Highlanders lost many men in the savage fighting that followed.

Of General Snow's three divisions attacking between Wancourt and Croisilles, very little was achieved apart from a small gain by the 50th Division. Snow, ever optimistic, recorded in his diary on 23 April:

> We are having a deuce of a fight today . . . We have taken a lot of prisoners, but not made the headway we hoped; however, perhaps we shall by evening. We've no doubt killed a lot of Boche today, but I hoped to walk right through them and thought we had at one time. Today is St George's Day and we ought to have luck on our side.[8]

But luck was in short supply all round, as the men of both sides could testify. After one bloody battle that day, the youngsters of the 16th (Church Lads) King's Royal Rifle Corps had finally managed to capture Fontaine Trench, near Fontaine-les-Croisilles, and they were just mopping up when a German suddenly appeared from a dugout. As Rifleman Robert Renwick later said:

[8] Snow papers, Imperial War Museum.

I think he was an engineer as he had been mending the telephone wires. He seemed to be thunderstruck at seeing the trench taken over by the British. He picked up a rifle and bayonet and had a go at a sergeant in the 2nd Queens who had somehow got mixed up with us. The Queens sergeant was stabbed in the shoulder, but he bayoneted the German a bit more severely – who then dropped the rifle and fell to the ground, losing blood rather badly. When this happened, our man just dumped his rifle and took out his water bottle, had a drink and then handed it to the German. He then got out his cigarette tin; taking two cigarettes out and lighting them, he handed one to the German. I heard him say, 'Come on, Jerry, we are both finished with this,' and he picked the German up. I watched the two men go out of the trench, the German being assisted by the Englishman and not the least sign of hatred on either face. I remember saying to myself, 'My God, Robert, what are we fighting for?'

For the loss of 10,000 of its best troops on 23 April, the British Army had made precious few gains apart from the villages of Gavrelle and Guémappe. But worse was to come, for the 23rd marked the start of two weeks of the bloodiest and most pointless fighting in the war.

19

The Right Thing

The Germans were puzzled about British plans. What great prize did Haig see in this narrow sector of the front? Why was he pressing on with the offensive here, sucking more and more German divisions into the bloody vortex of the Arras battle? Ludendorff himself 'took for granted that a great breakthrough was planned, and not merely a battle of attrition and diversion'.[1] Still, at least the new defensive system was working well, largely thanks to Colonel von Lossberg, the new Chief of General Staff, who had immediately revamped the *Abwehrschlact* (elastic defence) arrangements to great effect. Again and again, British troops advanced – only to find themselves caught in a trap. Indeed, on 23 April alone, the same tactics had caused the downfall of the 2nd Royal Scots, the 17th and 18th Manchesters, the 2nd Argylls and the Yorkshire and Durham battalions of 150 Brigade, as several battlefield cemeteries near Heninel silently testify.

What the Germans did not know, of course, was that Haig was being forced to continue the offensive because the spirit of the French Army had been broken. On 24 April, a Tuesday, Haig met Nivelle at Amiens to discuss strategy. Worried by the enemy's successful submarine campaign, Haig now wanted to turn his armies northwards and focus their attention on the Belgian ports; but this would be possible only if the French continued their offensive on the Aisne. That night Haig wrote in his dairy: 'Nivelle assured me that neither he nor his government had any intention of stopping the offensive.'[2] But Nivelle was on the point of being removed from power.

By Wednesday the 25th it had become clear that the French Government was in turmoil and the cause was disagreement over Nivelle's leadership. 'I believe Nivelle is done,' Sir Henry Wilson wrote that night following dinner with Painlevé.[3] Lord Esher,

[1] Ludendorff, *My War Memories*, vol. 2, p. 24.
[2] Blake, *The Private Papers of Douglas Haig*, p. 220.
[3] Callwell, *Sir Henry Wilson: His Life and Diaries*, p. 342.

another guest at the dinner, agreed: 'Painlevé told us that he had made up his mind to supersede Nivelle.'[4] In mid-battle, the French were about to sack their commander-in-chief. Sir Henry Wilson wrote:

> The French at the present moment are in an uncertain frame of mind. They have no man of really commanding presence and outstanding ability either in the government or the country or the army. They are sore at the failure of Nivelle's attacks as compared with the hopes they have entertained and this soreness is accentuated by our great successes.[5]

Prime Minister Ribot, 'a dear old thing' of eighty, admitted to Haig that 'in his opinion this was no time for making a change in the command,' but went on to ask what Haig thought of Pétain.

While the French continued to argue and debate the merits of possible replacements for Nivelle, the British grew ever more anxious and impatient. There was a flurry of letters and meetings over the next few days as British politicians and generals began to realize they were now in control; the one-time 'unification of command' was clearly over. On 26 April Sir William Robertson wrote to Haig: 'It seems to me the right thing to do is to keep on fighting.'[6] And Haig agreed; but he was in a dilemma. He wanted to launch his new offensive in the north, but he couldn't neglect the Arras front while the French were in their present disarray. As he informed the War Cabinet on 1 May: 'We cannot rely on adequate French offensive co-operation. The fact is deeply to be regretted, but it must be recognized. We must maintain the offensive for at least two or three weeks more.'[7]

By this time Nivelle's fate was sealed. He clung to power for a further two weeks; even when formally called upon to resign on 10 May, he refused to go. It was not until 15 May, amid shameful scenes of mutual recrimination at French High Command, that he was finally forced out of office. On 15 May Pétain took over as the French Commander-in-Chief. His first task was to quell a mutinous army.

The rot had set in long before Pétain arrived. Disheartened by the failure of the Aisne offensive, the French troops had fallen prey to the defeatists and extremists within their ranks. The resultant mutiny

[4] Esher, *Journals and Letters*, vol. 4, p. 109.
[5] PRO WO158/23.
[6] PRO WO158/23.
[7] Ibid.

eventually spread to 68 out of the 112 divisions of the French Army, although many troops in the affected divisions stayed loyal throughout.[8]

A great deal has been written about this period of strife within the French Army, but much of it is fanciful. According to some contemporary writers, the major cause of unrest was Nivelle's dismissal – but in truth the unrest began under his leadership. Other writers claim that the unrest was put down with unnecessary force, yet the only recorded instance of such repression was on 6 June, 1917, when a Colonel of the 42nd Infantry Regiment ordered a machine-gunner to open up on a rowdy demonstration by his soldiers; one man was killed and three were wounded.

The facts, as usual, are less dramatic. The first outbreak of mutinous behaviour had been recorded on 17 April – only the second day of the Aisne offensive – when seventeen men in the 108th Infantry Regiment abandoned their posts in the face of the enemy; twelve were sentenced to be shot, but were later reprieved. On 29 April, the day before they were due to return to the front, 200 men of the 20th Infantry Regiment deserted from their barracks at Châlons-sur-Marne and went into hiding in nearby woods. On 3 May the entire 21st Division of Colonial Infantry refused to go into the line; the ringleaders were removed, however, and two days later the division did go into action – only to be very nearly wiped out.

The dissent spread like wildfire; even some of the elite light infantry regiments refused to fight. Over 21,000 soldiers deserted outright, and according to one survey[9] there were 250 cases of 'collective indiscipline' – which included acts of minor disobedience as well as more serious incidents, everything from waving the Red Flag and singing the Internationale to uncoupling rolling stock on the railways or assaulting the Military Police. The most common act of mutiny was merely a blunt refusal to go over the top; although they would still man the trenches, many of the troops now resisted orders to take a more active part in the doomed offensive.

The average mutineer's complaints concerned the lack of leave and the low pay. During the ten-month agony of Verdun, for instance, the majority of the long-suffering *poilus* had received no leave at all. They lived in these terrible conditions, in mud and snow and extreme discomfort, continually at risk of violent death, while industrial workers elsewhere in France not only lived in safety at home with their families but also got higher wages.

[8] Figures taken from Pendroncini, *The Mutinies of 1917.*
[9] Ibid.

Fuelled by such injustices, the mutiny was unlikely to subside without strong measures – and the new Commander-in-Chief did not shrink from his responsibilities. But Pétain had no need to resort to repression. He used a shrewd mixture of tactics, applying both the carrot and the stick. He immediately raised morale by introducing a new roster that guaranteed the men seven days' leave (later ten days' leave) in every four-month period, and generally caused living conditions to be improved. He also made use of the court martial. What he did not approve of was the summary trial followed by a swift execution – which undoubtedly occurred, although details went unrecorded and the number of those who died in this fashion will never be known. According to the French Official History, out of the 412 death sentences imposed on mutineers between May and October, 1917, only fifty-five were ever carried out; the majority of sentences were commuted to hard labour.

And so, under Pétain's fatherly eye, the French Army gradually recovered its former confidence and determination. Meantime, of course, the French contribution to the great allied spring offensive had faded.

Following the bitter fighting of 23 April, it can be safely said that no one in the British Army, from field-marshal to private, wanted to attack again on the Arras front. But the British commanders knew that there was no alternative: the offensive must continue. On 26 April, while Haig himself was meeting the French Prime Minister, his Chief of Staff, Lieutenant-General Kiggel, was warning Allenby and Horne to expect no respite; however tired their troops and no matter how much they deserved a rest, they would have to carry on and 'cut their coats accordingly'.[10]

[10] PRO WO158/311.

20

Recipe for Disaster

On 28 April, to step up the momentum of the dwindling offensive, the British again went into action at Roeux. This time the attackers came from the 34th Division, recently replenished with inexperienced boys, and the 37th Division, some battalions of which were now just 200-strong. The day was a worse disaster than the 23rd. Because of dense fog, visibility was extremely poor and the artillery observers failed to spot enemy reserves coming forward. Between the River Scarpe and the village of Monchy, the 12th Division men who had made such a victorious advance over Observation Ridge on the 9th, and who were now attacking with 35 Brigade, came up against a storm of machine-gun fire from undamaged trenches and were driven back to the start line. At Gavrelle, the 63rd (Royal Naval) Division attacked outwards from the village, but were soon repulsed. At Oppy Wood, although one brigade penetrated the enemy line in sufficient depth to add support to the Canadians on the left, the 2nd Division attack was a general failure. The only bright spot of the day was the capture of Arleux by Currie's 1st Canadian Division, its losses of 9 April repaired with reinforcements.

On the morning of 30 April Haig held a conference with Allenby, Horne and Gough at Noyelle Vion, the new Third Army HQ. One day before he informed the War Cabinet, he wanted to be sure his Army Commanders understood the situation. The French could no longer be counted upon, and yet the offensive must be maintained 'for at least two or three weeks more'; and so Haig wanted his First, Third and Fifth Armies to consolidate their gains and advance to a given line which he believed would be equally well suited 'for a renewed offensive or for defence'.[1]

The three Army Commanders did not entirely agree with Haig's plan. Allenby wanted his Third Army to launch a central thrust along the River Scarpe, to be supported on either flank by the First and

[1] PRO WP158/23.

Fifth Armies; this, he said, 'would have a better chance of success and be less costly'. This was agreed, and the attack was set for Thursday, 3 May. But there now followed a dispute about timing. Knowing that his army was not trained for night attacks, Allenby wanted to wait until dawn. But Gough, mindful of the Australians' wishes, pressed for a night attack. Haig merely stressed that the three-pronged attack should begin simultaneously and left his Army Commanders to settle the matter between themselves. Unfortunately they came to a hasty and ill-considered compromise: zero hour would be at 3.45 a.m. on the 3rd, which was before first light – a night attack after all.

Conceived in haste, this last great thrust of the Arras offensive was doomed to failure. Although later known as the Third Battle of the Scarpe, it extended all the way from the Vimy–Acheville road in the north to Bullecourt sixteen miles to the south. It was an enormous frontage of attack. As Haig knew, the enemy had bolstered the Hindenburg Line's defences with seven fresh new divisions – whereas only two of the fourteen attacking divisions could be called fresh: the 18th (Eastern) and 31st Divisions. And there was just two days' notice of the battle; with preparations being skimped, some units did not receive their attack orders until one hour before zero. It was a recipe for disaster. As Cyril Falls said, many of those who witnessed the events of 3 May, 1917, considered that day to be 'the blackest of the war'.[2]

The 18th (Eastern) Division, which had been over one month in GHQ reserve, were now brought into the line opposite the village of Chérisy with the intention of forcing the Hindenburg Line at its strongest point. Having to advance over a ridge and then downhill towards the village meant that the objective would be totally out of sight. The assault battalions were clueless as to the lie of the land over which they were to attack – in utter contrast to their spending several months in the sector of the objective taken by them on 1 July on the Somme. Added to that was the problem of darkness.

At zero on 3 May, 1917, three British armies went over the top and attacked the German trenches in this, the last major effort of the Arras offensive. At first the infantry of the 18th Division got away well, but soon ran into trouble with a returning tank. It had been allocated to the neighbouring 21st Division but had got lost among the confused wave of 18th infantry. The war diaries of several battalions allege that a voice in the darkness shouted 'Retire!'

[2] *Official History, France and Belgium 1917*, p. 450.

whereupon several companies of the 7th Bedfords and 12th Middlesex ran back to the start line. In the words of one old 18th Division man, 'It was one bloody great balls-up.' Or as the divisional historian later recorded: 'The battle of Chérisy on 3 May, 1917, has sombre memories for survivors of the 18th Division. It was the first set fight in which the Division received a definite and substantial check.'[3] In layman's terms, 'check' means a sound defeat.

Right from the start the attack had been doomed, or so it seemed to Sergeant Jack Cousins, MM, of the 7th Beds:

> Our orders didn't get through until the last minute and then they were all garbled. No one, including our officers, seemed to know what we were supposed to be doing, or where we were going. Officers were supposed to have synchronized their watches in so far as it was possible at that time of day. At a certain time, our barrage was supposed to lift and we were to climb out of the trenches and go forward. Well we did – but it wasn't all at the same time! We were given false information and told the artillery had smashed the enemy defences and we would get through the wire – did we hell!

It was the same old story of uncut wire and enemy machine-gun fire. Among the many who died on the wire, Cousins particularly remembered Captain Bull, who was trying to rally the men; he had only returned to duty the day before, after recovering from serious wounds received on the Somme.

As the 12th Middlesex advanced in a wavering line, the enemy opened fire. Private Horace Ham was hit: 'Suddenly I felt a hammer blow in my hand and there it was, a lovely "Blighty" – a great big hole right through me hand. 'That's your lot, Horace,' I said, then I scarpered!' Corporal Joseph Price took cover in a shell hole, along with three Leicesters and another man; all five were pinned down for the rest of the day: 'Jerry knew we were there as he kept skimming around with bursts of fire.' But at dusk they eventually managed to escape and Corporal Price set off to find his own unit, collecting en route 'a dozen or so stragglers like me. When we got to the transport lines we were met by Sergeant-Major Warner who said "Where's all my Company?" and he turned around and burst into tears.'

Private Claude Kent, also of the 12th Middlesex, was more seriously wounded:

> Halfway across I was shot in my left leg, just below the knee-cap. I managed to get into a shell hole. The 3rd of May was my

[3] G. H. F. Nichols, *The 18th Division in the Great War*, p. 164.

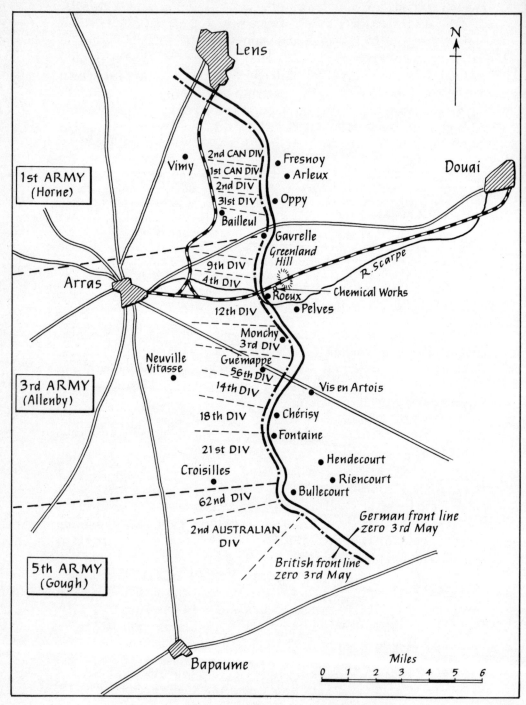

N

Lens

Douai

1st ARMY
(Horne)

Vimy

2nd CAN DIV

1st CAN DIV

2nd DIV

31st DIV

Bailleul

Fresnoy

Arleux

Oppy

Gavrelle

Greenland
Hill

R. Scarpe

9th DIV

4th DIV

Chemical Works

Arras

Roeux

Pelves

12th DIV

Monchy

3rd DIV

Neuville
Vitasse

Guémappe

56th DIV

14th DIV

Vis en Artois

3rd ARMY
(Allenby)

18th DIV

Chérisy

Fontaine

21st DIV

Croisilles

Hendecourt

Riencourt

62nd DIV

Bullecourt

German front line
zero 3rd May

2nd AUSTRALIAN
DIV

5th ARMY
(Gough)

British front line
zero 3rd May

Miles

0 1 2 3 4 5 6

9. THE INFANTRY ATTACK PLAN, 3 MAY, 1917.

mother's birthday and I thought of her and home. I lay there all day and later ate some chocolate, tied my wounded leg to the other one and crawled out to get a drink from the water bottles of the dead. Next morning it started to rain, so I put my mackintosh sheet over myself and went to sleep. I was awakened by a German officer[4] who asked me in French if I was wounded. I told him that I was and he blew a whistle and continued to talk to me. Very soon his Red Cross men came. I was due home on leave in a few days time for my commission and so had a number of German souvenirs on me. He suggested that I got rid of them, which I did. Four men carried me on a stretcher into Chérisy, where there are caves and I was taken into one of them. To my surprise, there was a bar with soldiers drinking. We then passed into a well-equipped hospital where they operated on my leg. I suppose being on the young side (I was eighteen) gave them the impression that we were hard up for soldiers.

But Claude Kent was by no means the only casualty to fall into German hands at Chérisy. Captain H. Perks of the 12th Middlesex, commanding a support company, somehow got into Chérisy village with sixty men. Here they held a small defensive flank at the southern crossroads. This small body of men gallantly fought the enemy off throughout the morning until driven out during the afternoon. Only eight came back. Perks, being badly wounded, was left for dead but taken prisoner. Incredibly, in spite of the confusion caused by the darkness, strong parties of 55 Brigade also got into the village but at 10 a.m., on being counter-attacked by a mere three enemy platoons, fell back to the start line.

On the left of the 18th Division, the 14th (Light) Division, met the same fate as the 18th and, with the depleted ranks being spaced ten yards apart in the darkness, chaos reigned. To add to the problems of these troops, they were enfiladed by machine-gun fire from beyond the Cojeul brook. Private John Coupland, MM, of the 42nd Machine-Gun Company arrived at the jumping-off trench to find it already full of wounded men 'due to them having been shelled':

I bandaged the arms and leg of a sergeant who gave me his water bottle which was full of rum. I had just taken a couple of large gulps when our officer shouted 'Let's go!' So I scrambled out of the trench and I think we had gone just fifty yards into the darkness when I was hit in the thigh, the bullet severing an artery. I jumped into the next trench, which must have been Jerry's first line, and cut my trousers open. Blood was spraying

[4] Probably of the 114th (Baden) Regiment, 199th Division.

199

everywhere. I just clamped my hand over the wound but the blood poured out of the exit wound in the back of my thigh. The dressing in my kit would not cover the exit wound, so I had to use two, getting one off a dead man next to me. Squeezing the artery with my fingers, I managed to stop the flow of blood. Feeling very weak I propped myself up and suddenly noticed in the increasing light that the trench was crowded with terrified youngsters. I shouted at them to get moving, 'Come on, you little bastards, get going now!'

But to Coupland's horror, his companions merely scuttled back to the safety of their own lines.

'Our battalion was cut to bits that day and we did not get very far at all,' recalled Captain T. C. Tanner of the 5th King's Shropshire Light Infantry. 'But I refuse to comment on the wisdom of the attack. How can I? The Generals are all dead now but I must maintain my silence. All I will say is that May 3rd was the worst day of my life.'

In the far north of the First Army front, the Germans were well aware of the impending attack and tried to fend it off by smothering the Canadians' forming-up areas with high explosive and gas. The Canadians swept forward regardless. Within a minute of zero hour the Germans had placed a blocking barrage across no-man's-land, causing heavy losses in the rear waves; but still the Canadians advanced, the 1st Canadian Brigade on the right and the 6th Brigade on the left, pressing steadily on towards Fresnoy.

Alarmed at this unstoppable advance, the defenders of Fresnoy – from the 15th and 25th Reserve Divisions – turned their machine-guns on the ever-approaching Canadians; and the 6th Brigade, held up by uncut wire, suffered the inevitable casualties. The enraged survivors now swarmed into the village, determined to avenge their comrades' deaths, and in the heat of the moment many of the Canadians allowed their rage free rein.

One young German machine-gunner, *Gefreiter* Harm Frerichs, 25th Machine Gun Company, had left the gun position to use a rifle instead, a chance decision that may have saved his life:

I fired into the advancing enemy until I was surrounded and had to surrender. Later, walking past our gun position, I noticed that my pals had been battered to death. The Canadian guard told me that they will kill any machine-gunners that they can find, or recognize by their uniforms. But it was my lucky day and I went unnoticed.

200

The capture of Fresnoy was the high-water mark of a series of successes achieved by the Canadians in the Arras battle; it was also the only bright feature of a terrible day for the British Army. General Horne had every right to be proud of his Canadians. Of his other two divisions, the 31st had faced the formidable barrier of the strongly defended Oppy Wood; here the division had been spotted by the enemy as it formed up, silhouetted by the light of the setting moon, and mercilessly shelled in its trenches. The battered 2nd Division, which had suffered so badly on 28 April, could muster only 1,800 men for the attack, hurriedly formed into a single 'Composite Brigade'. Like their comrades in the 31st Division, the men of the 2nd Division were shelled in their assembly trenches; yet somehow enough of them survived to raise a protective arm around the Canadians' southern flank in Fresnoy.

Far to their south, on the extreme right-hand flank of the attack were the Australians of Gough's Fifth Army. Ever since their misfortunes of 11 April at Bullecourt, the Australians had been eager to take another crack at the Hindenburg Line. On 3 May their chance had come. The 5th and 6th Brigades of the Australian 2nd Division advanced at 3.45 a.m., supported by the 62nd Division on the left. The Australians, whose commanders had instigated the idea of a night attack, found that the darkness caused some confusion, especially where men were bunching to get through gaps in the German wire and were suddenly hit by an intense cross-fire. Then, as at Chérisy, someone apparently gave the order to retreat. The 5th Brigade streamed back to the start line. It was, as the official historian so truly said, 'All a bloody mix-up'.[5]

The 6th Brigade on the left, however, found the wire demolished and rushed into the Hindenburg Trench while the 24th Battalion gallantly pushed on to the second German line. Brigadier-General Gellibrand, seeing the failure of the 5th Brigade, now took command of the whole Australian attack; he sent officers to rally the 5th Brigade survivors and lead them back into the fray. The 6th Brigade found that it now had a real fight on its hands and bombed its way forward to the second objective, the Fontaine-Quéant road, where they fought throughout the day, all efforts to relieve them having failed. At dusk the remainder of the 5th Brigade troops, who had been hiding in shell holes all day, now ran back to their start lines and in the dim light were mistaken for the enemy attempting to cut off the little force deep in the Hindenburg Line. Consequently orders were

[5] Bean, *The Australian Imperial Force in France*, p. 437.

eroneously issued for the remainder of 6th Brigade to withdraw; but the disbelieving Australians refused to pull out and give up their hard-won gains. At this time a British pilot, flying low over the Hindenburg Line and seeing the lodgement of khaki-clad infantry, dropped a message which read *'Well done Australia.'*

It was not until 1 a.m. on 4 May that the relieving battalions got through to what was left of the little party of 6th Brigade. It is said that the incoming troops, forced to trample on the dead in the narrow trenches, were at pains to avoid stepping on anyone whose sleeve carried the red and white patch of the gallant 24th Battalion, who had taken the position.

On the left, the failure of the 62nd Division had not helped this precarious Australian foothold on the Hindenburg Line and thereby forcibly changed the nature of the operations on this sector. For while the Third Battle of the Scarpe had lasted a mere twenty-four hours, the Australians were forced to fight on here for a further fourteen days in order to improve their hold on the position, so gallantly won at great cost of life by Gellibrand's brigade. This hard-won gain was of no tactical value whatsoever; but that episode on the extreme right of the offensive, coupled with the Canadian capture of Fresnoy on the extreme left, provided the only ray of light on a dark and sombre day. The whole of the Third Army attack had failed, apart from a small gain of 500 yards by a handful of Royal Fusiliers near Monchy where the worst nightmare of the fighting had been realized.

The 12th (Eastern) Division had been ordered to advance on a two-brigade front across the corpse-strewn downland between Monchy and the River Scarpe and halt at a line conspicuous by a line of telegraph poles, which included a sunken road running from Keeling Copse north-west towards Roeux. The Division's second objective, the village of Pelves, was not to be attacked until Roeux had been taken, thereby protecting the northern flank.

The task of capturing the Chemical Works and Roeux fell once more to the unfortunate 9th Division. This once-strong fighting unit had recently received some untrained and totally unsuitable drafts. The 8th Black Watch, for example, was ordered on 23 April, despite protests, to accept a draft of ninety-seven men – mainly unwilling transfers from the Army Service Corps, who had had no infantry training whatsoever. They were hastily put into kilts and given a crash course on how to load their rifles. In the darkness of the attack hour, some battalions became mixed up and fired on each other. The troops lost their sense of direction. It was utter chaos, and a total failure.

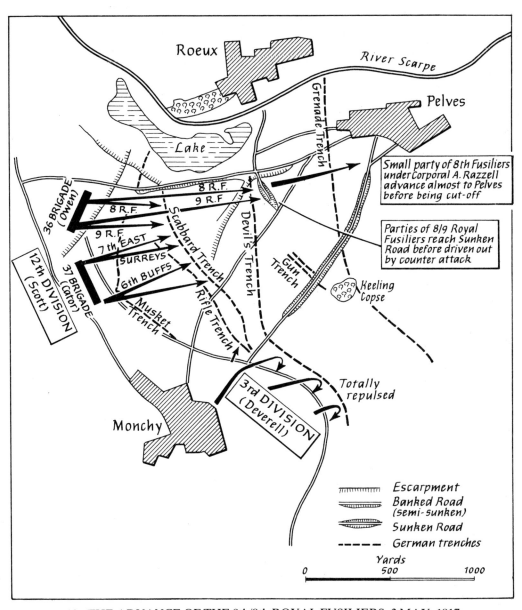

Roeux

River Scarpe

Pelves

Lake

Grenade Trench

36 BRIGADE (Owen)

8 R.F.

8 R.F.

9 R.F

9 R.F

7 th EAST

Scabbard Trench

Devil's Trench

Gun Trench

12 th DIVISION (Scott)

37 BRIGADE (Gator)

SURREYS

6 th BUFFS

Rifle Trench

Musket Trench

Keeling Copse

Small party of 8th Fusiliers under Corporal A. Razzell advance almost to Pelves before being cut-off

Parties of 8/9 Royal Fusiliers reach Sunken Road before driven out by counter attack

Monchy

3rd DIVISION (Deverell)

Totally repulsed

Escarpment

Banked Road (semi-sunken)

Sunken Road

German trenches

Yards

0   500   1000

10. THE ADVANCE OF THE 8th/9th ROYAL FUSILIERS, 3 MAY, 1917.

As the 8th Black Watch's own Lieutenant-Colonel Sir G. W. Abercromby later reported:

> Owing to heavy casualties, both in officers and men, it is impossible to collect anything like a correct story, but it appears likely that only a few scattered parties of men reached the German lines and these were captured or killed.[6]

So, with its left flank still unprotected, the 12th Division attack looked doomed before it even began. As Tim Collior, with the 8th Royal Fusiliers, later recalled:

> Two Battalions of Royal Fusiliers, the 8th and 9th, were leading in the attack by 36th Brigade. Our frontage was 1,000 yards and yet both battalions only totalled about 800 men – a pretty thin line. Before the attack, myself and four friends who were all bank clerks in civvy street had exchanged last letters to our families. Little did I know that it would be me who would send them all on – they being killed. On the given signal, we went over, we were on the left near the Scarpe and at first it seemed OK, but then we came under heavy machine-gun fire from across the Scarpe – from Roeux.

Corporal Alf Razzell, also with the 8th Royal Fusiliers, made slightly better progress towards Pelves, but he too saw many of his comrades falling at his side – including a new platoon commander: 'Mr Pride I think his name was, he was the same age as myself – twenty.' The young second-lieutenant was shot within seconds of 'going over', and as Alf Razzell remarked: 'What a waste – and he had never even seen a German!' But Razzell had no time to mourn:

> Someone said, 'Hey, here you are, Corp – a Jerry!' And he'd got a Jerry by the scruff of the neck. Well, I couldn't take him back, so I said to this Jerry 'Go, go!' pointing back towards our lines. I could well understand his fright; there in the grey dawn and illuminated by the flashes of light from ahead, were row after row of our troops with bayonets fixed, advancing up the slope. A fearsome sight. Suddenly he whipped away and ran off towards his own lines, zig-zagging like a rabbit. I threw up my rifle and drew a bead between his shoulders – but I could not shoot a man in the back.

Corporal Tom Bracey, MM, of the 9th Royal Fusiliers, did not recall such gentlemanly conduct:

[6]PRO WO95/1766.

204

Major Coxhead – who was killed later – comes up and says, 'Right, Corporal, get your gun set up and let's see what you can do.' We were in this sunken road and we set up the gun on the top of the bank. By now it was light and I remember seeing Colonel Elliott-Cooper[7] – we called him 'Dolly' – rounding up about thirty prisoners. He was only carrying his walking stick. Just then a Jerry stands up from a shell hole about fifty yards away and walks towards us, sort of half-hearted and still carrying his rifle, and one of our blokes says, 'It's that bloody sniper, let him have it!' And blimey, so they did – you should have seen that body jerk as the bullets hit him, they didn't give him a chance. Then we were ordered on, just as I'd set the bloody gun up. Well, we got into Rifle and Bayonet Trench, I think it were called, about 400 yards further on. There were a lot of dead Jerries there and Major Coxhead says, 'All bodies to be thrown over the parapet' – but we went through their pockets first of course!

By 5 a.m. the 8th and 9th Royal Fusiliers had advanced over 1,000 yards completely unsupported, deep into enemy territory. In the darkness they had passed over many pockets of the enemy hidden in shell holes who had fired into their backs as they advanced. Heavy casualties had also been steadily inflicted by enfilade machine-gun fire from the untaken village of Roeux on the north bank of the Scarpe. Ever mindful of their orders, small groups of men pressed on, some to be cut off and captured, others to disappear without trace. Tim Collior again:

I put up this periscope to see where the rest of our blokes were. No sooner had I put it up when a bullet went through it. Well, I nudged the bloke next to me and asked him what he thought. He didn't move; he was dead. I just lay there on my back all day and later one of our planes came over and fired a signal to our guns and they opened up and nearly blew us out of the ground. So I thought, 'I'm going to get out of this one,' and I scooted back as fast as I could – and eventually got back to our starting point where I saw a mate, Rex Williams, who was white as a sheet. He had been captured along with George Jarratt, another pal, and several others and put into a dugout. . . .

Twenty-five-year-old Corporal George Jarratt from Kennington, together with other wounded men of the 8th Royal Fusiliers, had been taken prisoner and placed under guard in a dugout. Later in the day

[7] Lieutenant-Colonel Neville Bowes Elliott-Cooper, DSO, MC, 8th Royal Fusiliers; won the VC at Cambrai on 30 November, 1917. Died of wounds in German hands, 11 February 1918. Buried Hamburg Cemetery.

the enemy had been driven back by a counter-attack by the 7th Royal Sussex in an effort to assist the Royal Fusiliers. A soldier of the Sussex had thrown a Mills bomb into the dugout and Jarratt, without hesitation, placed both feet over the bomb in an effort to limit the explosion, which blew off both legs. His comrades were safely removed to the British lines but George Jarratt was left in the dugout, dead. For this gallant act of self-sacrifice he was awarded a posthumous VC.[8]

One small party of Royal Fusiliers reached the outskirts of Pelves, and only one of them survived to tell the tale – Corporal Razzell:

> There were twenty-five of us including me old mate who I had joined up with, Bill Hubbard. I was the only NCO. We were not unduly alarmed as we thought other troops would follow on. I stopped the boys and told them to join up a line of shell holes, make a little trench, and I thought we would wait there until help arrived. We had just started digging when a cluster of stick grenades fell amongst us and exploded – and a group of Germans appeared from behind us, the way we had come! I realized then that we were right behind their lines and cut off. We started to retire down a grassy slope – only going the wrong way, even deeper into the enemy lines. But then I noticed how the old discipline held firm; our fellows were doing what they had been trained to do in such a situation – dashing back, then down on one knee, fired a volley into the enemy, then back a few more yards and down again, fired another volley . . . But I'm sad to say it was all over so quickly, we were completely outnumbered and they were shot down. I got into a shell hole and waited. The Germans just stood there picking our blokes off – finishing them all off. Well I was just thirty yards to the left and these Jerries made excellent targets. It was my heaviest bag of Germans ever. I just fired and reloaded as fast as I could. My rifle got so hot I remember spitting on the bolt to stop it jamming. My chief concern now was my own position, I couldn't understand what had happened to the rest of the battalion. I was surrounded by my dead pals, so I just lay there all day. When darkness came, judging by flares sent up by both sides, the position was back to what it was before we attacked. Pondering what to do and playing possum when the German ration and fatigue parties passed by my shell hole, daylight came once more. I heard a clanking noise and realized the Germans were coming. They stopped right by my shell hole. They were a digging party. After a spell of digging very near me, they stopped work. One of them was kneeling and he said 'Cigarettes.' He was evidently searching our dead. More of

[8] Corporal George Jarratt, VC, 8th Royal Fusiliers. No known grave. Commemorated on the Arras memorial to the missing.

them joined in, going through their pockets and haversacks. Suddenly one of them stepped into my shell hole, went on his knees and started fumbling with my pockets – so I stood up. He looked pretty startled. He looked at me and another one came up and I heard him say '*Unterofficer,*' then he said, '*Nix verwounded?*' and then, '*Komm.*' He led me for about fifty yards to where there was a manned trench and put me in the charge of an NCO. We went a few paces along the trench and I was greeted with, 'Hello Razz, am I glad to see you!' And there, lying on the floor of the trench, was Bill Hubbard. 'Hello Bill, how are you?' I asked. 'I've got a painful wound in my back and I've been lying here for two days and these bastards haven't helped me in any way. Will you have a look?' So I rolled him over carefully, cut through his blood-soaked tunic with my jack-knife, and I knew it was fatal. His intestines were hanging out of his back and there was earth and chalk in the wound. 'Is it bigger than the palm of me 'and?' he said. 'Oh no, nothing like that,' I lied. Actually, it was bigger than two palms; Bill had been hit by the explosions from the initial cluster of grenades thrown at us by the Germans from behind. I indicated for the nearest Germans to come and have a look and they merely shrugged their shoulders. They were battle-worn and surly. I asked 'Officer?' and they answered '*Nix.*' The field dressing we carried was useless for Bill's wound. In that filthy trench I was desperate to help him and I eventually cut off a large piece of his shirt, picked as much of the dirt and chalk from the wound as I could (my hands were filthy too), placed the shirt piece as a dressing, took off his puttees and with difficulty wound them around his waist to make a kind of corset. Poor Bill; by the time I had finished, perspiration was pouring down his face, such was his agony. He wanted a drink, and after ten minutes of sign language the Germans allowed me to get out of the trench and get a water bottle from of one of our dead. We remained in the trench throughout the night until the next day, when in the afternoon the Jerries were relieved – we were to go with them. With difficulty, I got Bill on his feet and out of the trench. Where our artillery had passed over, it resembled a moonscape with each shellhole touching the next. You can imagine the agony I inflicted on Bill when I gave him a fireman's lift over my shoulder and began to stagger across that awful surface. I hadn't gone far when Bill thumped me with his fists, screaming 'Put me down, I'd rather die!' I put him down. I could not handle him very gently because he was heavier than me. I hoped he would faint . . . The Germans were getting rather shirty. They had been relieved you see, and wanted to get out of it. They started swearing (I presume) and threatening me. 'Leave me, Razz, leave me,' he implored. Well, the Jerries were now pointing their rifles at me, so I left him in a shell hole. 'I'll get help, Bill, don't worry,' I told him. 'Goodbye, Razz,' he said. So I left Bill in that wilderness and have been haunted down the years by the very thought of it. Further on I saw two Germans, one with an empty stretcher going up the line. I went up to them but the extent of my German was '*Bruder*,' and 'Wounded', pointing in the direction where I had left Bill. There was a chorus of '*Ja's*' from the two. I gave one of them a ring which had been a gift from my mother. I had a faint hope they might find Bill and do something for him. Months later, in a prisoner-of-war camp, on a list of missing men posted from the Swiss Red Cross I saw Bill's photograph. I knew then he was never found. I wrote to his family from the POW camp and described in the letter how the Germans refused to help me carry him. The letter came back to me. It had been censored; '*Bei Karful*' was written across it in big letters. I never wrote again. It was a sad episode. I think of him every day.

21

The Boys who Really Did the Job

Officially, the Battle of Arras ended on 17 May – but in reality it ceased at the termination of the last major British attack, which was on 4 May, 1917. For most of the troops, however, the war still had a long, terrible path to follow.

On the Arras battlefront the village of Bullecourt finally succumbed to the 58th (2nd/1st London) Division on 17 May. Many of the worn-out divisions of Third Army were destined to be back in action at Arras before the end of the month. The dreaded Chemical Works and the village of Roeux, among the ruins of which lay the bodies of so many Highland soldiers, finally fell, after a crushing artillery bombardment, to the much-tried 4th Division on 11 May. When the 1st Hampshires stormed the ruins of Roeux Château, they were amazed to discover the enormous *Mebu* and other concrete emplacements hidden among the rubble of the outbuildings. Here was the prime cause of the failure of the 51st (Highland) Division to capture Roeux on 23 April and the 4th and 9th Divisions on 3 May. This huge structure, linked to other emplacements and the Chemical Works by tunnels, was the nerve centre of the brilliant enemy defence of Roeux. Boasting walls six feet thick and a roof seven feet thick, it had several machine-gun embrasures for multi-directional fire and was protected by a field of fire from neighbouring concrete machine-gun emplacements. The Highlanders who attempted to storm this fortress on 23 April never lived to tell the tale. Their dead lay piled nearby. The luckless 51st Division were sent in once more to Roeux on 13 May, to relieve the 4th Division and consolidate the remainder of the village, the Germans having cleared out. In the unusual absence of any fighting, 13 May was known to the Jocks as the 'meatless day'.

The enemy maintained pressure in this area throughout the following days by launching a series of counter-attacks, the brunt of the action being borne by the 51st Division. Again the Chemical Works changed hands twice, but remained a British possession. The fighting in the vicinity of Monchy continued sporadically until 30 May and a strip of the Hindenburg Line was seized further south by the 33rd Division. The main Third Army effort which formed the bulk of the Arras fighting from 9 April until 3 May, 1917, had been maintained for a period of twenty-five days.

In spite of management errors made at all stages in the battle and in particular the latter half, no one could criticize the British Army for its supreme effort in drawing and engaging thirty-six enemy divisions, some of which were fought to a standstill, or for capturing 20,859 prisoners and 254 guns. Within the scope of the original plan, although hampered by shocking weather, the first day was a wonderful and unexpected success; but the subsequent French failure to break through on the Aisne changed the purpose of the battle and created a new set of circumstances as to how it was to be fought, thereby turning it into an expensive expression of loyalty to the French.

Loyalty was not the only forte. The courage and grit displayed by the Infantry of both sides, who as always bore the greatest loss, was self-evident, twenty-five infantry VCs being won in the period 9 April–17 May, in which twelve of the recipients lost their lives. It was in the latter part of the battle that the smallest gains and the heaviest losses were recorded from the British point of view. It was then that the struggle called on the endurance, cheerfulness and will of the British soldiers as never before – but at what cost?

The most accurate British casualty figures available are those in the returns made by Lieutenant-General Sir G. H. Fowke, the Adjutant-General, for the months of April and May, 1917. They amount to 87,226 for the Third Army, 46,826 for the First Army and 24,608 for the Fifth Army – a total of 158,660 casualties for the three armies engaged at Arras (see Appendix I for a break-down of divisional casualties).

In this brief résumé of the battle casualties, it is interesting to record, as a testimony to the ferocity of the fighting at Arras as compared with the other three major *offensive* battles fought by the British Army in the First World War, that the Battle of Arras, 1917, with the highest average daily rate of casualties of them all was the most lethal.

It is not hard to calculate that had the Arras offensive been continued, as opposed to the switch to Flanders and the Third Battle of Ypres, and *supposing* the infantry divisions at Arras had been reinforced or replaced by fresh ones, as they were on the Somme the previous autumn, and *supposing* the battle had continued for 141

Battle	Duration (days)	Casualties (approx.)	Daily Rate
Somme, 1 July–18 November, 1916	141	415,000	2,943
Arras, 9 April–17 May, 1917	39	159,000	4,076
Ypres (third battle of), 31 July–12 November, 1917	105	244,000	2,323
Final Offensive, 8 August–11 November, 1918	96	350,000	3,645

days (the length of the Battle of the Somme), then on the same daily rate the casualties would have amounted to 574,716 – the highest for any British offensive in the war. One could imagine the uproar if a daily rate of casualties had reached 4,076 in the Falklands War!

The exact German losses for the Arras battle are difficult to determine because the returns made by battalions in the field did not include those 'Lightly wounded' or 'Wounded at duty' who were not removed from the Corps area. Captain Cyril Falls, the British official historian for the Arras battle, reckons that thirty per cent must be added to the German total for comparison with the British. Unlike the Somme battle, the Germans did not expose their soldiers to continuous fire, especially while under the wing of Colonel von Lossberg, the greatest tactician of the war, who by his interpretation of Ludendorff's new methods of defence undoubtedly saved the lives of many of his soldiers. The figures given by the German historical sources for the Sixth Army only, for April and May, 1917, amount to 79,418. To this should be added the figure of thirty per cent and the figures incurred to the south of Sixth Army by German units facing Gough's Fifth Army at Bullecourt. There are no definite figures available for these units and Falls is vague when he says that the total enemy casualties were 'probably fairly equal', but a general estimate would be in the region of 120,000.

The noise of the Arras battle had hardly died down when it started up again with the explosions at Messines on 7 June and the remainder of 1917 became dominated by the Third Battle of Ypres. It is to battles like this and the British defeat of 1 July, 1916, that the British people, with their peculiar trait for focusing on misery and loss, most remember the First World War. The magnificent achievements of the British citizen armies of 1916–18 have been forgotten. It is a significant fact that the British Army for the rest of 1917 fought the German

Army on the Western Front alone. With the exception of two local attacks, one at Verdun and the other at Malmaison on the Chemin-des-Dames, no assistance was obtained from the French Army at all. The mutinies had a more far-reaching and deeper effect than was realized at the time.

The massive British efforts in the spring and autumn of 1917 had left the Army in France considerably under strength. Although there were large numbers of men under arms in England, 'in case of invasion', Lloyd George refused to send these men out to replenish the depleted battalions. Taking his anti-Western Front stance, he purposely sought to prevent Sir Douglas Haig from launching new offensive battles in 1918, by keeping him dangerously short of men. In an effort to overcome this serious shortage, the Army tightened its belt by reducing each infantry brigade from four to three battalions, a total of 153 infantry battalions being disbanded or merged in February and March, 1918. This weakness in the British Army had not gone unnoticed by Ludendorff; the collapse of Russia had bolstered his Army with the arrival of divisions from the eastern front, and now he launched a massive infantry attack, following a lightning bombardment on the foggy morning of 21 March, 1918. The British defences in the forward zones were overwhelmed and the German infantry swept through Gough's Fifth Army and parts of Third Army, and for ten days maintained a steady advance, which at its farthest point reached thirty-five miles, almost to the town of Amiens.

Arras was well defended by some of the Third Army divisions that had fought there in April, 1917, although the enemy came close, Monchy-le-Preux falling in the initial surge. The biggest blow struck at Arras was on 28 March, 1918, called by Ludendorff 'Operation Mars'. Four British divisions in front of the city faced fifteen German divisions. Once again it was the 56th and 4th Divisions, reinforced with eighteen-year-old soldiers, who held up the bulk of the enemy attack. The subterranean galleries at Roeux and the Chemical Works were, this time, turned to British advantage, with battalions of infantry taking shelter from the plunging shellfire. By 30 March the German attack had been subdued, but to guarantee the safety of the city against further enemy attacks, the Canadian Corps, now under the command of General Arthur Currie, were employed to defend it.

While the German Army had been expending itself in violent attacks during the spring and summer of 1918, Haig had kept his nerve, carefully building up a strong reserve of the troops now released from Britain, in the hope of launching a mighty counter-offensive on the enemy when the opportunity arose. He was quick to seize his chance on 8 August, when Sir Henry Rawlinson's Fourth Army knocked the enemy back across the old Somme battlefield. Several sharp, powerful attacks by the Allies ended with a victory by American troops at St Mihiel on 12 September. On 29 September, once again using Canadian troops, Haig finally broke the Hindenburg Line and his army poured through. By November the Germans were beaten and unconditionally sued for peace, an armistice was signed and at 11 a.m. on 11 November, 1918, all fighting on the Western Front ceased.

Adopted by Newcastle-upon-Tyne after the war, Arras was a shambles. Her returning citizens set about a dedicated rebuilding programme, thereby restoring the ancient city, leaving little traces of the war. At first it was decided not to rebuild the beautiful cathedral, leaving it as a permanent sacred ruin; but this decision was over-turned and by 1932 the cathedral and spectacular Hôtel-de-Ville had been restored to their original Gothic splendour. The railway station has been rebuilt twice and is now surrounded by hotels and fronted by flower beds and fountains. The Grande Place looks the same now as it did to the British soldiers of 1917, but beneath the arches are fancy shops and restaurants. Some of the caves beneath the Grande Place which once shook with the concussion of exploding shells now echo to the beat of thunderous disco music; at night, young people are drawn to these old cellars to drink and dance, unaware that they were once occupied by swearing, sweating British soldiers. The huge caves beneath 'Barbed Wire Square' extending down to three levels, once a British hospital during the battle, are now a car park. A small part of the tunnels under the Hôtel-de-Ville have now been opened to the public, together with an excellent museum and exhibition of photo-graphs. On the Faubourg d'Amiens stand the British Military Cem-etery and Arras Memorial to the Missing, which records the names of the 35,928 missing of the Battles of Arras, 1917–18. It is the central British Memorial of the old Western Front and on the stone panels can be found the names of Private Bill Hubbard of the 8th Royal Fusiliers and Sergeant-Major Jack Renwick of the 9th Royal Scots.

The sleepy and seemingly deserted villages that surround the town, most of them totally flattened during the war, have been carefully restored on their original sites. Little evidence of the savage fighting that devastated the area in 1917 now remains. The village of Roeux still bears its scars. On the site of the old Château buildings stands the huge blockhouse captured by the 4th Division on 11 May, 1917. The

213

cries of children at play now echo within its massive walls and a close crop of new houses has recently sprung up to conceal the commanding field of fire that the German defenders of this old fortress once enjoyed. Near the station still stands the forbidding ruin of the old Chemical Works, overgrown with almost impenetrable tangles of bramble and dangerous to enter due to the presence of unexploded missiles, glass and rubble underfoot. Behind the Chemical Works can be seen the gentle slope of Greenland Hill, and nearby Browns Copse Cemetery contains the graves of many Scottish soldiers, killed here in April, 1917. The sunken road from which the 2nd Seaforths launched their tragic attack on the Chemical Works can be found at nearby Fampoux. Easily missed by the casual visitor to sleepy Monchy is the bronze caribou which stands on the roof of an old German blockhouse, a lasting memorial to the brief but gallant action of the Newfoundlanders, and nearby stands the attractive memorial to the 37th Division.

Few visitors come to the remote and tiny Houdains Lane British Cemetery near Feuchy, which overlooks Battery Valley and contains the graves of 12th Division troops killed here on 9 April, 1917. Yet this windswept spot affords an excellent panorama of the central Arras battlefield. The Point du Jour ridge dominates the northern skyline and a walk along the nearby railway brings one to the Railway Triangle. The rolling cornfields have changed little and one can easily find the route taken by 'Lusitania' and the remains of several concrete machine-gun emplacements knocked out by her six-pounder guns on the opening day of the battle. The remains of the old windmill of Wancourt Tower also provide an excellent vantage point, and it is from here that the value of the commanding position of Monchy can be appreciated. The remains of German fortifications can still be seen on Hill 90, dominating the valley leading to Wancourt. Hibers Trench Cemetery near the motorway bridge bears silent testimony to the forgotten sacrifice of the 7th King's Royal Rifle Corps. Tank Cemetery, to the north-west of Guémappe, on the site of an old forward dressing station used by the 15th (Scottish) Division during the battle, contains the trench grave of sixty-four men of the 7th Cameron Highlanders killed in a desperate attack on Cavalry Farm on 28 April. At the time of burial, in order to save space, the men were buried without blankets, in their kilts, lying on their sides with each man's arm placed around the body next to him – embracing his comrade in death.

The ugly scar of the A1 motorway now runs right along the old front line of April, 1917, and the traveller on it might notice in the freshly ploughed fields a profusion of tiny cemeteries, each with a cross of sacrifice standing like a sentinel to watch over the graves, surrounded by low flint walls which in places almost collide with the motorway itself. These are the only signs to the traveller, bound for some holiday spot in the south, that the British Army once stood here.

These beautiful cemeteries, which are lasting memorials to the Arras battles, were established by the Imperial War Graves Commission, now the Commonwealth War Graves Commission, during and after the Great War. There are 134 cemeteries on the Arras battlefield. Just after the war there were many more but some of the smaller ones were closed down and moved to the larger battlefield cemeteries. Wherever possible the names used by the soldiers for the resting places of their dead have been retained, hence 'Crump Trench' Cemetery and 'Happy Valley' Cemetery. For the work of reburial and searching for bodies, the front was divided into areas each covered by a party of some twelve men and a senior NCO. All the British battlefields were examined at least six times; in places where the fighting had been heaviest, as many as twenty. Between the Armistice and September, 1921, 204,654 bodies were exhumed and reburied by the War Graves Commission and any belongings sent to London to be traced if possible. *The Times* of 10 November, 1928 reported that a wrecked tank had been found at Monchy, with 'three of its crew dead and one of these unrecognizable':

> They were buried where they were found. Later a grave was located under the name of a man who had come out of the tank alive. From him it was learned he had left his kit in the tank as he got clear and was sure that it had been assigned to the unrecognizable one of the dead. By his aid, the other two graves were found and the identity of the third man settled.

Vimy Ridge Canadian Memorial on the site of Hill 145 was unveiled on 26 July, 1936, at a great gathering of veterans by King Edward VIII. The 270-foot twin pylons of this white colossus can be seen for miles and the memorial itself commemorates the 60,000 dead of Canada, 1914–18. On the walls are engraved the names of the missing – the 11,285 Canadians who fell in France and have no known grave. (The names of the 7,024 Canadians missing in Flanders are on the Menin Gate at Ypres.) A 248-acre park in which the memorial stands has been purchased and preserved by the Canadian Battlefields Commission and is one of the few remaining places where one can view the original shell holes, trenches and mine-craters.

Unfriendly, uniformed French security men are employed to guard this memorial and woe betide the innocent visitor who should stop his vehicle in any place other than the designated parking areas.

The countryside around Arras again saw action in the Second World War when Rommel's Panzer divisions fought a tough action with British rearguards protecting the roads to Dunkirk in May, 1940. Among the last of the British units to leave Arras itself were the Welsh Guards; but at the end of August, 1944, this same unit was one of the first to re-enter the town to a rapturous welcome. A grim reminder that the stout citizens of Arras played an important role in the underground movement of the Second World War can be seen at the sombre Mur des Fusilées, near the British memorial, which contains 200 memorial plaques along the Vauban walls, commemorating French patriots – some as young as fourteen – shot by the Nazis in this dismal place. A concrete post marks the execution spot.

Arras yet again suffered grievous damage in 1940 and after the D-Day landings in June, 1944, was subjected to several Allied bombing raids aimed at knocking out the railway complex. Once again the old tunnels under the town were re-opened and it is said that many of the townsfolk walked to work below ground to avoid the danger above.

As we race through the years into the twenty-first century, the First World War will become as remote as Waterloo. The last remaining survivors of the war will have long since faded away and the only reminder to that generation, forced to fight the 'war to end wars' will be the silent memorials left as a poignant token of their day. It is certain that a hundred years from now, the merits of the war and the aims of those who directed it will continue to be the source of much argument. The directors of the war, the generals and politicians, have long since gone, most of them before the Second World War, and it is towards the generals of the First World War that such a high level of venom has been directed by a succession of historians. The verdict of this writer is best summed up in the words of one old soldier, Sergeant Bill Wilson of the 2nd Royal Welsh Fusiliers:

> Let sleeping dogs lie. The generals are all dead now and it is noticeable how most critics waited until they were dead before tearing them to pieces. I believe that our generals were the best and did their job to the best of their ability. After all, we did win the war, didn't we?

One important truth has been recently pointed out by the notable historian John Terraine, who has done so much in recent times to

216

blow away some of the myths that have sprung up out of the literature of the war. He states:

> It is a simple historical fact that the British generals of the First World War, whatever their faults, did not fail in their duty.
> It was not a British delegation that crossed the lines with a white flag in November, 1918.
> No German Army of occupation was stationed on the Thames, the Humber or the Tees.
> No British Government was forced to sign a humiliating peace treaty. The British generals had done their duty. Their army and their country were on the winning side. That is the only proper, the only *sensible* starting point for an examination of their quality.[1]

Of the directors of the Arras battle of 1917, General Edmund Allenby, commander of the Third Army, was recalled to London on 5 June, 1917 and sent to command the British forces in Egypt and Palestine. At first, on hearing the news, Allenby was devastated, for he believed – as did many others – that he was being removed because of his failure to do better at Arras. But Allenby did brilliantly in Palestine, working closely with T. E. Lawrence (of Arabia), a junior officer whom Allenby shrewdly used to win over the support of the Arabs. Within six weeks Allenby had pushed forward the British front line by 350 miles and captured over 70,000 Turkish prisoners at a cost to the British of only 5,666 casualties. The capture of Jerusalem, Damascus and the Holy Land, which had been in Turkish hands for 400 years, is rated as one of the greatest feats of arms of the war but this great achievement for Allenby was marred by the news of the death of his only child, Michael, killed in action in Belgium.

Allenby returned to Britain a conquering hero and after the war a grateful country made him a Viscount and High Commissioner for Egypt together with an award of £50,000. On his return from Egypt in 1925, Allenby retired and bought a modest house in South Kensington where he spent much of his time in his aviary in the back garden, caring for his collection of rare exotic birds. He confined his public work to the schools cadet force and welfare of old soldiers. In May, 1936, he died suddenly while sitting at the desk in his study. He was seventy-five years old. His ashes were interred alongside the grave of Sir Hubert Plumer in Westminster Abbey, the only other First World War general to be so honoured.

General Sir Julian Byng, the victorious commander of the

[1] *The Smoke and the Fire*, p. 214.

Canadian Corps at Vimy Ridge, was promoted to succeed Allenby as commander of the Third Army, a position he held until the end of the war. After the war, Byng was awarded £30,000 by Parliament and raised to the peerage as Baron Byng of Vimy. In 1921 he was made Governor-General of Canada, a popular appointment in that country, but in 1926, just before he was due to return to England, he became embroiled in a bitter political crisis with the Canadian Government and left the country. In June, 1928, at the mature age of sixty-six, 'Bungo' was made Commissioner of the Metropolitan Police and introduced sweeping reforms into the force which had decreased in efficiency since the war. He is mostly remembered by the 'Met' for his system of patrolling and his introduction of police cars and telephone boxes. He retired from the force in September, 1931, and died suddenly on 2 June, 1935. He is buried in the churchyard of Beaumont-cum-Moze, Essex. His striking portrait hangs in the Hall of Commissioners at New Scotland Yard.

Sir Douglas Haig, although he had brought the war to a successful conclusion as Commander-in-Chief, bore the brunt of the blame for the heavy casualties incurred in defeating Germany – as he still does – and on the day he returned to Britain in 1919, he found himself redundant. Although he was granted £100,000 and given the title Earl Haig of Bemersyde, he was offered no worthwhile occupation. Haig no doubt half-expected this snub as Lloyd George was still Prime Minister; but it never seemed to bother him and he spent the rest of his spare time co-ordinating the work of the various ex-servicemen's associations. This reached its zenith with the formation of the British Legion in 1921 – the red poppies of remembrance still bear Haig's name. He died of a heart attack in London in January, 1928, and lies beside Sir Walter Scott in Dryburgh Abbey, near his beloved Bemersyde home.

After being sacked as Commander-in-Chief, General Robert Nivelle was given a command in North Africa – well away from the Western Front. At the end of the war, making a limited return to grace, he was nominated to represent France in the USA as a member of the Supreme War Council. He died in 1924, leaving no memoirs of the controversial and costly battle of April, 1917.

The cynical Tommies' song, 'Onward Joe Soap's Army' (to the tune of 'Onward Christian Soldiers') contains a particular line that rings out above all other: *'The boys who really did the job are dead and in their graves.'* And that line contains a nugget of truth, with 725,557 British and Commonwealth soldiers lying in the rich soil of France and Flanders. Of the fighting men who 'did the job' at Arras in April and May, 1917, there spring to mind that extraordinary soldier and brilliant General, Frank Maxwell, VC, DSO, killed four months later at Passchendaele; that brave young Sergeant-Major Jack Renwick, MC, MM, killed in the Chemical Works and his body never found; Captain Pat Blair, MC, the fatherly company commander of the 9th Royal Scots, killed while acting as a general's runner; and Captain Charles Whitley, MC, killed in a suicidal attack near Wancourt. The list is endless. Then there are the humble infantrymen, the Ned Mullalys, the Porky Flynns and the Bill Hubbards, all part of that great British Army of 1914–18.

And yet that same line is not the whole truth. For the majority of the boys who 'did the job' did come home – and whilst not forgetting their dead comrades, the British nation should always remember these men, to whom life in the post-war years was an anti-climax. Following the armistice, they were treated none too well by a nation that promised them a land 'fit for heroes' and many were unemployed for years. Some returned to the army, some turned to crime and some resorted to selling matches on the streets to earn a few pence. In the 1920s there were over four million British veterans of the 1914–18 War; now only a few are left. Some of them have made it their business to forget the terrible memories of the war years, while others have been unable to forget. Some committed these memories to paper, perhaps realizing that they had taken part in one of the greatest upheavals in the history of the world. Others kept the memory alive, which, born of the stark fear of battle, could never be erased. Of the survivors who fought at Arras, and lived on to a ripe old age, their memories have made this book.

Alf Razzell of the 8th Royal Fusiliers returned from the prisoner-of-war camp in December, 1918, a wiser, weaker man. He again took up his old profession as an electrical engineer and worked until he was seventy. He now lives in Watford and at the time of writing, was aged ninety-two, immensely proud at having been a Royal Fusilier and still being in perfect health. On 3 May, 1984, at the age of eighty-seven, he returned to the green fields between Monchy-le-Preux and Pelves where he had left his grievously wounded pal in a shell hole in May, 1917. On a grassy bank covered in red peppies he left a simple wreath inscribed 'In memory of my dear pal, Bill Hubbard.' He was, in his own words, 'putting my mind at rest'.

Albert Anderson, the fierce sergeant-major of the 4th Gordon Highlanders who fought to maintain a precarious foothold in Roeux on 23 April, 1917, was awarded the DCM for his fine leadership on

219

that day. Following the Battle of Arras, he won the Military Cross at Passchendaele and received a battlefield commission. In 1918, while serving in the Tank Corps, he was badly wounded when his Whippet tank was blown up near Cambrai. He left the army in May, 1919, and returned to 'civvy street' in Aberdeen. He died in May, 1982. His last comment on the Great War was that he was 'one of the lucky ones': 'I was young then and I can honestly say that, in spite of many hard times, I enjoyed every minute of it.'

Arthur Betteridge, of the 4th South African Infantry, following the crushing losses inflicted on the South African Brigade of Arras and being totally sick of the horror of the trenches, applied for a transfer to the Royal Flying Corps, which was approved in July, 1917. Following his training, he was commissioned in February, 1918, and posted to No. 3 Squadron, stationed near Doullens, France, flying Sopwith Camels. Betteridge took to flying like a duck to water and saw much aerial combat in 1918. He was also involved in several hair-raising exploits, one of which was in October, 1918, when he buzzed a football match being watched by 20,000 Allied troops. On his last swoop he hit the goal posts and crash-landed on to the pitch, where he was saved from certain lynching by Air Vice Marshal Sir John Salmond. Another daredevil stunt performed by Betteridge was to fly through a Zeppelin hangar. In 1919 he left the RAF and returned to South Africa and later became sales manager for South African Airways, retiring in 1956 on his sixtieth birthday. He died in Pretoria, following a fall, in January, 1983.

Of the Canadian soldiers, Neville Tompkins of the 26th Infantry Battalion took part in and survived all the remaining major engagements of the war. He returned to Vancouver in 1919 where he became a successful businessman. He died in February, 1982. His last letter to the author contained the following reflections:

> In closing I might say that, while I would not want to repeat my experiences in World War I (and certainly not at my present age), it was *the greatest adventure of my life*, the memories of which will remain with me for the remainder of my days, and I would not have missed it for anything. In the twilight of my advancing years, I frequently think of my forty-three months of army life, trench and open warfare, the battles of Vimy and Hill 70, the actions at Passchendaele, Amiens and the last hundred days of the war. And in particular I think of the loss of many good friends, including Ned Mullaly, killed by his own rifle grenades at Vimy, Roy Grencon (seventeen years old), a member of my machine-gun section and the victim of a sniper's

bullet at Hill 70, and many others who made the supreme sacrifice.

Bill Hay of the 'Dandy Ninth' should have the last word – he always did. Following his wound at Arras, he returned to the 9th Royal Scots at the end of May, 1917, when he was promoted company sergeant-major. His great rival, John Willocks, who had won the MM at Roeux on 23 April, had been promoted to the position following the death of Jack Renwick; but it was a position he did not hold for long – he was killed at Roeux on 27 May. Hay was next in action at Ypres in July and August, 1917, and at Cambrai in November, 1917. His luck finally ran out when he was captured on the banks of the St Quentin Canal on 22 March, 1918. Returning to Britain in 1919, he moved to London, where he pursued his trade as a coachmaker and through the years of hard work, while struggling to raise a young family, being bombed out of his home during the Blitz, he never forgot his pals of the 'Old 51st Highland Division' who he left in France.

In May, 1983, he made the first of several journeys to the battlefields, to visit the graves of Pat Blair, the Campbell brothers and to remember 'Jackie' Renwick at the Arras Memorial to the Missing. Bill Hay fought 'his' war to the very end, and at his little house in West Hampstead, appropriately named 'The Dugout', there was *always* a warm welcome to anyone who would lend an eager ear to his stories of the war. In his ninety-first year he entered hospital after suffering a stroke where he died peacefully on 1 December, 1985. Just before his death he wrote to the author:

> We that are left must never forget the debt we owe to the thousands of young men who gave their all that we should live in peace. God help me, how I am here I'll never know. I must have a guardian angel looking after me. After the episode at the Chemical Works when we got a right old bashing, and the rest of my pals were killed, I was left sadly alone. How I hate to be alone. When I get my checks I want to be scattered among my youthful chums, where I could have been. Memories, memories, the finest young men who ever breathed . . . My generation.

Bill Hay's last wish was duly carried out, somewhere on the old Western Front.

Appendix I:

Skeleton Order of Battle of British Divisions
Engaged in the Battle of Arras,
9 April to 17 May, 1917

Where available, total casualties are shown in brackets (figures taken from
Official History).

Third Army (General Sir Edmund Allenby)

3rd Division (Major-General C. J. Deverell):
   8, 9, 76 Brigades   (5,388)
4th Division (Major-General the Hon.
   W. Lambton):
   10, 11, 12 Brigades   (6,304)
9th (Scottish) Division (Major-General
   H. T. Lukin):
   26, 27 South African Brigades   (5,362)
12th (Eastern) Division (Major-General
   A. B. Scott):
   35, 36, 37 Brigades   (4,685)
14th (Light) Division (Major-General
   V. A. Couper):
   41, 42, 43 Brigades   (3,388)
15th (Scottish) Division (Major-General
   F. W. N. McCracken):
   44, 45, 46 Brigades   (*April only*: 6,313)
17th (Northern) Division (Major-General
   P. R. Robertson):
   50, 51, 52 Brigades   (4,478)
18th (Eastern) Division (Major-General
   R. P. Lee):
   53, 54, 55 Brigades   (2,404)
21st Division (Major-General
   D. G. M. Campbell):
   62, 64, 110 Brigades   (3,166)
29th Division (Major-General Sir H. de
   B. de Lisle):
   86, 87, 88 Brigades   (5,981)

30th Division (Major-General J. S. M. Shea):
    21, 89, 90 Brigades   (*April only*: 3,563)
33rd Division (Major-General R. J. Pinney):
    19, 98, 100 Brigades   (4,662)
34th Division (Major-General C. L. Nicholson):
    101, 102, 103 Brigades   (*April only*: 5,487)
37th Division (Major-General
  H. Bruce-Williams):
    63, 111, 112 Brigades   (*April only*: 6,286)
50th (Northumbrian) Division (Major-General
  P. S. Wilkinson):
    149, 150, 151 Brigades   (*April only*: 2,748)
51st (Highland) Division (Major-General
  G. M. Harper):
    152, 153, 154 Brigades   (6,477)
56th (1st London) Division (Major-General
  C. P. A. Hull):
    167, 168, 169 Brigades   (4,490)
1st Cavalry Division (Major-General
  R. L. Mullens):
    1, 2, 9 Cavalry Brigades   (*April only*: 104)
2nd Cavalry Division (Major-General
  W. H. Greenly):
    3, 4, 5 Cavalry Brigades   (*April only*: 174)
3rd Cavalry Division (Major-General
  J. Vaughan):
    6, 7, 8 Cavalry Brigades   (*April only*: 628)

First Army (General Sir Henry Horne)

2nd Division (Major-General C. E. Pereira):
    5, 6, 9 Brigades   (3,290)
5th Division (Major-General R. B. Stephens):
    13, 15, 95 Brigades   (4,905)
24th Division (Major-General J. E. Capper):
    17, 72, 73 Brigades   (1,498)
31st Division (Major-General R. Wanless
  O'Gowan)
    92, 93, 94 Brigades   (*May only*: 3,211)
63rd (Royal Naval) Division (Major-General
  C. E. Lawrie):
    188, 189, 190 Brigades   (4,284)
1st Canadian Division (Major-General
  A. W. Currie):
    1, 2, 3 Canadian Brigades   (6,221)

2nd Canadian Division (Major-General
    H. E. Burstall):
        4, 5, 6 Canadian Brigades   (5,657)
3rd Canadian Division (Major-General
    L. J. Lipsett):
        7, 8, 9 Canadian Brigades   (3,529)
4th Canadian Division (Major-General
    D. Watson):
        10, 11, 12 Canadian Brigades   (5,619)

Fifth Army (General Sir Hubert Gough)

Flanking operations round Bullecourt, April–May, 1917
7th Division (Major-General T. H. Shoubridge):
        20, 22, 91 Brigades   *(May only*: 2,341)
58th (2nd/1st London) Division (Major-General
    H. D. Fanshawe):
        173, 174, 175 Brigades   *(May only*: 1,938)
62nd (West Riding) Division (Major-General
    W. P. Braithwaite):
        185, 186, 187 Brigades   (4,233)
1st Australian Division (Major-General
    H. B. Walker):
        1, 2, 3 Australian Brigades   (2,341)
2nd Australian Division (Major-General
    N. H. Smyth):
        5, 6, 7 Australian Brigades   (3,898)
4th Australian Division (Major-General
    W. Holmes):
        4, 12, 13 Australian Brigades   (2,967)
5th Australian Division (Major-General
    J. J. T. Hobbs):
        8, 14, 15 Australian Brigades   (1,243)

Appendix II:

Skeleton Order of Battle of German Divisions
Engaged at the Battle of Arras,
9 April to 17 May 1917

3rd Guards Division
4th Guards Division
3rd Bavarian Division
5th Bavarian Division
14th Bavarian Division
16th Bavarian Division
4th Division
11th Division
17th Division
18th Division
26th Division
27th Division
35th Division
38th Division
56th Division
111th Division
185th Division
199th Division
207th Division
208th Division
220th Division
221st Division
1st Guards Reserve Division
2nd Guards Reserve Division
1st Bavarian Reserve Division
5th Bavarian Reserve Division
6th Bavarian Reserve Division
9th Reserve Division
12th Reserve Division
15th Reserve Division
17th Reserve Division
18th Reserve Division
26th Reserve Division
49th Reserve Division

79th Reserve Division
80th Reserve Division

Appendix III:

Victoria Cross Awards
for the Battle of Arras,
9 April to 17 May 1917

In alphabetical order. (P) = posthumous.

Temp/Captain Albert Ball, DSO & 2 Bars, MC (P). 7th Battalion. The Sherwood Foresters (Notts & Derbys) and Royal Flying Corps. For flying services rendered. Killed 7 May 1917. Buried Annoeullin Communal Cemetery, German extension.

Lance-Corporal Thomas Bryan, 25th (Tyneside Irish) Battalion, Northumberland Fusiliers. Near Roclincourt 9 April 1917. Died Doncaster, Yorks, 13 October 1945.

Sergeant Harry Cator, 7th Battalion East Surrey Regiment. Observation Ridge, near Arras, 9 April 1917. Died Norwich 7 April 1966.

Lieutenant Robert G. Combe, (P). 27th (Manitoba) Battalion C.E.F. Near Arleux 3 May 1917. No known grave. Vimy Memorial.

Corporal John Cunningham, (P). 2nd Battalion, The Leinster Regiment. Bois-en-Hache, near Vimy Ridge, 12 April 1917. Died of wounds 16 April 1917. Buried Barlin Communal Cemetery.

Private Tom Dresser, 7th Battalion Yorkshire Regiment. Near Roeux 12 May 1917. Died Middlesborough 9 April 1982.

Second Lieutenant Reginald L. Haine, MC & Bar. 1st Battalion, Honourable Artillery Company. Near Gavrelle 28 April 1917. Died London 12 June 1982.

Temp/Second Lieutenant John Harrison, MC (P). 11th Battalion, East Yorkshire Regiment. Oppy Wood 3 May 1917. No known grave. Arras Memorial.

Private Michael Heaviside, 15th Battalion, The Durham Light Infantry. Near Fontaine-les-Croisilles 6 May 1917. Died Durham 26 April 1939.

Temp/Captain Arthur Henderson, MC (P). 4th Battalion Argyll and Sutherland Highlanders. Near Fontaine-les-Croisilles 23 April 1917. Buried Cojeul British Cemetery.

Temp/Captain David P. Hirsch, (P). 4th Battalion, The Yorkshire Regiment. Near Wancourt 23 April 1917. No known grave. Arras Memorial.

Corporal George J. Howell, MM. 1st Battalion (New South Wales), Australian Infantry. Near Bullecourt 6 May 1917. Died Perth, Australia, 23 December 1964.

Corporal George Jarratt, (P). 8th Battalion Royal Fusiliers. Near Monchy-le-Preux 3 May 1917. No known grave. Arras Memorial.

Captain Thain W. MacDowell, DSO. 38th (Ottawa) Battalion C.E.F. Vimy Ridge 9–13 April 1917. Died Nassau, Bahamas, 29 March 1960.

Lieutenant Donald Mackintosh, (P). 2nd Battalion The Seaforth Highlanders. Near Roeux Station 11 April 1917. Buried Brown's Copse British Cemetery, Roeux.

Private William J. Milne, (P). 16th (Manitoba) Canadian Scottish Battalion C.E.F. Vimy Ridge 9 April 1917. No known grave. Vimy Memorial.

Lieutenant Rupert (Mickey) Moon. 58th (Victoria) Battalion, Australian Infantry, Bullecourt 12 May 1917. Died Australia 1986.

Lance-Corporal Harold S. Mugford, 8th Machine-Gun Squadron. Monchy-le-Preux 11 April 1917. Died Chelmsford, Essex, 16 June 1968.

Private John G. Pattison. 50th (Calgary) Battalion C.E.F. Vimy Ridge 10 April 1917. Killed Lens 3 June 1917. Buried La Chaudière Military Cemetery.

Second Lieutenant Alfred O. Pollard, MC & Bar, DCM. 1st Battalion, Honourable Artillery Company. Gavrelle 29 April 1917. Died Bournemouth, Hants, 5 December 1960.

Lance-Sergeant Ellis W. Sifton, (P). 18th Battalion C.E.F. Vimy Ridge 9 April 1917. Buried Lichfield Crater Cemetery, Thelus.

Private Ernest Sykes, 27th (Tyneside Irish) Battalion, Northumberland Fusiliers. Near Arras 19 April 1917. Died Lockwood, Yorks, 3 August 1949.

Private Horace Waller, (P). 10th Battalion, The King's Own Yorkshire Light Infantry. Near Heninel 10 April 1917. Buried Cojeul British Cemetery.

Lance-Corporal James Welch, 1st Battalion, The Royal Berkshire Regiment. Near Oppy Wood 29 April 1917. Died Bournemouth, Hants, 28 June 1978.

Sergeant Albert White, (P). 2nd Battalion, The South Wales Borderers. Monchy-le-Preux 19 April 1917. No known grave. Arras Memorial.

Acknowledgements

Research for a book of this nature demands a great deal of hard work and this, coupled with the interviewing of over three hundred veteran soldiers singlehanded, has taken me the best part of five years before I could even think of putting pen to paper. I must be honest and say that on several occasions during this period – often after following promising leads up blind alleys – I have felt like giving it all up. Continual encouragement came, however, from my family, friends and not least, veteran soldiers, with some of whom I developed a special friendship.

As an unknown tackling a complex military subject, help from military 'experts' was not readily forthcoming. The whole subject of the Western Front seemed to be a jealously guarded closed shop. Thankfully, I was thrown several lifelines. The first came in the form of Martin Middlebrook of Boston, Lincs (author of the compelling *The First Day on the Somme*, Allen Lane, 1971), who gave me valuable and friendly advice. The second came with a chance meeting, one hazy morning in Messines, with Rose Coombes, MBE, author of *Before Endeavours Fade*, who revealed to me many 'secrets' of the Arras battlefield and who told me of the tunnels of Roeux and Neuville Vitasse. Her knowledge of the battlefields of the Western Front is unsurpassed. The problem of finding a source of reading material on the battle – I was determined to read as many Regimental, Divisional and Battalion Histories I could lay my hands on – was solved by a fellow Metropolitan Police Officer, Peter Gilhooley of Canonbury Park. He possessed almost all of them and allowed me unlimited access to what must be one of the finest private collections of books on the Great War. Peter also made himself available at a moment's notice to carry out any piece of research for me. To the aforementioned three, I express my sincere gratitude.

My heartfelt thanks are also expressed to the following who have willingly assisted me in a variety of ways: Cyril H. J. Nicholls, (1921–1988) my father, great friend and regular companion to the battlefields. For his encouragement; Geoffrey Hull of Woodham, Surrey, who carefully read, edited and advised on my first manuscript; Eugenie Brooks of the Commonwealth War Graves Commission, for her unstinting help in letting me read the Cemetery Registers for the Arras area (and who has since joined the Metropolitan

Police!); Richard Dunning, Peter Scott, John Marshall and Ian Ronson of the Western Front Association; Irene Kaufman of Deanshanger, Otto Sander of Slough and Charles Day of Boreham Wood and the Metropolitan Police Diplomatic Protection Group who took on the difficult task of translating the German accounts; Clive Hughes, Phillip Powell and Mike Willis of the Imperial War Museum; the staff of the Public Record Office at Kew for their courteous and efficient service when they must have been sick of the sight of me; Charles Vincent of Vancouver and his old comrades of the 44th Battalion Association of Canada; Harry Hart, MBE, for putting me in touch with many old comrades of the 8/9th Royal Fusiliers; and likewise Harry Cohen of the 16th Royal Warwicks Old Comrades; Gerard Fitton of Deanshanger; Keith Collman of Hemel Hempstead for his photographic expertise; Ernest Slatter of Arcadia, Pretoria, South Africa; Paul Smith of Fairfield, Pennsylvania, USA; Richard Baumgartner of Huntington, West Virginia, USA; Paul Nicolas (who accompanied me to Germany), Gerald Lejuené and José Heussneur of the French Police Department, André Coilliot of Beaurains, Tom Fairgrieve of the Commonwealth War Graves Commission, Michel Fardel of Albert and Maurice Link of Mesnil; Percy Towergood, Veterans Affairs, The Canadian Embassy, London; A. J. (Jack) Smithers of Ickham, Kent, for his constructive advice and help; likewise my publisher, Leo Cooper; my fellow police officers and friends of West Hampstead and Hampstead Police Stations, many of whom have accompanied me on over twenty visits to the old Western Front; in particular, John Goodwin for his help in the initial stages of research; Dave Proctor, who took great pains in drawing the plans, and Michael Curtis and Douglas Mackenzie for their endless amusing banter which brightened up many a wet day in France; many other people, too numerous to mention, who kindly lent me letters and documents in response to my press campaign; and last but not least, a special word of thanks must go to my wife Linda and my son Gregory who have 'cheerfully sacrificed' much, to enable me to finish this book.

I would also like to thank the following British, German, Canadian and South African veterans, who in 1978–85 generously contributed their personal experiences of the Battle of Arras, 1917, and who gave this author a greater understanding of a soldier's life in the Great War, 1914–18. Without their help, this book could never have been written.

THE BRITISH ARMY
In alphabetical order of surname; ranks shown are those held during the Battle of Arras 1917.

Private S. Abbot, 11th Royal Fusiliers
Sergeant W. Ackland, Army Service Corps

Private W. Allman, 4th Machine Gun Corps
Private A. Allwood, 153rd T. M. Battery
Co. Sergeant-Maj. A. G. Anderson, MC, DCM, 4th Gordon Highlanders
Private D. C. Anderson, 78th Btn. (4th Canadian Division)
Private S. H. Appleby, 8th Royal Fusiliers
Gunner C. W. Archer, 5th Brigade RHA
Trooper S. B. Atkinson, Canadian Light Horse
Sergeant J. Attwood, 2nd Royal Fusiliers
Private R. Austin, 42nd Btn. (3rd Canadian Division)
Private W. Austin, 8th Royal Fusiliers
Private W. Ayers, 1st Gloucesters
Private J. Badger, 16th Royal Warwicks
Trooper S. Bailey, 1st Life Guards
Private C. Baines, 1st South African Infantry Battalion
2nd Lieutenant E. A. Baker, 13th Royal Scots
Major E. Barber, 4th Siege Bty, RGA
Private T. Barber, 16th Royal Warwicks
Private E. Barnes, 3/10 Middlesex
Private F. Barnett, 17th Royal Welsh Fusiliers (Not at Arras)
Private S. R. Barter, 8th Royal Fusiliers
Private W. E. G. Bartlett, 4th Gloucesters (Not at Arras)
Gunner F. Bate, 87th Siege Bty, RGA
Lieutenant A. E. Bath, 2nd Beds
Private W. Bayley, 7th Loyal North Lancs
Private T. Bazeley, 6th Northants
2nd Lieutenant F. W. Beadle, 159 Brigade RFA
Private R. J. Beale, ASC att. 2nd Cavalry Division
Corporal J. Beament, MM, 16th KRR Corps (Not at Arras)
Private J. Beeston, 13th Royal Fusiliers
Private H. Belrose, 102nd Btn, (4th Canadian Division)
Private L. Belston, 17th Kings
Private A. Belyea, 1st Canadian Division, Amm. Column
Private A. E. Betteridge, 4th South African Infantry Battalion
Private J. Blair, 4th Seaforth Highlanders
Private D. Block, 8th KRR Corp.
Private W. J. Boatman, 9th Royal Fusiliers
Private E. Body, 8th Btn, (1st Canadian Division)
Private A. Bonney, 2nd South Wales Borderers
Trooper B. Bowers, Herts Yeomanry (Not at Arras)
Private J. Bracegirdle, 50th Btn, (4th Canadian Division)
Corporal T. Bracey, MM, 9th Royal Fusiliers
Private R. Bradbrook, 17th Kings
Gunner J. U. Brade, 72nd Bty, South African Heavy Artillery
Private L. Brooks, 3rd Div. Canadian Field Ambulance
Private J. Broome, 1st Royal Warwicks

Sapper G. Brougham, Royal Engineers, 3rd Division
Private H. Brown, 11th Middx
Private S. Bryan, 16th Royal Warwicks
Private J. Buley, 8th T. M. Battery
Private W. Bullock, 1st Gloucesters
Private W. Burke, 1/4th London Regiment
Sapper G. A. Burns, Royal Engineers (12th Divison)
Private E. Burtenshaw, 2nd Notts & Derby
Private F. Butler, 4th East Yorks
Private E. Carolan, 1st Royal Berks
Trooper H. W. Carpenter, Oxfordshire Yeomanry
L/Corporal J. Carr, 3rd Army Military Police
Private A. H. Carter, 5th Canadian Mounted Rifles
Private F. P. Caulton, 2nd Royal Fusiliers
Gunner J. Chalmers, 2/1st Lowland Heavy Battery RGA
Sergeant L. G. Charles, Mounted Military Police, 3rd Army
Private J. Chester, 1/2nd London Regiment
Corporal M. Cistel, 1st South African Infantry Battalion
Private F. Clarke, 5th Northants
Private G. Clarkson, 44th Btn (4th Canadian Division)
Private C. Cleale, 18th Kings
Gunner J. Cobb, 36 Bty, RA
Private H. Cohen, 16th Royal Warwicks
Private W. M. Collior, 8th Royal Fusiliers
Private W. A. Cook, 27th Brigade Field Ambulance
Private G. H. Cooper, 17 Corps, Troop Supply Column
Private J. W. Coupland, MM, 42nd Machine Gun Company
Sergeant J. J. Cousins, MM, 7th Beds
Private H. Cowley, 8th Royal Fusiliers
Private E. Crane, 6th Beds
Private A. Crisp, 8th Btn (1st Canadian Division)
Private P. Curtis, 1/4th London Regiment
Private W. G. Cuttle, 44th Btn (4th Canadian Division)
L/Corporal A. Davies, 7th Middx
Corporal J. de Cruyenaere, DCM, 1st Canadian Mounted Rifles
Private A. Denholm, 9th Royal Scots
Private A. Dickinson, 10th Lincs
Private J. Dobie, 9th Seaforth Highlanders
Private E. Drinkwater, 16th Royal Warwicks
Private L. A. Dunn, 1st East Yorks
Gunner S. Dunning, RGA
Gunner P. Dyke, 4/5 Howitzer Bty, RND, RA
Private T. Easton, 21st Northumberland Fusiliers
Private A. Ellingham, 42nd Field Ambulance, RAMC
Private F. Ellis, 7th Rifle Brigade

Private W. Erander, 10th Lincs
Private R. Eveling, 7th Border Regiment
Private C. W. J. Farlie, 9th Royal Fusiliers
Private W. I. Fawcett, 78th Btn (4th Canadian Division)
Bombardier H. Fayerbrother, DCM, RGA
Corporal J. Fell, 21st West Yorks
L/Corporal H. Fellows, 12th Northumberland Fus (Not at Arras)
Sergeant J. Ferguson, 9th Royal Scots
L/Corporal A. Fisher, MM, 8th Black Watch
Private C. Fisher, 10th Royal Welsh Fusiliers
Able Seaman J. Fitch, Drake Battalion
Gunner V. M. Flemmer, 74 Siege Bty, South African Heavy Artillery
Private E. Fletcher, 11th Suffolks
Private A. E. Flynn, 4th Gordon Highlanders
Private D. Flynn, 4th Seaforth Highlanders
Private F. J. Ford, 6th Duke of Cornwalls Light Infantry
Gunner R. Ford, 157th Brigade, RFA
Private G. J. Forrester, 1st London Scottish
2nd Lieutenant J. Foster, MM, 16th Manchesters
Private H. Fowler, 1st London Scottish
Private E. Francis, 16th Royal Warwicks
Private W. W. Francis, 7th Kings Shropshire Light Infantry
Private S. T. Fuller, 8th Suffolks
Sergeant D. B. Gardner, 9th Royal Scots
Trooper C. H. Garnett, Essex Yeomanry
Private G. J. Giggins, 62nd Machine Gun Company
Sapper B. Gill, 3rd Army Corp, Royal Engineers
Private H. Gilmour, 7th Gordon Highlanders
Private B. Good, 9th Black Watch
Gunner G. Goodbody, 133 Siege Bty, RGA
Private H. Goodby, 1st London Scottish
Trooper P. Goodman, Bedfordshire Yeomanry
Private A. Graham, MM & Bar, 1st Northants (Not at Arras)
Private D. Graham, 7th Black Watch
Corporal R. Graham, 9th Royal Scots
Private K. H. Grant, 7th Btn (1st Canadian Division)
Private W. A. Grant, 7th Btn (1st Canadian Division)
Private C. W. Graves, DCM, 6th Royal Berks
Private R. C. Gray, 11th Suffolks
Lieutenant H. Green, 54th Btn (4th Canadian Division)
Sapper J. Greenwood, Special Brigade, Royal Engineers
Sergeant W. Greggain, 72nd Btn (4th Canadian Division)
Private H. C. Gregory, 6th Royal West Kents
Gunner J. W. Greig, 123rd Bty, RGA.
Gunner N. Grey, 53rd Brigade, RFA

Private E. Grisdale, 54th Btn (4th Canadian Division)
Private W. H. A. Groom, 1st London Rifle Brigade
Private R. E. Gyton, MM, 29th Division Signals
Lieutenant G. H. Hadley, 16th Royal Warwicks
Private H. G. Ham, 12th Middx
Trooper The Reverend G. H. Hambley
Lieutenant C. B. Hamm, MM, 7th Btn (1st Canadian Division)
L/Corporal W. Harper, 12th Rifle Brigade (Not at Arras)
Sergeant A. W. Hart, MM, 44th Btn (4th Canadian Division)
Corporal H. Hart, 9th Royal Fusiliers (Not at Arras)
Private E. Hartman, 9th Royal Fusiliers
Sergeant W. Hay, 9th Royal Scots
Private M. Heath, 44th Btn (4th Canadian Division)
Private J. H. Herdman, 26th Northumberland Fusiliers
Private W. Hodgson, 2nd Duke of Wellington's (West Riding) Regiment
Private F. Hollingworth, 4th Seaforth Highlanders
Private H. Holt, 8th Royal Fusiliers
Private L. C. Horton, 1st London Scottish
Private F. Hunt, RFC attchd. 81st Heavy Artillery
Private E. Impey, 35th Kite Balloon Section, RFC
Private A. R. Inman, 1st Lancashire Fusiliers
2nd Lieutenant H. Instone, RHA
Private J.J. Jamieson, 9th Gordon Highlanders
Private E. Jenkins, 8th Royal Fusiliers
Private D. Johnston, 1/16th London Regiment
Trooper A. Karr, South Irish Horse
Private G. P. Kay, 7th Border Regiment
Private F. Kechego, 20th Btn (2nd Canadian Division)
Bombardier T. Kellham, 21st Heavy Bty, RGA
Private P. J. Kennedy, MM, 18th Manchesters
Private C. Kent, 12th Middx
Private A. Kindell, 42nd Btn (3rd Canadian Division)
Private C. C. King, 44th Btn (4th Canadian Division)
Trooper C. Kingswell, 4th Hussars
Corporal A. Kirk, 2nd Royal Scots
Gunner R. P. Knappitt, MM, 41st Brigade, RFA
Private C. A. Lacey, 1st East Lancs
Private R. Langley, 8th Royal Fusiliers
2nd Lieutenant G. I. Larkins, 10th West Yorks
Sub. Lieutenant T. M. Lawrie, Howe Battalion
Private J. A. Lees, 2nd Duke of Wellington's (West Riding) Regiment
Private G. Liddle, 38th Btn (4th Canadian Division)
Signaller E. H. Lilley, 17 Corps, Royal Engineers
Gunner W. Lockhart, 150th Brigade, RFA
Private J. Luxon, 'D' Btn, Heavy Branch, Machine Gun Corps

Private A. D. McCrindle, 24th Battalion (2nd Canadian Division)
Private J. Mackay, 6th Gordon Highlanders
Private N. Mackechnie, 1st London Scottish
Sergeant A. Manson, 44th Btn (4th Canadian Division)
Private W. Marshall, 9th Royal Fusiliers
Private T. A. Matthews, 2/5th Royal Warwicks (Not at Arras)
Sergeant A. E. Mayhew, Mounted Military Police, 3rd Army
Private N. Mollast, 89th Brigade, Machine Gun Corps
Captain R. d'A. G. Monypenny, 2nd Essex
Private E. Moody, 9th Royal Fusiliers
Private R. Moore, 16th Royal Warwicks
Private H. Morgan, 10th Royal Welsh Fusiliers
Bombardier W. J. Muir, 63rd (Royal Naval) Division, RFA.
Leading Seaman J. Murray, Hood Battalion
Private F. Murrell, 1/8th Middx
Private A. Musson, 2nd Lincs
Private D. A. New, MM, 72nd Btn (4th Canadian Division)
Private W. Nicholls, 7th Wilts (Not at Arras)
Private J. Nicholson, 19th Btn (2nd Canadian Division)
Private W. Nutley, Machine Gun Corps
Private D. Ogilvie, 4th South African Infantry Battalion
Private J. O'Neil, 2nd Royal Dublin Fusiliers
Private W. J. Onions, 9th Royal Scots
Corporal S. Parker-Bird, 29th Division Sanitary Section
Private D. Parry, 16th Manchesters
Sergeant W. Partridge, 7th Middx
Gunner E. P. Pearson, 36th Brigade, RFA
Private W. C. Pearson, 15th Btn (1st Canadian Division)
Gunner H. Pegg, 96th Siege Bty, RGA
Captain H. Pegrum, 10th Lancashire Fusiliers
Rifleman A. H. Pennington, 16th KRR Corps
Private A. Peters, 7th Kings Shropshire Light Infantry
Sapper F. Pickett, Royal Engineers
Private A. C. Pinkney, 6th Duke of Cornwall's Light Infantry
Corporal P. G. Pinneo, 8th Btn (1st Canadian Division)
Private L. G. Plumridge, 1st Kings Shropshire Light Infantry
Private F. Poulter, 9th Div. ASC Dispatch Rider
Corporal J. Price, 12th Middx
2nd Lieutenant F. W. J. Quinn, 19th Kings
Lieutenant B. B. Rackham, MC and Bar, Hawke Battalion
Private B. Rands, 4th Beds
Private C. Rayner, 8th KRR Corps
Corporal A. E. Razzell, 8th Royal Fusiliers
Gunner F. Read, 150th Brigade, RFA
Rifleman R. Renwick, 16th KRR Corps

Private A. Richards, 'C' Battalion, Heavy Branch Machine Gun Corps
Private E. C. Richards, 4th South African Infantry Battalion
Private F. H. Richards, 8th Royal Fusiliers
Private S. Ridgeway, 5th Royal Berks
Sergeant F. H. Robbins, 13th Rifle Brigade
Private W. A. Robbins, 25th Btn (2nd Canadian Division)
Private A. C. Roberts, 16th Royal Warwicks
Private A. Rossington, 7th Lincs
Private T. Rourke, MM, 8th Durham Light Infantry
Private C. Rowland, 17th West Yorks
Bombardier W. H. Rowley, 232th Mobile Brigade, RFA
Sapper C. Rushby, 3rd Field Squadron, Royal Engineers
Private F. Sargent, ASC
Private C. Sayers, 1st South African Field Ambulance
Private E. Schofield, ASC
Private A. E. Scriggins, 7th Suffolks
Private A. Scrimgeour, 2nd South African Infantry Battalion
Private G. Shaves, 7th KRR Corps
Private C. Shea, 1st Btn (1st Canadian Division)
Corporal F. Shepherd, 9th Royal Fusiliers
Private G. P. Shepherd, RAMC 56th Division
Private J. Shields, 17th Royal Fusiliers
Trooper L. G. Shurrock, 3rd (Kings Own) Hussars
Gunner S. L. Sidwell, Warwickshire Battery, RFA
Private A. Sillitoe, 7th Kings Shropshire Light Infantry
Rifleman M. Silverman, 2nd Rifle Brigade
Captain C. M. Slack, MC and Bar, 1/4th East Yorks
Gunner D. Smart, London Brigade, RGA
Private S. Smart, 1st Canadian Mounted Rifles
Private A. M. Smith, 8th Royal West Kents
Private A. W. Smith, 7th Gordon Highlanders
Private G. P. Smith, 1st Lancashire Fusiliers
Private J. W. Smith, 1st Lancashire Fusiliers
Gunner W. J. Smith, 44 Siege Bty, RGA
L/Corporal J. W. Spears, 44th Btn (4th Canadian Division)
Sapper A. A. Spofforth, Royal Engineers
Private R. Stanbridge, 7th East Surreys
Private J. Stephens, 16th Royal Warwicks
Private C. Stewart, 6th Cameron Highlanders
Gunner L. C. Stewart, 222nd Siege Bty, RGA
Private A. Stuart-Dolden, 1st London Scottish
Private R. E. Tandy, 4th South African Infantry Battalion
Captain T. C. Tanner, 5th Kings Shropshire Light Infantry
Private W. H. Tapper, 38th Btn (4th Canadian Division)
Gunner A. Taylor, 128 Bty, RFA

Trooper B. Taylor, Northants Yeomanry
Private B. Taylor, 7th Sussex
Trooper C. V. Taylor, South Irish Horse
Private J. Thain, 6th Seaforth Highlanders
Private V. A. Theobald, 11th Suffolks
Private A. L. Thomspon, RAMC 30th Division
Sapper W. Thurston, Canadian Engineers
Private J. W. Thwaites, 107 Btn (Pioneers) (1st Canadian Division)
Private N. C. Tompkins, 26th Btn (2nd Canadian Division)
Private W. Townsend, 2nd Wilts
Sergeant F. G. Udall, MM and two Bars, 1/4th London Regiment
Private L. C. Urquart, 44th Btn (4th Canadian Division)
Private W. Vallence, 4/5th Royal Scots Fusiliers (Not at Arras)
Private L. A. Vassiere, 8th Royal Fusiliers
Private F. W. Vogts, 2nd South African Infantry Battalion
Private W. Walker, 9th Royal Scots
Corporal W. B. Walker, 6th Beds
Private J. Wallis, 2nd Royal Berks (Not at Arras)
Bugler B. A. Ward, 24th Btn (2nd Canadian Division)
Private S. Ware-Lane, 7th East Surreys
Private F. Warner, 16th Royal Warwicks
Sergeant E. C. Warren, 1/12th London Regiment (Rangers)
Corporal D. A. M. Watson, 9th Royal Scots (Not at Arras)
Private R. A. Watts, 10th Royal Dublin Fusiliers
Sergeant V. W. Wheeler, 50th Btn (4th Canadian Division)
Private J. Wieder, 1/3rd London Regiment
Private E. H. Wilford, 11th Royal Warwicks
Private E. Williams, 2/5th Kings Own R. L. Reg (Not at Arras)
2nd Lieutenant R. H. Williams, 4th Royal Fusiliers
Private W. Williams, 2nd Royal Fusiliers
Corporal R. P. Willson, MM, 4th Beds
Sergeant W. T. Wilson, 10th Royal Welch Fusiliers
Sergeant W. Wright, Machine Gun Corps
Private V. W. Yorke-Hart, 3rd South African Infantry Battalion

THE GERMAN ARMY
Musketier H. H. Andreson, 164th (Hamelin) Regiment
Musketier F. Auhagen, 73rd (Hanover) Regiment
Infanterist A. Beerman, 25th Regiment
Unteroffizier A. Bernardini, 23rd Regiment
Musketier F. Bokohn, 76th (Hamburg) Regiment
Infanterist F. Bomhauer, 230th Reserve Regiment
Gefrieter H. Frerichs, 3rd and 25th Machine Gun Company
Musketier L. Friestarif, 230th Reserve Regiment
Leutnant H. Garbe, 420th Minenwerfer Company

Kanonier F. Godry, 405th Field Artillery
Gefreiter A. Honig, 73rd Regiment
Soldat A. Kamper, 99th Reserve Regiment
Musketier E. Kann, 84th Reserve Regiment
Leutnant O. Klüsener, 3rd Guard Minenwerfer Company
Gefreiter R. Kolesch, 13th Infantry Regiment
Musketier H. Kraft, 263rd Reserve Infantry Regiment
Musketier E. Langwost, 73rd (Hanover) Regiment
Fusilier H. Lutmer, 90th Fusilier Regiment
Leutnant E. Majewski, 61st Regiment
Gefreiter C. A. Maroth, 84th Reserve Regiment
Gefreiter E. P. Nicholas, 89th Grenadiers
Musketier O. Noack, 31st Regiment
Soldat W. Oellerich, 121st Reserve Regiment
Infanterist K. W. Paul, 18th Bavarian Regiment
Kanonier W. Paulmann, 2nd Guards Artillery Regiment
Gefreiter G. Petsch, 51st Infantry Regiment
Musketier H. Schulze, 94th Regiment
Leutnant H. Sulzbach, 63rd Field Artillery Regiment (Not at Arras)
Oberleutnant E. Volker, 119th Regiment

Other Acknowledgements

Acknowledgements for permission to include quotations from *The Official History of the War, France and Belgium 1917* and from Crown copyright records in the Public Record Office are made to the Controller of H.M. Stationery Office; to the Imperial War Museum for the Maxse Papers and the Snow Papers and the accounts of L. Gameson, W. Vignoles, J. Williamson, and G. Christie-Miller; from *Canon's Folly* by Martin Andrews, to Michael Joseph; from *The Private Papers of Douglas Haig* edited by Robert Blake, to Eyre & Spottiswoode; from *The Memoirs of Lord Chandos* to Bodley Head; from *A Passionate Prodigality* by Guy Chapman and from *Journals and Letters* by Lord Esher, to Nicolson & Watson; from *Three years with the 9th (Scottish) Division* by W. D. Croft, to John Murray; from *The First World War* by Cyril Falls, to Longmans; from *The War Dispatches* by Sir Phillip Gibbs, to Anthony Gibbs & Phillips; from *The Fifth Army* by General Sir Hubert Gough, to Hodder & Stoughton; from *Storm of Steel* by Ernst Jünger, to Chatto & Windus; from *The Kaiser* by Joachim von Kurenberg, to Cassell; from *My War Memories 1914–18* by Erich von Ludendorff, to Hutchinson; from *The Middle Parts of Fortune* by Frederick Manning, to Peter Davies; from *The Australian Victories in France in 1918* by Sir John Monash, to Angus & Robertson; from *Prelude to Victory* by Sir

Edward Spears, to Jonathan Cape; from *The Smoke and the Fire* by John Terraine, to Sidgwick & Jackson; from *No Mans's Land* by Victor Wheeler, to the Alberta Historical Resources Foundation; to *Punch* Magazine for permission to include illustrations.

The Press
Many newspapers and magazines published my appeals for participants in the Battle of Arras 1917 and I am pleased to record my thanks for this kind help.

UNITED KINGDOM: *Aberdeen Evening Express, Accrington Observer, Acton Gazette and West London Times, Boreham Wood and Elstree Post, Bournemouth Times, Brighton and Hove Gazette, Bristol Evening Post, Bucks Advertiser, Buckingham, Towcester and Brackely Advertiser, Burton Daily Mail, Bury St Edmunds Free Press, Bury Times, Cambridge Evening News, Camden Journal, Corby Leader, Coulsden and Purley Advertiser, Dundee Evening Telegraph, Dunstable Gazette, Dover Express and East Kent News, East Fife Mail, Eastbourne Herald, East Anglian Daily Times, Edgware, Mill Hill and Hendon Times, Edinburgh Evening News, Folkestone and Hythe Gazette, Glasgow Herald, Gloucester Journal, Grimsby Evening Telegraph, Hampstead and Highgate Express, Harrow Observer, Hemel Hempstead Gazette, High Wycombe Observer, Herts Advertiser, Hexham Courant, Ilford Recorder, Kent Messenger, Kilburn Times, Leek Post and Times, Lincolnshire Echo, Liverpool Daily Post, London Evening Standard, Luton News, Maidenhead Advertiser, Manchester Evening News, Milton Keynes Observer, Newcastle Evening News, Northampton Chronicle and Echo, Oxford Mail, Sheffield Morning Telegraph, Shrewsbury Chronicle, Shropshire Star, Slough and Hounslow Evening News, Southend Evening Echo, Stirling Observer, Walsall Observer, Watford Evening Echo, West Byfleet News, West Herts and Watford Observer, West Lancashire Evening Gazette, West London Observer, Wiltshire Times, Wolverhampton Express and Star, Wolverton Express, Yorkshire Evening Press, Yorkshire Post.*
ALSO: *National Association of Retired Police Officers Journal, Royal Engineers Journal, Royal British Legion Journal, The Job (The Journal of the Metropolitan Police), Police Review, Royal United Services Institution Journal, The Green Howards Gazette, The London Scottish Gazette, Stand To! (The Journal of the Western Front Association), The Gallipolian (Journal of the Gallipoli Association).*
REPUBLIC OF IRELAND: *Cork Examiner, Dublin Evening Press, Limerick Advertiser, Wexford People.*
CANADA: *Calgary Herald, Edmonton Journal, Hamilton Spectator, London Free Press, Medicine Hat News, Montreal Gazette, Ottawa Journal, Owen Sound Sun Times, Sarnia Observer, Sakatoon Star Phoenix, St Catherine Standard, St John Telegraph, Toronto Daily Star, Vancouver Sun, Victoria Colonist, Winnipeg Free Press, The Legion.*

SOUTH AFRICA: *Cape Times, Cape Town Argus, Die Burger, Johannesburg Daily Star, Pretoria News, Rand Daily Mail, The MOTH Magazine.*

GERMANY: *Badische Neuste Nachrichten, Berliner Morgen Post, Coburger Tageblatt, Dusseldorfer Nachrichten, Flensburger Tageblatt, Frankfurter Rundschau, Hamburger Abendblatt, Lubecker Nachrichten, Neue Westfalische, Nordsee Zeitung, Rheinische Post, Saarbrücker Zeitung, Stuttgarter Zeitung, West Deutsche Zeitung, Wormser Zeitung.*

Bibliography

Official Histories

Bean, C. E. W., *The Australian Imperial Force in France, 1917*, Sydney 1933
Falls, Cyril, *Military Operations France and Belgium 1917*, Macmillan 1940
Jones, H. A., *The War in the Air*, Oxford University Press 1934
Nicholson, G. W. L., *Canadian Expeditionary Force (Official History of the Canadian Army in the First World War, 1914–19)*, Ottowa 1962
Die Osterlacht Bie Arras 1917, Reichsarchiv, Berlin 1929
Les Armées Françaises dans la Grande Guerre, Service Historique, Paris 1929

Other Publications

Andrews, Martin, *Canon's Folly*, Michael Joseph 1968
Baker-Carr, C. D., *From Chauffeur to Brigadier*, Ernest Benn 1930
Bewsher, F. W., *The History of the 51st (Highland) Division 1914–18*, William Blackwood & Sons 1921
Bishop, W. A., *Winged Warfare*, Penguin Books 1938
Blake, Robert (ed), *The Private Papers of Douglas Haig 1914–1919*, Eyre and Spottiswoode 1952
Boraston, J. H. (ed), *Despatches of Field Marshal Earl Haig*, Dent 1919
Buchan, John, *The South African Forces in France*, Nelson 1923
Callwell, C. E., *Field Marshal Sir Henry Wilson*, Cassell 1927
Carrington, C. E., *Soldier from the Wars Returning*, Hutchinson 1965
Carter, V. Bonham, *Wully, Soldier True*, Mullen 1963
Chandos, Viscount, *The Memoirs of Lord Chandos*, Bodley Head 1962
Chapman, Guy, *A Passionate Prodigality*, Nicolson & Watson 1933
Charteris, John, *At G.H.Q.*, Cassell 1931
Churchill, Sir Winston, *The World Crisis*, Odhams 1938
Colliot, André, *Mai 1940 (Région d'Arras)*, private publication 1980
Coombes, Rose, *Before Endeavours Fade*, Battle of Britain Prints International 1976
Croft, W. D., *Three Years with the 9th (Scottish) Division*, Murray 1919
Crutwell, C. R. M. F., *A History of the Great War 1914–18*, Oxford University Press 1934
Cuddeford, D. W. J., *And All For What?*, Heath Cranton 1922

Duff Cooper, *Haig*, Faber 1935

Esher, Lord, *Journals and Letters* (4 vols), Nicolson & Watson 1934

Ewing, John, *History of the 9th (Scottish) Division 1914–18*, John Murray 1921. *The Royal Scots, 1914–1919*, Oliver and Boyd 1925

Falls, Cyril, *The First World War*, Longmans 1960

Farrar-Hockley, Anthony, *Goughie*, Hart-Davis Macgibbon 1975

Gardner, Brian, *Allenby*, Cassell 1965

Gibbs, Sir Phillip, *The War Dispatches*, Anthony Gibbs and Phillips 1966

Gillon, Stair, *The Story of the 29th Division*, Nelson 1925

Glubb, Sir John, *Into Battle*, Cassell 1977

Gough, Sir Hubert, *The Fifth Army*, Hodder & Stoughton 1931

Horne, Alistair, *The Price of Glory, Verdun 1916*, Macmillan 1962

Jerrold, Douglas, *The Royal Naval Division*, Hutchinson 1927

Junger, Ernst, *The Storm of Steel*, Chatto & Windus 1929

Kurenberg, Joachim von, *The Kaiser*, Cassell 1954

Lawrence, T. E., *Seven Pillars of Wisdom*, Jonathan Cape 1973

Liddell Hart, Sir Basil, *History of the First World War*, Cassell 1970

Lloyd George, *War Memoirs* (2 Vols), Odhams 1936

Ludendorff, Erich, *My War Memories 1914–18*, Hutchinson 1919

McKee, Alexander, *Vimy Ridge*, Souvenir Press, 1966

Macksey, Kenneth, *The Shadow of Vimy Ridge*, William Kimber 1965

Manning, Frederick, *The Middle Parts of Fortune*, Peter Davies 1977

Mitchell, F., *Tank Warfare*, Nelson 1923

Monash, Sir John, *The Australian Victories in France in 1918*, Angus and Robertson 1936

Murray, Joseph, *Call to Arms*, William Kimber 1980

Nichols, G. H. F., *The 18th Division in the Great War*, Nisbet 1922

Pendroncini, G., *The Mutinies of 1917*, Paris 1967

Robertson, Sir William, *Soldiers and Statesmen 1914–18* (2 Vols), Cassell 1926

Rupprecht, Crown Prince of Bavaria, *Mein Kriegstagebuch*, Munich 1929

Scott, Sir Arthur B. and Bramwell P. Middleton, *History of the 12th (Eastern) Division in the Great War*, Nisbet 1923

Shakespear, John, *The 34th Division 1915–1919*, Witherby 1921

Sixsmith, E. K. G., *Douglas Haig*, Weidenfeld & Nicolson 1976

Slack, Cecil M., *Grandfather's Adventures in the Great War 1914–18*, Arthur H. Stockwell 1977

Smithers, A. J., *Sir John Monash*, Leo Cooper 1977

Spears, Sir Edward, *Prelude to Victory*, Jonathan Cape 1939

Steele, Harwood, *The Canadians in France, 1915–1918*, T. Fisher Unwin 1920

Stewart, J., and Buchan, John, *The Fifteenth (Scottish) Division 1914–1919*, Blackwood 1926

Swinton, Sir Ernest, *Twenty Years After* (3 Vols), George Newnes 1938

Talbot-Kelly, Richard, *A Subaltern's Odyssey*, William Kimber 1980

Terraine, John, *The Western Front*, Hutchinson 1964. *The Road to Passchendaele*, Leo Cooper 1977. *The Smoke and the Fire*, Sidgwick & Jackson 1980

Thomas, Alan, *A Life Apart*, Victor Gollancz 1968

Ward, C. H. Dudley, *The 56th Division*, John Murray 1921

Wavell, Sir Archibald, *Allenby – A Study in Greatness*, Harrap 1940

Wheeler, Victor W., *No Man's Land*, the Alberta Historical Resources Foundation 1980

Williams, John, *Mutiny 1917*, Heinemann 1962

Williams-Ellis, C. and A., *The Tank Corps*, George Newnes 1919

Wood, Herbet Fairlie, *Vimy!*, Macdonald 1967

The Army Quarterly, Vol. XXXV, No. 2, January 1938

The Cavalry Journal, Vol. XXI, No. 82, October 1931

The 10th Royal Hussars Gazette, Vol. XXI, No. 5

Pilgrimage, The Royal British Legion, 1928

Register of the Victoria Cross, This England Books 1981

Index

Abercromby, Lieut-Col Sir G. W., 204
Achicourt, 66
Achiet-le-Grand, 13
Adams, 2nd-Lieut J., 59, 71, 92
Agny Military Cem, 131
Aisne, Battle of, 2, 168, 192, 210
Alberich, 7, 10
Albert, 19
Alberta, 43
Allenby, Gen Sir Edmund, 23, 24, 25, 30, 62, 66, 68, 118, 123, 129, 131, 135, 136, 137, 139, 148, 154, 160, 164, 172, 176, 194, 195, 196, 217
America, 40, 60, 213
Ancre Valley, 10, 12, 13, 184
Anderson, CSM, A. G., 45, 177, 219
Andrews, Rev Martin, 64
Arleux, 195
Arras, 2, 8, 19, 20, 22, 28, 30, 31, 32, 34, 35, 36, 37, 43, 44, 47, 52, 53, 57, 60, 64, 66,. 98, 101, 102, 104, 106, 109, 110, 118, 123, 127, 137, 141, 213, 215, 219
Arras, Battle casualties, 210
Arras Memorial, 213, 221
Artillerie Mulde, 22
Artois, 19, 167
Asbury, Lieut, 186
Ashburner, 2nd Lieut T.B., 46
Asquith, Cmdr A., 183, 184, 185, 186
Asquith, Raymond, 183
Athies, 102, 125, 149
Auckland, 21

Bailleul, 103, 136
Baker, 2nd Lieut E., 110

Ball, Capt A., 36, 43
Balloon Hill, 23
Banchory, 173
Bantams, 28, 29
Bapaume, 16, 18
Barbed Wire Square, 213
Baron, 2nd Lieut, 120
Batter Trench, 86, 87
Battery Valley, 22, 106, 112, 113, 129, 214
Baudimont Gate, 57
Bean, C. E. W., 157, 160, 201
Beaumetz, 164
Beaumont-cum-Moze, 218
Beckett, Lieut-Col S., 49, 50
Beeston, Pte J., 140
Belston, Pte L., 72
Benyon, Maj, 128
Bennett, Cmdr, 184
Bernardini, Unt Off A., 141
Betteridge, Pte A., 37, 103, 104, 220
Berlin, 13, 52
Bewsher, Maj, 172
Bishop, Billy, 43
Black, Maj P., 157
Black Line, 27, 78, 79, 93, 100, 103, 110, 115
Black Watch Museum, 110
Blair, Capt P., 58, 59, 161, 176, 219, 221
Blake, Robert, 165
Blangy, 53, 107, 128
Blenpense Ditch, 82
Blue Line, 27, 79, 80, 94, 98, 100, 103, 108, 110, 115, 172, 189
Bluff, 84
Boiry, 144
Bois-du-Vert, 165
Bonval Wood, 81, 85

Boom Ravine, 12
Bourassa, Henry, 42
Bracey, Corp T., 32, 107, 204, 205
Briscoe, Capt R., 84
British Army
  Armies
    First, 27, 35, 44, 69, 89, 196,
      200, 210, 223,
    Third, 17, 25, 28, 32, 33, 34,
      35, 44, 60, 66, 69, 91, 131,
      135, 139, 154, 170, 172, 195,
      202, 210, 222
    Fourth, 16, 25
    Fifth, 16, 25, 34, 35, 156, 160,
      196, 201, 224
  Corps
    I, 32
    IV, 22
    VI, 31, 113, 127
    XVII, 129
  Infantry Divisions
  First Army
    2nd, 164, 195, 201, 223
    5th, 81, 223
    24th, 27, 223
    31st, 201, 223
    63rd (Royal Naval), 37, 164,
      172, 183, 195, 223
    1st (Can), 80, 91, 94, 195, 200,
      223
    2nd (Can), 81, 82, 85, 223
    3rd (Can), 84, 85, 224
    4th (Can), 47, 48, 50, 85, 86, 88
  Third Army
    3rd, 113, 114, 116, 117, 129,
      139, 222
    4th, 44, 123, 125, 127, 128, 137,
      153, 154, 170, 209, 212, 213,
      222
    9th (Scottish), 27, 46, 63, 101,
      102, 105, 123, 202, 222
    12th (Eastern), 107, 112, 113,
      115, 116, 127, 129, 202, 204,
      222
    14th (Light), 117, 154, 222
    15th (Scottish), 27, 104, 106,
      107, 113, 127, 129, 139, 141,
      172, 188, 214, 222
    17th (Northern), 165, 187, 188,
      222
    18th (Eastern), 7, 11, 12, 13,
      196, 197, 199, 222

    21st, 117, 196, 222
    29th, 164, 172, 188, 214, 222
    30th, 117, 164, 172, 223
    33rd, 164, 210, 222
    34th, 96, 98, 99, 100, 101, 103,
      131, 181, 195, 223
    37th, 127, 129, 137, 139, 141,
      145, 164, 172, 195, 223
    50th (Northumbrian), 164, 189,
      223
    51st (Highland), 57, 58, 91, 95,
      98, 99, 170, 172, 173, 179,
      181, 187, 188, 209, 223
    56th (1st London), 24, 66, 117,
      119, 135, 212, 223
  Fifth Army
    2nd (Aus), 18, 22, 201, 224
    4th (Aus), 156, 158
    58th, 209
    62nd, 201
  Infantry Brigades
    4th (Aus), 158
    7th (Can), 69
    8th, 115
    9th, 115
    10th, 148, 152
    11th, 127, 137
    11th (Can), 86, 87
    12th, 137, 159
    12th (Can), 86
    13th, 81
    26th, 104, 105
    27th, 46, 101, 103, 123
    28th, 102
    36th, 110
    37th, 147
    44th, 107, 108
    45th, 107
    71st, 30
    76th, 115, 116
    101st, 100
    103rd, 98
    150th, 191
    152nd, 96, 98
    153rd, 91, 181
    154th, 58, 91, 92, 180
  Infantry Battalions
    Anson Battalion, 183
    2nd Argyll & Sutherland
      Highlanders, 191
    7th Argyll & Sutherland
      Highlanders, 93, 95, 96, 178

14th Australian, 159
16th Australian, 157, 159
24th Australian, 202
4th Bedfords, 183, 187
6th Bedfords, 143
7th Bedfords, 12, 97
7th Border, 187, 188
6th Black Watch, 176
7th Black Watch, 176
8th Black Watch, 105, 156, 202, 203
9th Black Watch, 107, 109
6th Cameron Highlanders, 62, 109, 140
7th Cameron Highlanders, 189, 214
1st Canadian, 80
3rd Canadian, 79
8th Canadian, 89
20th Canadian, 85
22nd Canadian, 42
24th Canadian, 42, 65, 85, 89
26th Canadian, 50, 68, 76
38th Canadian, 89
42nd Canadian, 42, 85
44th Canadian, 41, 88
47th Canadian, 89
50th Canadian, 43, 88
54th Canadian, 47, 49
72nd Canadian, 47, 49, 86
73rd Canadian, 47, 48, 49
75th Canadian, 47, 49
78th Canadian, 90
85th Canadian, 87
87th Canadian, 86
102nd Canadian, 86
1st Canadian Mounted Rifles, 72, 83
Drake Battalion, 183, 184, 187
7th East Surreys, 112
1st Essex, 165, 166
2nd Essex, 44, 123
9th Essex, 112, 113, 116
1st Gordon Highlanders, 115, 116
4th Gordon Highlanders, 45, 95, 96, 177, 219
6th Gordon Highlanders, 181
7th Gordon Highlanders, 175, 173
1st Hampshire, 209
2nd Hampshire, 165, 166

Hawke Battalion, 183, 187
1st Hon. Artillery Co. 183
Household Battalion, 153
Hood Battalion, 183, 184, 186
Howe Battalion, 37
17th Kings, 72
1st King's Own, 137
6th King's Own Scottish Borderers, 103
7th King's Royal Rifle Corps, 154, 155, 214
16th King's Royal Rifle Corps, 189
5th King's Shropshire L.I., 117, 118, 200
7th King's Shropshire L.I., 115, 116
7th Lincolns, 188
10th Lincolns, 60
1/3rd London, 121
12th London (Rangers), 119, 120, 121, 122
1st London Scottish, 73
17th Manchesters, 191
18th Manchesters, 191
21st Manchesters, 8
8th Middlesex, 121
7th Middlesex, 62, 121, 170
11th Middlesex, 72, 110
12th Middlesex, 13, 197, 199
Nelson Battalion, 183, 184
7th Norfolks, 112
21st Northumberland Fus, 131
24th Northumberland Fus, 98
25th Northumberland Fus, 98
26th Northumberland Fus, 99, 182
27th Northumberland Fus, 182
2/1st Oxford & Bucks L.I., 16
1st Rifle Brigade, 127
8th Rifle Brigade, 155
5th Royal Berks, 112, 113
4th Royal Fusiliers, 64
8th Royal Fusiliers, 63, 65, 110, 112, 113, 202, 203, 213, 219
9th Royal Fusiliers, 107, 110, 204, 205
13th Royal Fusiliers, 139, 140
1st Royal Irish Fus, 149, 154, 153, 154
Royal Marine L.I., 183, 187
Royal Newfoundland Regiment, 165, 166

British Army – *cont.*
    2nd Royal Scots, 191
    8th Royal Scots, 70
    9th Royal Scots, 58, 59, 70, 91,
      92, 93, 160, 170, 172, 178,
      213, 221
    11th Royal Scots, 66
    13th Royal Scots, 107, 110
    16th Royal Scots, 98
    7th Royal Sussex, 72, 110, 206
    1st Royal Warwicks, 153
    11th Royal Warwicks, 143
    16th Royal Warwicks, 81, 82
    10th Royal Welsh Fus, 115
    7th Royal West Kents, 7
    6th Scottish Rifles, 46
    10th Scottish Rifles, 113
    2nd Seaforth Highlanders, 148,
      149, 151, 152, 153, 154, 161
    4th Seaforth Highlanders, 59,
      67, 75, 91, 94
    6th Seaforth Highlanders, 94,
      181
    9th Seaforth Highlanders, 102
    10th Sherwood Foresters, 6
    1st Somerset L.I., 41, 137
    1st South African, 46
    4th South African, 37, 103, 161,
      220
    8th South Staffords, 187, 188
    11th Suffolks, 100
    17th West Yorks, 28
    4th Worcesters, 165
    Artillery (R.F.A., R.G.A.), 32,
      33, 66
    Cavalry, 24, 34, 132, 137, 138,
      144, 146, 147, 223
    Cyclists, 127
    Heavy Branch Machine Gun
      Corps, 34, 81
    Military Police, 17
    New Zealand Tunnelling
      Companby, 21, 28, 29, 30
    Pigeon Section, 35
    Royal Engineers, 18, 21, 33, 35,
      84, 85
    Royal Flying Corps, 8, 37, 43, 83,
      112, 148
British Legion, 218
Brown, Pte, H., 72
Brown Line, 27, 103, 112, 115, 129,
  135

Browns Copse Military Cem, 152,
  214
Bruce-Williams, Maj-Gen, 139
Bryan, Corp T., 99, 100
Buffalo Lake, 43
Bulkeley-Johnson, Brig-Gen, C.,
  144, 146
Bullecourt, 39, 156, 158, 160, 201,
  209
Burstall, Maj-Gen H. E., 81
Bury, Lieut-Col, 155
Byng, Gen Sir Julian, 27, 69, 217,
  218

Calais Conference, 2, 32
Cambrai, 27, 98, 167, 220, 221
Campbell, Brig-Gen, 176, 181
Campbell, Pte G., 59, 71, 93, 221
Campbell, Pte J., 59, 71, 93, 221
Canadian Battlefields Commission,
  215
Candle Factory, 66
Carton de Wiart, Brig-Gen, 137
Cator, Sgt H., 112
Cavalry Farm, 189, 214
Chandos, Lord, 40, 157
Chapel Hill, 115
Chaplin, Lieut, 144
Chapman, Guy, 179
Charles, Sgt L. C., 17, 18
Charlton, Able-Seaman, 186
Charteris, Brig-Gen J., 24
Chemical Works, 22, 136, 137, 139,
  148, 149, 154, 161, 162, 163, 170,
  173, 176, 178, 180, 181, 182, 202,
  209, 214
Chemin-des-Dames, 168, 212
Chérisy, 196, 197, 199, 201
Chinese Barrage, 53
Christie-Miller, Capt G., 16
Clark, CSM C., 120, 122
Cojeul stream, 154, 199
Collior, Pte W. M., 63, 65, 110,
  204, 205
Commonwealth War Graves
  Commission, 215
Compiègne Conference, 55, 56
Cooke, Sub-Lieut, 186
Cooper, Capt G. R., 84, 85
Cousins, Sgt J. J., 12, 197
Coupland, Pte J., 61, 199

248

Crane, Pte E., 142
Craonne, 168
Crest Trench, 7
Crinchon Sewer, 28, 29
Crinchon Valley, 115
Croft, Lieut-Col, 66
Croisilles, 27, 71, 189
Crump Trench, 177, 178, 215
Cruyenaere, Corp J. de, 72
Cuddeford, Capt D. W. J., 146
Cunningham, 2nd Lieut, 120
Curll, Corp M., 88
Currie, Maj-Gen A., 78, 80, 85, 91,
  96, 195, 212
Cuthbert Crater, 46, 47

Davies, Sgt A., 121, 122
Davis, Corp G. W., 147
Dawson, Brig-Gen, 104, 181
Dawson, Lieut-Col W., 147
Dead Man's Corner, 57
Deodar Lane, 119
Delville Wood, 102, 103, 162
Deverell, Maj-Gen C. J., 115, 116
Diffenbach, Gen, 39
Dobie, Pte J., 102
Douai, 20, 22, 75, 104, 128, 136
Douaumont, Fort, 1
Drake-Brockman, Lieut-Col E., 159
Dunkirk, 216
Dunn, Pte L., 71
Durgan, Maj J., 28, 30, 31

Easton, Pte T., 131
Ecurie, 59
Edinburgh, 58
Edward VIII, 215
Elliot-Cooper, Lieut-Col N. B., 205
Ellis, Lieut-Cmdr, 184
Esher, Lord, 191, 192
Etaples, 101
Eveling, Pte R., 187

Falls, Capt Cyril, 129, 130, 177, 196,
  211
Falkenhayn, Gen Von, 40
Fampoux, 126, 128, 136, 145, 148,
  149, 161, 162, 176
Farbus, 27

Fasbender, Gen Von, 39
Fasbender Tower, 23
Faubourg d'Amiens, 213
Fellowes, Capt H., 148, 149
Ferguson, 2nd Lieut W., 92
Fergusson, Lieut-Gen C., 161, 173,
  176
Fermie, Corp, 93
Feuchy, 108, 128, 214
Feuchy Chapel, 116
Feuchy Chapel Redoubt, 112, 113
Feuchy Redoubt, 108
Feuchy Switch Trench, 106
Fisher, Corp A., 105, 106
Flanders, 1, 215, 219
Flying Circus, 36
Flynn, Pte G., 59, 219
Fontaine-les-Croisilles, 117, 160,
  189
Fontaine Trench, 189
Forbes-Robertson, Lieut-Col J.,
  166
Fowke, Brig-Gen G. H., 210
Fowler, Pte H., 73
Francis, Pte E., 81
Frankl, *Leutnant* W., 37
Fraser, Capt A., 95
Fred's Wood, 108
French Army, 20, 21, 192, 193
Frerichs, *Gef* H., 200
Fresnoy, 200, 201, 202
Freybourg, Cmdr, 183

Gameson, Capt, 30
Gardner, Sgt D., 76
Garnett, Tpr C., 144, 145
Gavrelle, 136, 172, 183, 184, 186,
  190, 195
Gavrelle Windmill, 187
Gellibrand, Brig-Gen, 201, 202
German Army
  Gruppe Arras, 39
  Gruppe Souchez, 39
  Gruppe Vimy, 39, 100
  1st Bavarian Res Div, 39, 89,
    92
  3rd Bavarian Div, 137
  11th Inf Div, 106
  14th Bavarian Div, 39
  15th Res Div, 200
  18th Inf Div, 148

German Army – *cont.*
  25th Res Div, 200
  26th Inf Div, 148, 189
  79th Res Inf Div, 81, 89
  2nd Bavarian Res Inf Reg, 92
  3rd Bavarian Res Inf Reg, 82
  8th Res Inf Reg, 23
  23rd Bavarian Inf Reg, 141,
    165
  25th Bavarian Inf Reg, 101
  31st Inf Reg, 136, 148, 152
  51st Prussian Inf Reg, 53, 106,
    110, 112
  73rd Fus Reg, 15
  76th Res Reg, 115
  84th Res Reg, 37, 143
  86th Fus Reg, 153, 175
  90th Fus Reg, 185
  124th Inf Reg, 157
  125th Inf Reg, 187
  161st Inf Reg, 175
  162nd Inf Reg, 118
  163rd Inf Reg, 121
  180th Reg, 12
  405 Artillery Battalion, 52
Germany, 40
Gilmour, Pte H., 173
Godry, Knr F., 53
Gommecourt, 24, 120
Goodbody, Gnr G., 33
Gordon-Canning, Capt, 138, 144
Gosling, Brig-Gen C., 148, 153
Gough, Gen H., 16, 156, 157,m
  160, 195, 196
Graham, Corp R., 93
Grand Place, 28, 31, 213
Gray, Pte R., 100, 131
Green, Lieut-Col J., 160
Green Line, 27, 91, 96, 98, 101, 123
Greenland Hill, 126, 139, 148, 161,
  172, 173, 181
Greenwood, Spr J., 33
Greggain, Sgt W., 86
Groupe des Armés du Nord, 11
Guemappe, 128, 144, 190,
  214

Habarq, 127
Haldane, Lieut-Gen Sir A., 31, 113
Haig, Field-Marshal Sir Douglas, 2,
  18, 22, 23, 34, 54, 57, 129, 135,
    164, 167, 168, 169, 191, 192, 194,
    196, 212, 218
Ham, Pte H., 13, 197
Hamilton, Brig-Gen, 180
Hamm, Lieut C. B., 89
Hangstellung, 88, 135
Harp, The, 115, 117, 118
Harper, Maj-Gen G., 57, 91, 96,
  173, 176, 182
Hay, Sgt W., 58, 70, 92, 221
Heinrich, *Leutnant* R. L., 111
Herbert, A. P., 183
Hermon, Lieut-Col E., 98
Hibers Trench Military Cemetery,
  155, 214
Hill 90, 154, 155, 214
Hill 135, 81
Hill 145, 48, 86, 87, 88, 215
Hindenburg, Field-Marshal von, 109
Hindenburg Line, 8, 25, 117, 122,
  135, 157, 158, 104, 172, 196, 201
Holland, Maj-Gen E. A. E., 24, 25
Hollingworth, Pte F., 68, 75, 94, 96
Horne, Gen Sir H., 25, 90, 135,
  172, 195
Houdain Lane, 112
Houdain Lane British Cemetery,
  214
Hubbard, Pte W., 206, 207, 208,
  213, 219
Huddle Trench, 149
Huntley, Capt, 99
Hutcheson, Capt, 181
Hyderabad Redoubt, 126, 127, 137,
  148, 152, 154, 163

Imperial War Graves Commission,
  215
Irles, 113

Jarratt, Corp G., 205, 206
Jerome, Lieut, 141
Joffre, Gen, 1, 2
Junger, Ernst, 15

Kaiser, The, 40, 54
Kaji, Sgt, 43
Kann, 2nd Lieut, 180
Keegan, Lieut K. F., 166, 167

250

Keeling Copse, 202
Kemball, Lieut-Col A., 49, 50
Kent, Pte, 197, 199
Keyser, Musk H., 37
Kiggel, Lieut-Gen, 194
King, Pte C. C., 41
Kircaldy, Lieut-Col J., 90
Kloke, Sgt, 185
Kraft, Musk H., 83
Kreuznach, 101, 130
Krumbach, 101

Labyrinth, 91, 94
Lahore Artillery, 89
Lambton, Maj-Gen W., 123, 153
Larasset Huts, 160
Latham, Sgt, 108
Lawrence, T. E., 217
Lawrie, Sub-Lieut T., 37, 184
Layton, Lieut-Col, 139
Lean, Capt, 176
Leane, Lieut-Col R. L., 159
Lee, Maj-Gen R. P., 12
Leishman, Sgt J., 59, 71, 92
Lens, 104
Les Tilleuls, 81
Leslie, Lieut E., 94, 95
Lewin, Lieut F., 7
Liddle, Pte G., 80
Lihons, 16
Lille Road, 21, 68, 94, 97
Lipsett, Maj-Gen, 84
Livens Projectors, 33, 53
Lloyd George, David, 1, 56, 169,
    212, 218
Loch, Brig-Gen, 122
London Colney, 36
Lone Copse, 137, 187, 188
Loos, 102
Lossberg, Col von, 191
Lowther, Capt J., 128
Lucas, Lieut F., 7, 8, 13
Ludendorff, 10, 16, 39, 101, 130,
    136, 191, 212
Luke Alley, 8
Lukin, Maj-Gen H. T., 101, 102,
    161, 162
Lusitania, 108
Lutmer, Fus H., 185
Luxon, Dvr J., 118
Lyttelton, O., 40

Mackay, Pte J., 180
Macdonald, Lieut-Col S., 181
Macdonall, Brig-Gen A. G., 69
Mackintosh, Lieut D., 151, 152, 153
Maison Rouge, 112
Malmaison, 212
Maltby, Maj, 83
Mannock, M., 43
Manning, F., 170
Maroeuil Huts, 59
Marr, Pte H., 175
Mars, Operation, 212
Mason, Brig-Gen, J42
Maude, 2nd-Lieut G., 110, 111
Maxse, Lieut-Gen, 11
Maxwell, Brig-Gen F. A., 46, 47,
    98, 101, 102, 103, 104, 123, 127,
    161, 162, 163, 219
McCracken, Maj-Gen F. W. N.,
    106, 107
McCrindle, Pte A., 42, 48, 65
McGill University, 65
Meikle, Sgt, 87
Menin Gate, 215
Mercatel, 121
Messines, 130, 211
Miraumont, 13
Monash, Gen J., 130
Monchy-le-Preux, 20, 22, 23, 27,
    129, 135, 137, 138, 139, 140, 141,
    142, 144, 145, 146, 147, 154, 165,
    166, 167, 187, 202, 210, 212, 214,
    215, 219
Monchy windmill, 165
Monypenny, Capt R., 44, 123, 125,
    126
Morris, Corp, 83
Moselle, River, 9
Mount Pleasant Wood, 23, 170, 177
Mugford, Corp H., 144
Mullaly, Pte F., 69, 219
Munich, 92, 101
Mutiny, French, 192, 193, 194

Neuville Mill, 23, 121
Neuville St Vaast, 81
Neuville Vitasse, 9, 23, 116, 117,
    118, 120, 121, 122
New Brunswick, 68
New Scotland Yard, 218
Nichols, G. H. F., 164

Nicholson, Maj-Gen C. L., 98, 131
Nickalls, Maj, 128
Niebelung Saga, 10
Nivelle, Gen Robert, 1, 2, 10, 11,
    16, 25, 54, 55, 164, 167, 168, 169,
    191, 192, 218
Noack, *Soldat* O., 136, 152
Noel, Sgt J., 180, 181
Norman, Lieut-Col W., 8
Norwest, Pte H., 43

Observation Ridge, 22, 107, 110,
    112
Odlum, Brig-Gen V. W., 86, 87, 88
Ogilvie, Pte Don, 104
Oppy Wood, 195, 201
Orange Hill, 22, 129, 137, 144, 145
Orr, Maj N. C., 151
Oundle School, 154
Owen, Pte, H., 78, 79

Painlevé, M., 191, 192
Parrot's Beak, 104
Partridge, Sgt W., 62, 72, 121, 122,
    170
Passchendaele, 3
Pearson, W., 76, 78
Peck, Lieut-Col J. H., 159
Pelves, 202, 206, 219
Perks, Capt H., 199
Pétain, Marshal, 192, 194
Petit Bois, 168
Petit Miraumont, 7
Petit Place, 28
Phillips, Brig-Gen, 184
Pimple, The, 27, 86, 87, 88, 135,
    164
Pine Lane, 120
Pinneo, Corp P. G., 89
Plumer, Gen H., : 17
Plumridge, Pte L. G., 41
Poincaré, Pres, 55
Point-du-Jour, 91, 96, 98, 101, 103,
    123, 214
Pont-à-Mousson, 9
Port-de-Fer, 31
Poulter, Corp F., 63
Poser Weg, 70
Price, Corp J., 197
Prince Arnulf Tunnel, 84

Quebec, 42

Rackham, Sub-Lieut B. B., 187
Railway Triangle, 53, 104, 106, 107,
    108, 109, 110
Rauchenburger, Gen von, 100
Rawlinson, Gen Sir Henry, 213
Razzell, Corp A. E., 111, 112, 113,
    204, 206, 207, 208, 219
Reay, Maj T., 99
Redbourn, 12
Red line, 78, 79, 80, 81, 82
Renwick, CSM J., 71, 93, 178, 219
Renwick, Rfmn R., 189, 213, 221
Richards, Pte A., 119
Ribot, Prime Minister, 55, 192
Richmond, BC, 86
Richtofen, Manfred von, 36
Riding Mill, 99
Riencourt, 157, 158, 160
Robertson, Brig-Gen, 159
Robertson, Maj-Gen P. R., 188
Robertson, Gen Sir William, 2, 55,
    169, 192
Roclincourt, 70
Roclincourt Military Cemetery, 93,
    98
Roclincourt Valley Cemetery, 93
Rodgers, Lieut-Col J. B., 80
Roeux, 22, 128, 136, 137, 139, 147,
    148, 170, 176, 177, 178, 179, 180,
    181, 182, 188, 195, 202, 205, 209,
    213, 219, 221
Roeux Château, 154, 176, 209, 213
Roeux Station, 182
Roeux Wood, 23, 170, 172
Ronville, 27, 28, 31, 61
Ross, Pte A., 151
Rossington, Pte A., 188, 189
Rowland, Pte C., 28
Rupprecht, Crown Prince, 10, 39
Russia, 1
Rutherford, 2nd Lieut, 31

Scarpe, Second Battle of, 172
Scarpe, Third Battle of, 196, 202
Scarpe, River, 19, 20, 32, 39, 98,
    101, 102, 126, 128, 129, 140, 145,
    172, 187, 195, 202, 205
Schlensog, Leutnant R., 112

Schissler, Corp, 49
Scholer, Gen von, 106
Schwaben Redoubt, 12
Schwaben Tunnel, 81
Schwerk, Sgt, 111
Scott, Maj-Gen A. B., 106, 112
Sector Arnulf, 81
Shakespear, J., 99
Siegfried Stellung, 8, 9, 10, 22
Simonsen, Haupt, 153
Skinner, Brig-Gen, 155
Smart, Pte S., 83, 84
Smith, Pte A., 173, 174
Snow, Lieut-Gen T. d'O., 117, 120,
    122, 135, 163, 189
Somme, Battle of the, 1, 3, 9, 11,
    12, 23, 27, 32, 34, 59, 98, 101,
    111, 121, 130, 151, 196, 210, 211,
    213
Soissons, 168
Souchez, 32, 39
Spears, Maj E., 55, 129, 160, 167
Speck, *Feldwebel* W., 143
Spider Corner, 108
St Albans, 12, 142
St Eloi, 75
St Laurent Blangy, 102, 104
St Mihiel, 213
St Nicholas, 103, 162
St Pol, 57, 129, 135
St Quentin, 10
St Quentin Canal, 221
St Rohart Factory, 172
St Sauveur, 27, 28, 31
Stewart, Pte C., 62, 63, 109, 140
Stitt, Lieut J., 173, 174, 175
Stockholm, Pte A., 103, 104
Stokes, Capt, 147
Studdert Kennedy, Rev, 65

Talbot-Kelly, 2nd-Lieut R., 163
Tank Cemetery, 214
Tanner, Capt T. C., 117, 118, 200
Tapper, Pte W., 89
Taylor, Gnr A., 66
Taylor, Pte B., 72
Taylor, Sgt B., 128, 145
Taylor, Tpr C. V., 24
Telegraph Hill, 118
Terraine, John, 216, 217
Thacker, Brig-Gen, 8

Tilloy-les-Mofflaines, 115
Times, The, 215
Tommy Trench, 96
Tompkins, Pte N., 68, 76, 218
Tottenham Tunnel, 86, 87, 88
Towcester, 128
Thelus, 82, 91
Thiepval, 12
Thomas, 2nd-Lieut A., 147
Thomas, 2nd-Lieut E., 131
Trones Wood, 11
Tyler, Corp G., 96

Vallières, Gen de, 167
Vauban, 19
Vauclerc Plateau, 168
Verdun, 1, 20, 34, 193, 212
Vickerman, Capt, 29, 31
Victor-Smith, 2nd Lieut L., 179
Vignoles, Maj W., 60, 69
Villers-au-Bois, 50
Villers Station Cemetery, 50
Vimy Memorial, 215
Vimy Ridge, 19, 20, 25, 27, 32, 34,
    39, 42, 43, 47, 51, 53, 57, 68, 69,
    71, 75, 76, 78, 82, 83, 84, 85, 89,
    90, 91, 130m, 135, 164, 215, 218
Vis-en-Artois, 164
Volker Tunnel, 84

Waley, Capt A., 35
Walker, Corp W. B., 138
Walter Trench, 8
Walton, Pte A., 59, 71, 92, 93
Wancourt, 23, 147, 154, 155
Wancourt-Feuchy Switch trench,
    112, 113, 115, 189
Wancourt Tower, 214
War Cabinet, 155
Ward, Bglr B., 89
Ward, Maj R., 82
Warren, CSM E., 119, 120, 122
Watford, Maj-Gen D., 86, 87, 88
Wavell, Lord, 23
Weber, 2nd-Lieut C., 108, 109
West Hampstead, 221
Wheeler, Sgt V., 43
Whitley, Capt C., 155, 219
Whitmore, Lieut-Col, 146, 147
Wilford, Pte E., 142

Wilhelm, Crown Prince, 54
Williamson, Capt G., 154, 155
Williamson, 2nd Lieut K., 155
Williamson, Sgt J., 21, 28, 29, 30
Willocks, Sgt J., 58, 70, 221
Willson, Corp R. P., 185, 186
Wilson, Sgt B., 216
Wilson, Gen Sir Henry, 22, 191, 192

Ypres, 19, 58, 84, 210, 211, 221
Yser Canal, 61

Zouave Valley, 20
Zwischen Stellung, 76, 77
Zwolfer Weg, 78